Screenwriters and Screenwriting

Screenwriters and Screenwriting

Putting Practice into Context

Edited by

Craig Batty
School of Media and Communication, RMIT University, Australia

First published 2014 by
PALGRAVE MACMILLAN

Palgrave Macmillan in the UK is an imprint of Macmillan Publishers Limited,
registered in England, company number 785998, of Houndmills, Basingstoke,
Hampshire RG21 6XS.

Palgrave Macmillan in the US is a division of St Martin's Press LLC,
175 Fifth Avenue, New York, NY 10010.

Palgrave Macmillan is the global academic imprint of the above companies
and has companies and representatives throughout the world.

Palgrave® and Macmillan® are registered trademarks in the United States,
the United Kingdom, Europe and other countries.

ISBN 978–1–137–33892–1

This book is printed on paper suitable for recycling and made from fully
managed and sustained forest sources. Logging, pulping and manufacturing
processes are expected to conform to the environmental regulations of the
country of origin.

A catalogue record for this book is available from the British Library.

A catalog record for this book is available from the Library of Congress.

Contents

Figures

Foreword

INT. SOMEWHERE – DAY OR MAYBE NIGHT

Late. Friday night. That clock on the television says 12.14. Actually, I guess that makes it Saturday morning. I'd just finished watching a movie and fell asleep here on the sofa. I could tell you the name of the movie but, try as I might, I don't recall who wrote it.

Come to think on it, maybe that's wrong. Maybe it's not night at all. Maybe I'm daydreaming. Maybe I've been reading this book, *Screenwriters and Screenwriting*, and here I am inside it, both writing this and written into this book, like a character. Weird, especially as two guys to the left seem to be filming me writing this, while three, four, maybe five people – a couple of women I recognise from the university bookshop, a guy I think is Craig Batty – are contemplating me as I write this, while the cinematographer behind a shimmering gold 35mm-film spool (What?! It's possible! Hey, it's my daydream!) seems perplexed by my choice of costume. I don't see why: I'm dressed as a combination of Mark Zuckerberg, Salvador Dali and Warren Buffet, as surely befits a book about writing for the screen.

Screen art is a kind of dream. Or, according to enthusiastic anecdotal record and earnest scientific studies, a dream is a kind of screen art. On the one hand, what a wonderful opportunity for any writer to be empowered to write a dream. What dream would you write? For my part, I appear to have opted for writing one involving a foreword to a book entitled *Screenwriters and Screenwriting*. On the other hand, if screen art is a dream, then it is a dream that might involve the complex commercial world of the mass media or the aesthetic commitments of the experimental artist, or perhaps some combination of these. As a writing project that isn't unusual: all writers have to navigate the territories of audience interest and the writer's personal intention and belief. All of us think at some point about our actions and the potential reactions when someone reads, or watches, something we have (largely) created. Why and how and to what effect we make creative compositional decisions remains an area of research requiring much more investigation. But we know we make them, and it seems at very least that if we start with the actions of writing themselves and move then to the texts those actions of writing produce, we get closest to the decisions made, nearest to our creative and critical knowledge.

When speaking about *creative* writing, screenwriting has not always found a home as easily in the community of creative and critical writing discussion as poetry or prose writing has found such a home. This fact has as much to do with the origins, history and location of the formal study of creative writing as with any differences between screenwriting and the writing of a poem or, indeed, between the screenplay and a novel, for example. *Screenwriters and Screenwriting* demonstrates well why such an historical lack of attention to writing for the screen has been to the detriment of those creative writing discussions. Whether with regard to structure and form, individuals within/associating with a culture, or the interactions between creators and receivers of final works, writers gain from explorations that are not limited by post-writing critical determinations – which were what previously limited how screenwriting was received in what can broadly be called 'literary' circles.

By 'post-writing critical determinations' I am, of course, referring to aspects of critical study that begin by addressing the existence of a written text. A writer cannot begin that way, because all creative and critical determinations a writer must make are brought about by the pragmatics of having to create a piece of writing in the first place. While questions of whether we create or recreate texts as audiences are about more than simple semantics, the literal and situational logic of a creative writer's formational role is nevertheless undeniable. The contributors to *Screenwriters and Screenwriting* recognise that fact. That's one of the reasons why this book should be read and read again. It's also interesting that while the writers' references bear clear evidence of the distinctiveness of writing for the screen, it is also true that they draw from a wider range of influences, from ideas defined not by post-writing territorial lines but by writerly preference, usefulness, thought and need.

When we discuss creative writing by focusing on the actions of writing, and discussion of the many results of those actions follows this, we are discussing what best informs during composition. Placing critical understanding in the position of informing how writers respond to the actions of writing resituates any final texts by reconfirming they are part of an evidential trail created by the writer in such a personal compositional history. These texts incorporate understanding and bear individual creative writer's knowledge in multiple ways; but they also represent the imagination, fortuitousness, cultural influence and individual belief. The writers in *Screenwriters and Screenwriting* show an engaged understanding of this.

I recall clearly that I began writing for the screen for two reasons. Firstly, it seemed exotic. The more I found out, the more exotic it became, with what seemed like secret codes of presentation and an alternative view of words where the final result was a guide to creating another art form, but equally had a written identity of its own. Writing for the screen asked for distinctive writing skills, as well as a willingness to see creative writing as innately about collaborative human exchange. This seemed immediately valuable but had largely been untaught in the educational places I had been to that point. Secondly, I began writing for the screen in my mid-twenties because if there was any other form of art and mode of communication I seemed immersed in, other than creative writing itself, it was film and television. Simply, I was watching a whole lot of it! After publishing my first novel, and because of winning an award for it, I ended up funded onto a short scriptwriting course for new, published novelists at the Australian Film, Television and Radio School (AFTRS), from which a number of notable international film and television directors had graduated. At the very first script workshop I found that anything I thought I knew about writing, based that is on my fiction writing, was barely adequate to address screenwriting. The workshop leader verbally and thoroughly shredded my first effort. From that point I was both intrigued by what I didn't know and, in a word, hooked.

Had I read a book like *Screenwriters and Screenwriting*, my first scriptwriting efforts would have been more successful. Had I at least had access to such a book, I might not have begun the activities of scriptwriting with so very little understanding of what those activities entailed, or of how I might develop a creative and critical knowledge of them. But, as Craig Batty points out in his Introduction, until the last five years or so maybe such a book wouldn't have found someone willing to publish it. 'How to' books all but monopolised the writing for screen market for so many years. Actually, and worse still, they all but monopolised how we were encouraged to understand and receive writing for the screen. It is only relatively recently that a wider and deeper consideration of the screenwriter and screenwriting has taken place.

Screenwriters and Screenwriting makes a wonderful contribution to the evolution of a field of practice and critical investigation. It is a book in the emerging tradition of talking about creative writing from the point of view of the actions of creative writers themselves, where creative and critical knowledge is applied to writerly situations and in that application ideas about writing are formed and reformed. We find in this book evidence that we have reached a point where the slugline can read INT. SCREENWRITERS AND SCREENWRITING and the scene is now truly about exactly that.

Graeme Harper

Contributors

Craig Batty is Creative Practice Research Leader in the School of Media and Communication at RMIT University, Australia. He is a writer and script consultant, and has worked on various short film, feature film, television and online projects. He is co-author of the books *Writing for the Screen: Creative and Critical Approaches* (2008), *Media Writing: A Practical Introduction* (2010) and *The Creative Screenwriter: Exercises to Expand Your Craft* (2012), and author of the books *Movies That Move Us: Screenwriting and the Power of the Protagonist's Journey* (2011) and *Screenplays: How to Write and Sell Them* (2012).

Peri Bradley is Lecturer in Media Theory at Bournemouth University, UK. She was part of the 1970s British Film project group at the University of Portsmouth and co-organiser of the 2008 international conference, British Culture and Society in the 1970s. She has chapters included in *Dark Reflections, Monstrous Reflections: Essays on the Monster in Culture*; *Don't Look Now? British Cinema in the 1970s*; *Culture and Society in 1970s Britain: The Lost Decade*; *LGBT Identity in Non-Western Worlds*; and *Queer Love in Film and Television*. She has also contributed a significant piece of research to *British Film Culture in the 1970s: The Boundaries of Pleasure*.

Elisabeth Lewis Corley has taught screenwriting at Emory University and the University of North Carolina at Chapel Hill, USA. Her screenplay *The Death of Innocents*, based on the Sister Helen Prejean book that followed *Dead Man Walking*, is currently in development. She wrote the screenplay for John David Allen's short film *Love and Roadkill*, which screened internationally. Her short film *About Time*, directed by Joseph Megel, has been screened at film festivals across the USA. She holds an MFA in poetry from the Warren Wilson Program for Writers and a BA with highest honours in poetry from UNC-CH. She is a member of the Dramatists Guild, Actors' Equity Association and SAG-AFTRA.

Graeme Harper is a Professor of Creative Writing and Dean of The Honors College at Oakland University, Michigan, USA. A writer of fiction and a scriptwriter, he is an honorary professor in the United Kingdom and was inaugural Chair of the Higher Education Committee at the UK's National Association of Writers in Education (NAWE). He is the editor of *The Companion to Creative Writing* (2013) and author of *Inside Creative Writing: Interviews with Contemporary Writers* (2012) and *On Creative Writing* (2010). Editor of *New Writing: The International Journal for the Practice and Theory of Creative Writing*, his latest book is *The Future for Creative Writing* (2014).

Kate Iles lectures in film and television production at both Roehampton University and Southampton Solent University, UK. Prior to teaching she ran an independent production company, Compulsive Viewing Ltd. There, she co-produced the Lloyds Bank Channel Four Film Challenge, the pioneering scheme showcasing the work of new writers and directors, which ran between 1995 and 2000, as well as producing single documentaries and documentary series, also for Channel Four. She has worked as a script consultant for various broadcasters, and the UK Film Council until its demise in 2010, and continues to produce independent drama and documentary projects.

Ann Ingelstrom is a PhD student at Bangor University, UK. She holds an MA from Umea University, Sweden, where she also attended a three-year practice-based screenwriting programme. Her research involves relating narrational theories from film and literature to the published screenplay text. The specific focus of her thesis is to examine how specific traits of the screenplay text-format serve narrational ends, and how a screenwriter communicates the potential film and its story to the reader.

Helen Jacey is a screenwriter and script consultant, and works as Senior Lecturer in Scriptwriting at Bournemouth University, UK. Her research interests include creative and critical approaches to screenwriting, the role of the screenwriter and screenplay in the film production process, screenwriting and gender, and screenwriting genre theory. As a professional writer, she has written numerous film, television and radio projects for UK, US and European production companies. She is a story consultant for international filmmakers and film agencies and author of *The Woman in the Story: Writing Memorable Female Characters* (2010).

Hester Joyce is Senior Lecturer in the Media Arts: Sound and Screen programme at La Trobe University, Australia, and has professional credits in acting, scriptwriting and consulting in theatre, film and television. Her research interests include national cinemas and indigenous cinema; scriptwriting theory, policy and practice; screenplay narrative, aesthetics and formal analysis; and creative project assessment. She has co-authored, with Trisha Dunleavy, the book *New Zealand Film & Television: Institution, Industry and Cultural Change* (2011), and contributed a chapter titled 'Making Nation: *Utu*' to *Making Film and Television Histories: Australia and New Zealand* (2012).

Shaun Kimber is Senior Lecturer at Bournemouth University, UK. His interests include horror cinema, film violence and film cultures. He has published a book, *Controversies: Henry: Portrait of a Serial Killer* (2011), and book chapters including an examination of the UK regulation of *The Passion of the Christ* and an analysis of UK media and film education using the lexicon of zombiedom. Forthcoming work includes an examination of *A Serbian Film* and transgression, and an investigation of film adaptations of the Henry Lee Lucas story. He is also co-editing *Snuff: Real Death and Screen Media,* and co-writing (with Craig Batty) *Writing & Selling Horror Screenplays.*

Susan Liddy lectures in the Department of Media and Communications at MIC, University of Limerick, Ireland. Her research interests include gender issues in the development process, and the representation of older women in screen narratives. She has produced a number of television documentaries for *Puddle Films.* Her feature-length script has received funding from the Irish Film Board and is currently in development with a Dublin-based production company. Forthcoming work includes an analysis of the representation of mature female sexuality in British and Irish film, and an exploration of recent work by Irish female screenwriters.

Alec McAulay teaches screenwriting at Yokohama National University and Gakushuin University, Tokyo, Japan. He holds an MA in screenwriting from Bournemouth University, where he is currently undertaking a practice-based PhD. His short films *The Errand* (2006) and *Three Days in Kamakura* (2012) have screened and won awards at various international film festivals. His feature production credits include *Starfish Hotel* (2006), *Backdancers!* (2006), *Sugar and Spice: Fumi Zekka* (2006) and *Tenshin* (2013). He consulted on J-Pitch, a Ministry of Trade and Industry project that advised Japan film projects on attracting international co-financing.

Joseph Megel has spent the last 25 years focusing on the direction and development of new works for theatre, film and video. He is currently a resident artist in Performance Studies at the University of North Carolina at Chapel Hill, USA, where he directs the Process Series: New Works in Development, and is Co-Artistic Director of the StreetSigns Center for Literature and Performance. He holds an MFA from the Peter Stark Motion Picture Producing Program at the University of Southern California, an MA from the University of Cincinnati's Conservatory of Music and a BS in Speech from Northwestern University, and is a member of SDC.

Margot Nash is Senior Lecturer in Communications at the University of Technology, Sydney, Australia, where she coordinates the postgraduate writing programme. She holds an MFA from COFA UNSW. Her areas of research include the theory and practice of screenwriting, developing subtext and Australian independent film history. Her films include the experimental shorts *We Aim To Please* (with Laurie, 1976) and *Shadow Panic* (1989), the documentary feature *For Love Or Money* (with McMurchy, Oliver and Thornley, 1982), and the feature dramas *Vacant Possession* (1994) and *Call Me Mum* (2005). In 2012 she was Filmmaker in Residence at Zürich University of the Arts.

Eva Novrup Redvall is Assistant Professor in the Department of Film and Media Studies at the University of Copenhagen, where, with Ib Bondebjerg, she is head of the Research Priority Area on Creative Media Industries. She holds a PhD in screenwriting as a creative process and has published a number of articles and chapters on Nordic film and television. She is also on the editorial board for the *Journal of Screenwriting*. Her latest book is *Writing and Producing Television Drama in Denmark: From* The Kingdom *to* The Killing (2013).

Díóg O'Connell is Lecturer in Film and Media Studies at the Dun Laoghaire Institute of Art, Design and Technology, Ireland. She is the author of *New Irish Storytellers: Narrative Strategies in Film* (2010) and co-editor of *Documentary in a Changing State: Ireland Since the 1990s* (2012).

Christopher Pullen is Senior Lecturer in Media Theory at Bournemouth University, UK. He is the author of *Documenting Gay Men: Identity and Performance in Reality Television and Documentary Film* (2007) and *Gay Identity, New Storytelling and the Media* (2012), editor of *LGBT Transnational*

Identity and the Media (2012) and co-editor of *LGBT Identity and Online New Media* (2010) and *Queer Love in Film and Television: Critical Essays* (2013).

Marilyn Tofler trained at UCLA's Graduate School of Film, Television and Theatre, and then RMIT University, Australia. She has worked as a script assessor in Australia for Village Roadshow, ABC Television (Comedy) and Film Victoria, and in the USA for Twentieth Century Fox and NBC Entertainment, where she helped to find new writers for shows such as *Seinfeld, Frasier, Mad About You* and *Friends*. She co-created and wrote the television comedy *Whatever Happened to That Guy?* and is currently developing the sitcom *Best Intentions*. Marilyn lectures in screenwriting at Swinburne University of Technology, Melbourne, and before this helped to set up the Master of Screenwriting course at the Victorian College of the Arts, University of Melbourne.

Paul Wells is Professor and Director of the Animation Academy, Loughborough University, UK, and has published widely in the field of animation, including *Understanding Animation, Re-Imagining Animation* and *The Animated Bestiary*. He is also an established writer and director in film, television, radio and theatre, and conducts workshops and consultancies worldwide based on his book *Scriptwriting*. He is Chair of the Association of British Animation Collections (ABAC).

Introduction

Craig Batty

We have experienced what we might call a 'screenwriting turn' in the last five or so years. By this I mean that in the fields of screen and cultural studies, we have begun to both understand and appreciate the role of the screenwriter much more than we have in the past. We are finally, and thankfully, moving beyond a director-centric critical appraisal of screen texts, and are beginning to truly acknowledge the importance played by creators, writers, showrunners, storyliners and script editors in the conception, development and execution of film and television drama. This is in part related to the work of the Screenwriting Research Network, whose annual conferences and *Journal of Screenwriting* have shed significant light on the world of screenwriting. It is also in part related to the fact that screenwriting has become a growth area across colleges, universities and film schools around the world, where not only are students demanding content relevant to them, but where those teaching are becoming increasingly interested in research, keen to understand screenwriting practice within an academic context.

Recent books helping to define the 'screenwriting turn' include *Me and You and Memento and Fargo: How Independent Screenplays Work* (Murphy, 2007), *Writing for the Screen: Creative and Critical Approaches* (Batty and Waldeback, 2008), *Screenwriting: History, Theory, and Practice* (Maras, 2009), *The Screenplay: Authorship, Theory and Criticism* (Price, 2010), *The Woman in the Story: Writing Memorable Female Characters* (Jacey, 2010), *Analysing the Screenplay* (Nelmes, 2010), *Movies That Move Us: Screenwriting and the Power of the Protagonist's Journey* (Batty, 2011), *The Psychology of Screenwriting: Theory and Practice* (Lee, 2013), *The Screenwriter in British Cinema* (Nelmes, 2013), *Screenwriting Poetics and the Screen Idea* (Macdonald, 2013), *Writing and Producing Television Drama in Denmark: From The Kingdom to The Killing* (Redvall, 2013), *A History of*

1

the Screenplay (Price, 2013) and *Screenwriting: Creative Labour and Professional Practice* (Conor, 2014). Along with articles found in, for example, the *Journal of Screenwriting*, the *Journal of Media Practice, New Writing: The International Journal for the Practice and Theory of Creative Writing*, the *Media Education Research Journal* and *TEXT: Journal of Writing and Writing Courses*, these works are quickly strengthening the presence of screenwriting in academia.

Hundreds more screenwriting books have been published throughout history, but they are almost exclusively 'how to' in nature. Screenwriting experts such as Syd Field, Linda Seger, Robert McKee, Christopher Vogler, Michael Hague and Linda Aronson have all written internationally successful guides to the practice of screenwriting, aimed predominantly at the emerging screenwriter market but also used frequently by more experienced writers and film and television development agencies. Even the BBC's former Controller of Drama Production and New Talent, John Yorke, has joined this group of authors with his book, *Into the Woods: A Five Act Journey into Story* (2013). Many of these guides have come under attack by academics, who view them as restrictive, content thin and serving capitalistic modes of screen production. Most of these guides also have a one-voice approach, where scholarship is limited and the tendency is for the author to advocate their own methods only.

Arguments against the guides undoubtedly carry weight, but as a screenwriting author as well as an academic myself, I find I am in an interesting predicament. On the one hand, I understand that critical texts generally serve a different purpose to professional or mainstream texts, and that it is the responsibility of the academic to create and disseminate new knowledge based on research and analysis. On the other hand, for a field whose central concern is practice – the screenwriter *writes*, and screenplays are *written for production* – I find it somewhat disappointing that many academics quickly write off anything intended to aid writing practice. It seems that anything aimed at helping screenwriters with their screenplays is beneath academic value. This is particularly problematic at a time when we talk a lot about practice-based or practice-led research, where the aim is, or should be, not to *theorise* practice per se, but to *interrogate* and *intellectualise* practice in order to generate new knowledge *and* new ways to practice.

As Harper notes in relation to creative writing, practice-based research should create its own 'site of knowledge' that has its concerns in process and practice, not 'post event' speculation (2006: 3). Furthermore, such research should be concerned with linking the individual (i.e. the understanding and approach of the individual writer) with the holistic (i.e. understanding of genre, form, convention, the market, the audience). There are similarities here between the post-event analysis of literature, film, theatre and other art forms, but the difference is plain enough: the critical understanding employed is used to assist the creative writer in the construction of a work at hand, and/or of their future work.

(Harper, 2007: 19)

This is where I see tensions arising between 'how to' books and what we might call 'screenwriting studies'.[1] The word 'studies' might be seen to speak solely to an academic audience, just as 'a guide to' apparently speaks solely to a commercial audience. As Brien and Williamson argue, 'many [concerns] are magnified when dealing with newer academic discipline areas such as the creative arts [...where] emergent research practice seeks to legitimise alternative forms of knowledge production that do not always sit comfortably alongside accepted norms of research' (2009: 1–3). This is exactly what I see happening in screenwriting: a clash between not only what is and what is not research but also what is accepted and what is rejected by screenwriting academics.

Obviously it comes down to an individual's position and what they want to achieve with their work. If, for example, an academic wants to be respected in the field of film and television studies for advancing theoretical knowledge about the practice of screenwriting, then this is one thing. If, on the other hand, an academic wants to speak to a wider audience, and wants his or her work to have an impact within the community of practice (screenwriters, script developers, script editors, etc.), then this is something quite different. In the end, it comes down to being honest about what one is trying to achieve, and for there to be mutual respect. Unfortunately, I have witnessed much snobbery towards academics who want their work to speak primarily to communities of practice.

In my view, it might be useful to reconfigure what we mean by screenwriting studies, to set it apart from film, television or cultural studies, for example. Screenwriting studies might be better thought of as being concerned with the act of writing and with the creative processes undertaken by the screenwriter. Screenwriting is an activity, not an end product, and so arguably it is more productive and more authentic to talk not just *about* practice, but also *for* practice. New knowledge should be generated alongside new methods of practice, where we do not merely *understand* a topic, but can offer *practical insights* to act on the topic. There still exists in academia a dilemma around these issues, but with every dilemma comes an opportunity. Therefore, it is the intention of this book to respond to such a dilemma.

It was at the 2011 Screenwriting Research Network conference in Brussels when the idea for this edited collection came about. The distinction between theory and practice was stark, and although, as in many other disciplines, there had been much talk about practice, and an encouragement to integrate theory with practice, I was left feeling that many of the presentations did not fit comfortably in what could be an exciting and innovative discipline. I was drawn most to papers that promised to be about practice and, as stated above, was also in anticipation that they would be *for* practice. As has been my experience of many conferences over the last decade, papers that leant more towards this attracted very few questions and, in some cases, criticism for not being sufficiently academic. On the contrary, academic papers, whilst well developed and interesting, left me feeling underwhelmed and, in some cases, inadequate. I sat with this feeling for a few days before deciding to do something about it.

This resulting book, then, seeks to address a lack of material in screenwriting studies that is not just about practice, but that is for practice. A collection of 16 chapters and 17 authors, it aims to provide practical insights into screenwriting practice as well as intellectual discussions of it. The word 'context' was deliberate in the title, suggesting that the essays are not trying to theorise screenwriting, but are attempting to situate screenwriting practice in relevant frameworks. Whether these contexts are related to process, industry, critical reception, or otherwise, the point is that each chapter is about understanding an aspect of practice through an intellectual lens. This is similar to the approach offered by Jason Lee in his recent book, *The Psychology of Screenwriting: Theory and Practice*, where 'screenwriting studies is combined [...] with more general writing studies, philosophy, film and literary studies, enhancing reflective creative thinking and practice' (2013: 2). This book is also about reflective creative thinking and practice, and by putting practice into a variety of relevant contexts, the chapters combine to create a collection that will be valued by both academics and practitioners.

There are three parts to this book: 'Screenwriters and their Screenplays', 'Screenwriting and the Development Process' and 'Screenwriting and Authorship'. As well as this structure mirroring aspects of a screenplay's journey – writing, development and reception – the structure was also dictated by the excellent topics proposed by the contributors. I initially thought it would be difficult to pull together a collection like this, but it was fortuitous that the chapters offered made the task a relatively easy one.

The first part of the book is concerned with the specific act of writing for the screen, and brings together chapters that explore practices of telling a story that will move from the page to the screen. In their chapter on screenwriting and poetry, Elisabeth Lewis Corley and Joseph Megel argue that much can be felt and understood about a story by the way it is presented on the page, in terms of both language and layout. Ann Ingelstrom's chapter dovetails neatly with this, wherein she examines the narrational voices at play in the screenplay. By exploring the specifics of language and point of view, she provides some exciting new insights into screenwriting practice. In his chapter about the relationship between theory and practice, Shaun Kimber uses the horror genre as a lens through which to argue that writers can benefit greatly from understanding their work in broader cultural and industrial contexts. His excellent study results in some very practical outcomes that can be employed by the screenwriter. This is followed by a chapter by Hester Joyce on New Zealand filmmaker Gaylene Preston. It focuses specifically on screenplays that are about real events and real people, suggesting that creative interpretations of history inevitably come into play, especially when the history being written is one's own. My own chapter concludes this part of the book, and examines how the physicality of costume can be seen to represent the character arc. By offering a case study of the film *Connie and Carla* (2004) through the lens of the Hero's Journey, it suggests ways in which screenwriters can usefully visualise emotional transformation.

The second part of the book presents a range of chapters concerned with aspects of script development, wherein the screenwriter negotiates both their own process and those imposed by others. Margot Nash's chapter examines 'the unknown', arguing that writers and directors should be allowed to undertake an exploratory approach to development where the imagination can roam free and dramatic 'gold' might be found. In her chapter on the Irish Film Board, Díóg O'Connell highlights some of the important changes in script development policy that have benefited both the craft and the careers of local screenwriters. This is followed neatly by Susan Liddy's study of Irish screenwriters who have had their first feature films produced. With insightful and entertaining interview material, her chapter illuminates both the challenges and the rewards experienced by new writers. Paul Wells then goes on to discuss the under-examined area of script editing, and in particular the role of the script editor in animation. By reflecting on both research and his own experiences in the industry, he provides rich material that adds to our knowledge in this area. This part of the book is concluded by a fascinating chapter by Peri Bradley, who compares recent scripted-reality television shows with the work of Mike Leigh, suggesting that there is much to be learned from improvisation in the context of 'social realist' texts.

The third and final part of the book asks questions about screenwriting and authorship, and whether there are practical ways for writers to influence how their screenplays and eventual produced screen texts are experienced. Alec McAulay's chapter explores notions of authorship as experienced through the script development process. Drawing on his own struggles of writing a short film for a director, he offers some fascinating insights into the perils of collaboration. In her chapter on British screenwriter Sarah Phelps, Kate Iles draws on rich interview material to provide an extensive account of the authorial intentions of the successful television writer. This is followed by Eva Novrup Redvall's discussion of writers' rooms, in particular the writers' room for Danish television series *Borgen* (2010–). Based on her ethnographic study, she is able to write convincingly about collaboration and authorship in what has traditionally been regarded a factory-like, mass-produced form.

Helen Jacey goes on to discuss screenwriting and gender, and in particular, representations of men in the bromance and bromedy genres. Drawing on both theoretical and practical material, she argues that the screenwriter has a duty to play in the formation of cultural discourse, one that is bound up with notions of authorial intent. Marilyn Tofler's chapter also discusses screenwriting and gender, and uses Nancy Meyers' screenplay *Something's Gotta Give* (2003) to examine how a writer might construct the satirical female voice. She offers practical tools for the screenwriter who is interested in writing strong female protagonists. The book concludes with a chapter by Christopher Pullen, who uses the writing of Tennessee Williams and Gore Vidal, and Joe Orton and Clive Exton, to explore how contentious representations of homosexuals have been offered in the mainstream cultural domain. His detailed study offers potential for writers to indirectly reference the self in their screenplays, embracing notions of authorship to challenge dominant ideologies.

Overall, this book seeks to be innovative, fresh, lively and, most importantly, useful for screenwriting practice as well as academic debate. It is a distinctive collection of chapters from creative-critical academics who are passionate about screenwriting. With its focus on what screenwriters do and how they do it, the book aims to be thought provoking, stimulating and an enabler of creative and professional practice.

Note

1. In relation to this, Palgrave Macmillan now has a book series called Studies in Screenwriting, developed by members of the Screenwriting Research Network and launched in 2013.

References

Batty, C. (2011) *Movies That Move Us: Screenwriting and the Power of the Protagonist's Journey*, Basingstoke: Palgrave Macmillan.

Batty, C. and Waldeback, Z. (2008) *Writing for the Screen: Creative and Critical Approaches*, Basingstoke: Palgrave Macmillan.

Borgen (2010–) Cr. Adam Price, Wrs. Various, Dirs. Various, Denmark.

Brien, D.L. and Williamson, R. (2009) 'Supervising the Creative Arts Research Higher Degree: Towards Best Practice' in *TEXT: Journal of Writing and Writing Courses*, (special issue 6), available at http://www.textjournal.com.au/back.htm [retrieved 19 August 2011].

Connie and Carla (2004) Wr. Nia Vardalos, Dir. Michael Lembeck, USA, 98 mins.

Conor, B. (2014) *Screenwriting: Creative Labour and Professional Practice*, Abingdon: Routledge.

Harper, G. (2006) 'Introduction' in Graeme Harper (ed.) *Teaching Creative Writing*, London: Continuum, pp. 1–7.

Harper, G. (2007) 'Creative Writing Research Today' in *Writing in Education*, (43), 64–66.

Jacey, H. (2010) *The Woman in the Story: Writing Memorable Female Characters*, Studio City, CA: Michael Wiese Productions.

Lee, J. (2013) *The Psychology of Screenwriting: Theory and Practice*, London: Bloomsbury.

Macdonald, I.M. (2013) *Screenwriting Poetics and the Screen Idea*, Basingstoke: Palgrave Macmillan.

Maras, S. (2009) *Screenwriting: History, Theory, and Practice*, London: Wallflower Press.

Murphy, J.J. (2007) *Me and You and Memento and Fargo: How Independent Screenplays Work*, New York: Continuum.

Nelmes. (2013) *The Screenwriter in British Cinema*, Basingstoke: Palgrave Macmillan.

Nelmes, J. (ed.) (2010) *Analysing the Screenplay*, Abingdon: Routledge.

Price, S. (2010) *The Screenplay: Authorship, Theory and Criticism*, Basingstoke: Palgrave Macmillan.

Price, S. (2013) *A History of the Screenplay*, Basingstoke: Palgrave Macmillan.

Redvall, E.N. (2013) *Writing and Producing Television Drama in Denmark: From The Kingdom to The Killing*, Basingstoke: Palgrave Macmillan.

Something's Gotta Give (2003) Wr./Dir. Nancy Myers, USA, 128 mins.

Part I

Screenwriters and Their Screenplays

1
White Space: An Approach to the Practice of Screenwriting as Poetry

Elisabeth Lewis Corley and Joseph Megel

Introduction

Despite contrary and eminently reasonable claims of many prominent experts in the field of screenwriting, such as Syd Field, we side with those who take the position that screenwriting can be an art form in and of itself; and we argue that, if the writing is approached and practised as an art, immeasurable benefits accrue. This is not to say that the writing of the screenplay is an end in itself, but that the approach to the writing can have wide-ranging influence on the quality of a finished film.

One of the most powerful tools at the disposal of the screenwriter, we argue, is one seldom employed to the fullest in the haste to create formulaic screenplays that appeal to a wide audience: the careful contemplation of the implications of script format and the language used to create visual description. As with the formal requirements of poetic forms, from the sonnet to the sestina, the strictures of form and precision of language can have liberating effects and profound implications. Like most who have instructed beginning writers, we believe technical language that pulls the reader's attention out of the story can largely be avoided by sophisticated use of the formatting norms already in place.

The aim of this chapter, then, is to discuss the potential of screenplay format and, very briefly, the language of its visual description to contribute to the creation of screenplays that are not simply read, but, as with poetry, are received on many levels. The ultimate goal of our focus on the format and language of the screenplay is to liberate the screenwriter to create something as polished and resonant as a well-crafted poem and in so doing to increase the presence of poetry in filmmaking.

The 'spec' screenplay as art

We are accustomed to hearing films described as cinematic poetry. For example, virtually everything written about Terrence Malick resorts to poetic equivalences at some point. A.O. Scott's review of Malick's *To the Wonder* (2013) in the *New York Times* asserts that the film 'spins visual poetry not only out of prairies and creek beds but also out of less obviously sublime facts of the landscape'. Hearing films described as poetry is commonplace, but few expect poetry of the screenplay or regard the choices of the screenwriter as meaningful in the way we assume that the choices of poets are.

Most of the focus of our work has been on one form of writing for the screen: the creation of a 'spec' screenplay for a narrative, full-length feature film. The spec script, one written speculatively by a writer who chooses to do so other than at the behest of a studio or producer as a work for hire, is a distinct form of screenwriting and one perhaps most likely to be a starting point for those who have no meaningful connection with the industry. David Trottier's *Dr. Format Answers Your Questions* offers clear distinctions between the norms of spec screenplay writing and the shooting script (2002: 67–69), primary among them the necessity to tell the story clearly, movingly, and to eschew anything that takes the reader out of the story. We do not need to hear about dolly moves if we can create a rhythm on the page that makes the film unspool in the mind of the reader as it does in the mind of the screenwriter. If it is difficult to find prominent examples of the kind of work for which we are advocating, it may be because so few spec screenplays are made into films; or, possibly, because most of the screenplays that are widely available are shooting scripts (Trottier, 2002: 18). Trottier also reminds us that industry norms change, albeit slowly, and formatting norms change (2002: 67–68). Change may accelerate as the means of making films move closer to the hands of the originating filmmakers. The 2012 independent film *King Kelly*, for example, was shot almost entirely on cellphone cameras (Holden, 2012).

In *The Screenwriter's Workbook*, Syd Field recalls his mentor, the legendary filmmaker Jean Renoir, as having claimed that screenwriting cannot be considered an art because a film is not the work of one person. According to Field, Renoir said, 'Art should offer the viewer the chance of merging with the creator' (2006: 1–2). It is well beyond the scope of this chapter to take on the question of what constitutes art, but the notion that, to qualify as art, a work must be in some way tied to an individual's private effort merged with a public audience seems difficult to defend. Whilst many have spoken to the issue of process and the importance of process, no one has supported the view that art can be traced to any one process in particular. As poet and theorist of poesy Samuel Taylor Coleridge writes,

> In every work of art there is reconcilement of the external with the internal; the conscious is so impressed on the unconscious as to appear in it; as compare mere letters inscribed on a tomb with figures themselves constituting the tomb. He who combines the two is the man of genius and for that reason he must partake of both. Hence there is in genius itself an unconscious activity; nay, that is the genius in the man of genius. And this is the true exposition of the rule that the artist must first eloign himself from nature in order to return to her with full effect. Why this? Because if he were to begin by mere painful copying, he would produce masks only, not forms breathing life.
>
> (cited in Krasny, 2004: 38)

It is those 'forms breathing life' to which we rightly aspire, and too often what results from a formulaic process is more like masks. Coleridge is also speaking of the role of the unconscious in getting to a place where the writing feels alive. No one argues that the unconscious can be summoned but we do argue that there are ways, long established in the writing of poetry, that make its entry and influence more generative.

As Wallace Stevens writes in his essay, 'The Irrational Element in Poetry',

> what I have in mind when I speak of the irrational element in poetry is the transaction between reality and the sensibility of the poet from which poetry springs [...] What interests us is a particular process in the rational mind which we recognize as irrational in the sense that it takes place unaccountably.
>
> (1957: 216–218)

What we are looking for in seeking more attention to the language of visual description in screenplays, and more conscious, less mechanical, use of format in screenwriting, is a benefit to the end product of the screenplay: the film itself. We freely acknowledge that, whatever this benefit may be, the means of its arrival are unaccountable.

Throughout their book *Writing for the Screen: Creative and Critical Approaches* (2008), Craig Batty and Zara Waldeback refer to 'the art of screenwriting'. We agree that screenwriting can be, is, and should always be, at least in aspiration, an art. Even if Renoir is right and individual creation is crucial, the time spent creating the screenplay is, after all, often the work of one person (even if that person is working with collaborators), and that person has an opportunity to raise the work to the level of art through careful use of language and a profound understanding of the form and the format. Given the requirements of the film industry, the writing process, especially of the spec screenplay, may be the only time that this kind of quiet attention is focused on the project. The result has to be strong enough to survive the armies of people who will shape the project once it leaves the screenwriter's hands.

A screenplay, then, should be not merely a set of technical notations for 'a story told in pictures' – Syd Field's oft-repeated definition (2006: 3) – but a legitimate work of art in itself. Story structure and format, the rules of screenwriting, are for some restraints that are paradoxically liberating, and for others a source of anxiety. William Wordsworth's *Nuns Fret Not at their Convent's Narrow Room* is instructive here.

> Nuns fret not at their convent's narrow room;
> And hermits are contented with their cells;
> And students with their pensive citadels;
> Maids at the wheel, the weaver at his loom,
> Sit blithe and happy; bees that soar for bloom,
> High as the highest Peak of Furness-fells,
> Will murmur by the hour in foxglove bells:
> In truth the prison, unto which we doom
> Ourselves, no prison is: and hence for me,
> In sundry moods, 'twas pastime to be bound
> Within the Sonnet's scanty plot of ground;
> Pleased if some Souls (for such there needs must be)
> Who have felt the weight of too much liberty,
> Should find brief solace there, as I have found.

> (cited in Perkins, 1967: 290)

The point of this is that whilst the screenplay does come with some clear rules and guidelines, those restrictions can be as liberating as the sonnet form proved for poets like Wordsworth, Keats, Shakespeare and countless others who created opportunities for the arrival of the unaccountable.

What format does

Format is more than rules; but there are some simple rules that seem to be universally accepted in most screenwriting circles. Batty and Waldeback give a wonderfully concise overview of some of these (2008: 5–6), and Christopher Riley's *The Hollywood Standard: The Complete and Authoritative Guide to Script Format and Style* (2009) and David Trottier's *Dr. Format Answers Your Questions* (2002) delve into them in meticulous detail. What we would like to address here are the implications of some of these requirements and to suggest ways of using them to assist the screenwriter in visualising the finished film more clearly, and also to propose that there may be attendant benefits on such precision and care.

Batty and Waldeback stress the importance of correct formatting for purposes of professional appearance and for the accuracy of predictions of screen time, since the general rule of thumb is that one page of a printed screenplay translates to one minute of screen time (2008: 5). There are other reasons why the formatting might be worthy of close attention.

Scene headings

Everyone agrees that each new scene begins with a scene heading, although there are disagreements about what constitutes a new scene or what kinds of subheading might legitimately appear under a single master shot scene heading. The scene heading begins with an abbreviation for either interior (INT.) or exterior (EXT.), followed by the location (BEDROOM), which should remain exactly the same each time the same location is used, and then time of day (DAY). When it is crucial, the quality of the light can be suggested (DUSK) in place of the third element, instead of DAY or NIGHT. This technical language is understood as essential for planning purposes as a screenplay goes into production. Scheduling and budgeting programs designed to search for these cues, such as Movie Magic and Gorilla, help prepare for the compressed period of principal photography when the goal is to put together on the same day or night as many scenes in the same location as are feasible to shoot in the time allowed. It seems obvious that a new scene heading would be required with every change in location or time, including whenever time is not absolutely continuous. This concept is easy enough to grasp but is surprisingly often forgotten or misunderstood.

There are great advantages to rigorous observance of this rule, not just in preparing films for production but in helping the reader of a screenplay subconsciously receive information about the rhythm of the story. For example, at the moment of maximum disintegration near the end of Alan Ball's screenplay *American Beauty* (1999), when time is whirling for the protagonist, the very text on the page seems fractured and fragmented as well, and the reader receives a distinct sense of jaggedness in time simply by *looking* at the page and observing the proliferation of scene headings.

EXT. WOODS — NIGHT

In BLACK & WHITE: Eleven-year-old Lester looks up, pointing excitedly at:

His POV: A DOT OF LIGHT falls across an unbelievably starry sky.

> LESTER (V.O.)
> For me, it was lying on my back at Boy
> Scout camp, watching falling stars...

INT. BURNHAM HOUSE — JANE'S BEDROOM — NIGHT

Ricky and Jane lie curled up on Jane's bed, fully clothed. We HEAR a GUNSHOT from downstairs. They look at each other, alarmed.

EXT. SUBURBAN STREET - DUSK

In BLACK & WHITE: Maples trees in autumn. Ghostly LEAVES FLUTTER slowly toward pavement.

> LESTER (V.O.)
> And yellow leaves, from the maple
> trees, that lined my street...

INT. BURNHAM HOUSE — POWDER ROOM — NIGHT

Angela stands in front of the mirror, fixing her make-up. We HEAR the GUNSHOT again. Angela turns, frightened.

INT. SUBURBAN HOUSE — DAY

In BLACK & WHITE: CLOSE on an ancient woman's paper HANDS as they button a cardigan sweater.

> LESTER (V.O.)
> Or my grandmother's hands, and the way
> her skin seemed like paper...

EXT. BURNHAM HOUSE — NIGHT

Carolyn walks slowly toward the RED DOOR, drenched to the bone, clutching her PURSE tightly. We HEAR the GUNSHOT again.

EXT. SUBURB — DAY

In BLACK & WHITE: A 1970 PONTIAC FIREBIRD in the driveway of a suburban home. The SUN'S REFLECTION in the windshield FLASHES BRILLIANTLY.

(Ball, 1999: 98)

When looking at this page, before one has read a word of it, there is a dizzying sensation that closely approximates the feeling engendered in the viewer at that moment in the film (1999). On this one page there are seven new scene headings, which equates to a change of scene roughly every eight and a half seconds. For the screenwriter, whose job it is to visualise as a film an emerging story on the page, the parallel between the jaggedness on the page and the quick rhythm of cutting in the film has the advantage of increasing the likelihood of the film coming to life in the mind of the reader in a way that closely resembles its life in the mind of the screenwriter.

In film, the story can go where it needs to go. The screenwriter can skip steps, move from one side of the planet to the other in a blink, or jump around in time. Skilful use of the scene heading can keep the reader in the story and keep the reader visualising the same story the writer is creating. Scene headings one after another speed up the rhythm of the sequence, along with one-line visual descriptions. The finished film will have its own rigorous visual logic. So, too, must the screenplay. The screenwriter conceiving the film, meticulously charting its progression scene by scene, helps to ensure that it does by careful attention to the visual elements of the page.

Ball has chosen to underline his scene headings, which is non-standard; and even though it does, perhaps, support the visual jaggedness of the page in this instance, there is no reason to think it would be valuable to depart from the norm in this way. If a writer wishes to mine derivative benefits from elements of form, it is important to observe norms so that departures from those norms have weight. James Longenbach, in *The Art of the Poetic Line*, underscores the power of these departures: 'As in all accomplished poetry, there is a tension [...] between pattern and variation [... We] feel this tension as pleasure' (2008: 6). We do, that is, if it is meaningfully and not arbitrarily employed.

Capitalisation

Like many screenwriters, Ball has his own style of employing capital-isation. Some uses are standard; some standards are changing. It was once customary, and not terribly distracting for the reader, to capitalise sounds. This served to alert the editor and sound editor that a sound effect might be needed. For example:

```
INT. BURNHAM HOUSE — JANE'S BEDROOM — NIGHT

Ricky and Jane lie curled up on Jane's bed, fully clothed.
We HEAR a GUNSHOT from downstairs. They look at each other,
alarmed.
```

(Ball, 1999: 98)

Here, Ball has chosen to capitalise both the verb, 'hear', and the sound, 'gunshot'. He does this consistently throughout the screenplay. It makes sense to capitalise 'gunshot' both as a sound effect and for intensity of sound, but as new norms for the spec screenplay develop, the uses of capitalisation change. According to Trottier, it is no longer necessary to capitalise for sound (2002: 67–68) and this seems to be in accord with the general trend towards less technical intrusion and more focus on the story and the readability of the screenplay. Riley, in his 'com-plete and authoritative guide', still calls for them (2009: 31–32) although for Trottier this might be a difference between shooting script and spec script formats (2002: 67–68). One thing to consider before eliminating them completely is the effect they have on the reader. If they are not turned into white noise by excessive use, then they do function to dis-tinguish a description of sound from what is otherwise primarily visual description.

Many screenwriters capitalise action verbs and other action-laden words in action scenes, as Quentin Tarantino does in *Kill Bill*:

```
INT. HOUSEWIFE'S NICE HOME — DAY

The white woman and the black woman FLY into the center of the
living room, CRASHING onto her coffee table in front of
the sofa.

These two wildcats go at each other savagely, TUMBLING OVER the
couch, clawing and scratching all the way, landing together on
the plush carpet.

The HOUSEWIFE KICKS The Bride, sending her CRASHING backwards
into the small table where the phone, a note pad (for
messages), and the mail is kept.
```

Given that there are already several things that the capitalisation of text is intended to signal in the screenplay, and that these are norms most screenwriters observe, it seems problematical to add others as Tarantino does here, capitalising both action verbs and the names of the characters at every mention. However, what all of these capitalisations seem to do in a Tarantino screenplay is give the kind of comic book pop and explosiveness he may be intending to create. Whatever the intent, the effect for the reader is of someone shouting or illustrating the text in brightly-coloured thought balloons. *Kill Bill* the film is not without its mix of camp and highly stylised violence. As Wallace Stevens writes, 'A change of style is a change of subject' (1957: 171). Everything matters, and whether subtle and unconscious or a Tarantinoesque bold stroke, the impact of both language and format should not be underestimated.

The primary uses of capitalised text in screenplays are for scene headings, character names above dialogue, sound effects, character names the first time a character is seen and sluglines. All of this is covered in detail in numerous books about screenplay format, including those previously mentioned, but we will take a brief look at how these things function in a couple of instances, first returning to *American Beauty*.

INT. BURNHAM HOUSE — MASTER BEDROOM — CONTINUOUS

We're looking down at a king-sized BED from OVERHEAD:

LESTER BURNHAM lies sleeping amidst expensive bed linens, face down, wearing PAJAMAS. An irritating ALARM CLOCK RINGS. Lester gropes blindly to shut it off.

(Ball, 1999: 1)

Here we see that capitals are used for the name 'Lester Burnham', the protagonist. Hereafter when his name is mentioned, other than above his dialogue, his name will not be capitalised. This, too, is a rule with reason. Capital letters are used to alert the casting director that an actor will be needed, and once the actor has been found, the role does not need to be cast again. The capitalisation of Lester's name is a signal to the casting director, and the capitalisation of the ringing alarm clock is a signal to the sound department or subsequently to the sound editor or Foley artist. If the argument is that these elements are more appropriate to the shooting screenplay than the spec screenplay, and that the purpose of the spec screenplay is to persuade someone to make a film, thus demanding of the spec screenplay that it be easy to read and engaging; then some might argue the time had come to stop the capitalisation of the names of characters at their first introduction in the same way that some argue for an end to capitalisation for sound. However, we should consider their usefulness for the reader of the screenplay who can, by capitalisation, be alerted to the fact that the reader is meeting a character for the first time. If the screenplay were carefully written with consistent use of format, the reader would be assisted by the subliminal information and not pulled out of the story.

It certainly seems potentially distracting to capitalise the bed and the pajamas, but this seems to be Ball's style. He capitalises nouns as frequently as Tarantino capitalises verbs. Focusing on nouns in an imagistic screenplay like *American Beauty* can be understood to be a cue to the way the film works visually. Focusing on verbs in a stylised action film like *Kill Bill* sends a very different, and stylistically appropriate, signal. We feel in general that when it is used for too many different things, capitalisation can become white noise. However, it is instructive to study its effects in the clearly interesting, functional and quite different choices of Ball and Tarantino.

The slugline

The term 'slugline' is often used interchangeably with the term 'scene heading' (Batty and Waldeback, 2008: 5), and some use the term 'master shot' to mean the same thing; others make a distinction. It can be useful to distinguish between scene headings that describe master shots and lines, often short lines, fully capitalised, which are meant to emphasise action or camera movement within a scene to focus attention on the most important or highly dramatic moments or images. We use the term 'slugline' for such lines. A slugline can be as brief as a couple of words of a sentence that continues on the line below, after a space, highlighting a single image or action. The use of such sluglines can simplify capitalisation in the screenplay and thereby streamline the reader's receiving of the story, making the use of technical jargon unnecessary.

Since we are always working to make the experience of reading the screenplay on the page mimic the experience of watching the actual film, it is important to match the rhythm on the page with the rhythm of the film we are trying to write. This can be greatly aided by skilful use of white space in action or visual description roughly every time there would be a cut or a camera move. We simply mean dropping down a space typographically, leaving white space on the page. As Longenbach puts it, 'The drama of lineation lies in the simultaneous making and breaking of our expectation for pattern' (2008: 70). If the pattern is to give white space when the camera moves, then if we use sluglines for moments of high tension or unexpected action, we match the drama on the page with the anticipated drama on the screen.

In his 1997 screenplay *The Sixth Sense*, M. Night Shyamalan's control of suspense is masterful and it may seem absurd to anatomise his stylistic choices. There are, however, opportunities here for comparison of different effects.

```
INT. HALL — NIGHT

Cole enters the DARK HALLWAY. He gets startled by the SOUND OF
HIS PUPPY GROWLING.

Sebastian comes racing down the hall and scurries past Cole.
Cole watches his puppy dart into the living room and under a
couch.

Cole slowly turns back and looks down the hall.

THE DOOR TO COLE'S ROOM SITS AT THE END OF THE CORRIDOR. IT'S
ALMOST SHUT. COLE WATCHES AS THE DOOR BEGINS TO OPEN VERY
SLOWLY. IT OPENS WIDE. COLE DOESN'T MOVE AN INCH.

SUDDENLY IN THE STILLNESS AND THE DARKNESS, A SMALL FIGURE
SCURRIES FROM ANOTHER BEDROOM INTO THE BLACKNESS OF COLE'S ROOM.
IT HAPPENS LIKE A FLASH.

Cole stops breathing.

THE FIGURE SLOWLY STEPS OUT FROM COLE'S DOORWAY.

IT'S A BOY. A FEW YEARS OLDER THAN COLE.

THE BOY WHISPERS IN A LOW HOARSE VOICE.

                         BOY
              Come on...I'll show you where my
              dad keeps his gun...Come on.

THE BOY TURNS. WE SEE THAT THE BACK OF HIS HEAD IS MISSING AS
HE DISAPPEARS INTO THE DARKNESS OF COLE'S ROOM.

Cole is too terrified to move.

                                              CUT TO:
                                    (Shyamalan, 1997: 81—82)
```

This is typed in Courier here for consistency, since formatting norms demand this font, partly by tradition as it looks like the old typewriter font, and because one page of the screenplay equating to one minute of screen time would not be as consistent if different fonts were used. Shyamalan appears to have used Times New Roman, and he has also indented his dialogue much more than standard indentations.

Everything is single-spaced, with one space left between elements, for example, between the end of dialogue and the beginning of action or visual description, as in normal script format; but he inserts transitions like 'CUT TO:' between every scene. In contemporary spec screenplay format, right-justified transitional elements are infrequently used, and never for normal transitions between scenes where a cut is assumed: 'Occasionally scene transitions are stated at the end of a scene, such as "fade to" and "dissolve to". The general advice here is that unless the transition has to be specific, then nothing needs to be said; a cut is implied with the start of a new scene' (Batty and Waldeback, 2008: 5). We only feel the need to call attention to the transition if it is a special kind of transition, or a great leap in space or time; something used sparingly so that its use, when it occurs, is effective.

Here is the same passage from Shyamalan's *The Sixth Sense* with the moments of swiftest action rendered in sluglines rather than larger blocks of text in full capitals:

```
INT. HALL — NIGHT

Cole enters the dark hallway. His puppy GROWLS.

Sebastian comes racing down the hall and scurries past Cole.
Cole watches his puppy dart into the living room and under
a couch.

Cole slowly turns back and looks down the hall.

The door to Cole's room sits at the end of the corridor.
It's almost shut.

THE DOOR

begins to open very slowly.

IT OPENS WIDE.

Cole doesn't move an inch. Suddenly in the stillness and the
darkness,

A SMALL FIGURE SCURRIES FROM ANOTHER BEDROOM

into the blackness of Cole's room.

Cole stops breathing.

THE FIGURE

slowly steps out from Cole's doorway.

IT'S A BOY
```

```
a few years older than Cole.

The boy whispers in a low hoarse voice.

                        BOY
            Come on...I'll show you where my
            dad keeps his gun...Come on.

The boy turns.

THE BACK OF HIS HEAD IS MISSING

as he disappears into the darkness of Cole's room.

Cole is too terrified to move.
```

Reading only the fully capitalised words, the reader can follow the main action of the scene and the moments of greatest tension have their own tension suspended on the line surrounded by white space. This use of the slugline may not match precisely the expected uses of fully capitalised lines as they are defined for scene headings or sub-scene headings, nor is it exactly used as an indicator of camera movement in the sense that Riley describes it (2009: 30). However, what this use of the slugline does suggest is that screenwriters can exploit screenplay format in new ways, as long as that new convention gestures to the historical norm and as long as it has a function that is not achievable in the same way using other means. The old saying, 'You have to know the rules in order to break them,' might be better said, 'Break the rules with a loving appreciation for the structure that allows you to diverge from them.'[1]

Since we know that technical cues risk pulling the reader out of the story, and that the art of the screenplay is to keep the reader in the story, we know we should not describe camera angles or movements. The reader should follow the story, and to further that goal screenwriters need to ensure that the reader is anchored visually at all times. In action scenes, where the picture will change almost constantly, lines of action or visual description could become concomitantly more fragmented with the use of sluglines as we have described them.

A slugline used in this way can be also be helpful for focusing on something small, something a viewer might otherwise miss; the way an 'INSERT' might be used, or a moment focused on a character's face, or a sudden action. For example, in order to slow down a scene sufficiently for a viewer to read a sign, the screenplay might usefully render it as a slugline, thus avoiding the distancing 'INSERT' with its following 'BACK TO SCENE'. If the audience needs to read something on the screen, it has to be there a little longer, and so putting this information on a line of its own with some white space to establish additional 'hang' time can be effective. Sluglines draw attention to critical images and suggest that we might be seeing them in close up or extreme close up, thus conveying a suggestion subliminally with no distracting jargon to take us out of the story. As indicated earlier, the slugline does not have to be a complete sentence; the sentence can continue normally after the element the screenwriter wishes to emphasise has been established.

Pace

Screenwriting experts are unequivocal about their preference for economy and speed. For Trottier, 'Paragraphs of narrative description should not exceed four lines' (2002: 104), and for Riley, 'Settings must be described in a handful of vivid words. Characters must be introduced in a single pithy sentence. Actions must be painted with extreme economy of language' (2009: 32). But what about films that want to move slowly? Wes Anderson has his own inimitable style, both in writing screenplays and in filmmaking. For example, let us consider this typical passage from his screenplay *Moonrise Kingdom*:

EXT. SCOUT CAMP. NIGHT

Scout Master Ward zips up his tent and turns off the light.
Crickets chirp. Bats circle. The wire-haired terrier digs
carefully through a pile of trash.

EXT. NARROW STREAM. DAY

The next morning. A fast current runs along a shallow ravine
deep in the forest. The boy from the snap-shot rows a
mini-canoe painted with Native American tribal symbols and
severely over-loaded with boxes, bags, and blankets. He wears a
pellet gun slung on a strap over his shoulder and his coon-skin
cap. He smokes a pipe. A sash across his chest is decorated
with numerous small, embroidered patches. There is a woman's
enameled brooch pinned to his shirt. It is a jeweled, black
scorpion. He whistles to himself quietly as he steers under a
fallen tree-trunk and winds through gentle rapids. He is Sam.

EXT. RIVER BANK. DAY

An eddy under a willow tree. The end of the canoe is tied to a
branch, and the cargo is stacked on the shore. Sam covers the
boat with a camouflage net and dresses the top with
pine-needles.

```
EXT. ROCKY GORGE. DAY

Sam hikes through a pass wearing an extremely large back-pack
with stakes, metal poles, and two bed-rolls strapped to the
bottom. He wears a compass on a string around his neck.

CUT TO:

A binocular shot of Sam emerging from the woods into a wide
meadow. The grass comes up to his chest and flows in waves.
He pauses to check his compass. He spins slowly one direction
and then back the other while he stares at the dial. He looks
up again. He walks onward. He stops.

EXT. WIDE MEADOW. DAY

Suzy lowers her binoculars. She stands at the end of a path cut
through the high grass. She has a leather folder in one hand,
the portable record player in the other, plus a small suitcase
and her kitten in a basket at her side. Sam takes his coon-skin
hat slowly off his head. He strides across the meadow. Suzy
watches him approach. She swallows. Her lips part. Sam comes
onto the path. He stops ten feet away from Suzy.
```
                                          (Anderson and Coppola, 2012: 18)

Like Ball and Tarantino, Anderson is a writer-director who is able to use his own methods and styles of screenwriting, however idiosyncratic they may be. Nevertheless, if we keep in mind Stevens' notion that 'A change of style is a change of subject' (1957: 171), it is instructive to look at what Anderson is doing. Simply by looking at this page of text, we would likely know not to expect a swift-moving film. From the proliferation of visual details, we would probably be expecting something careful, lapidary, with a precision of image and tone: exactly the film Anderson made.

The movement of the lines, whether in swift blasts or blocks of text that work to slow the reader to the pace of the film, possesses the capacity to bring the work to life. 'Whatever shape it takes, this kind of movement is what makes a poem feel like an act of discovery rather than an act of recounting of an event that happened prior to the page' (Longenbach, 2008: 113); and we would argue that this can be true of screenwriting as well as poetry. This 'act of discovery' might be compared to Coleridge's 'breathing forms' and the bare 'recounting' to Coleridge's 'masks'. From our perspective, we want the reader of the screenplay to disappear into the imagined film, and to experience it immersively.

The language of visual description

Most of the attention in screenwriting discourse is given to story, and this is necessary given the requirements of the industry and the pressures put on a screenplay as it travels through the complex, condensed, financial and inter-personal high-wire act that is film production. If the story is not robust and if the structure is not sound, it will not hold up. For high-concept films or tent-pole movies that are built on familiar characters and themes, it may not matter as much *how* a story is written on the page; but for stories that are more delicate, and that emerge from the individual consciousness of a screenwriter, everything matters, not just to whether it is successfully made into a film but in regard to what kind of film it turns out to be.

We argue that common filler phrases like 'we see' and 'we pull back to see', or in the example from *American Beauty*, 'we're looking down' (Ball, 1999: 1) are as distancing as direct references to camera angles and movements. Batty and Waldeback speak convincingly of 'implying the shot': 'Including camera directions distances the reader from the story and takes them out of the action, forcing them to *interpret* emotion rather than *connect* to it' (2008: 54, emphasis in original). Each time the screenwriter uses 'camera' or 'shot' or 'we see', the writer is reminding the reader that the screenplay is a creation of a writer defining what to see and hear. The reading experience would be more powerful if the reader simply imagined the story and found the characters to be as real as they had become to the writer. In the case of a spec screenplay the screenwriter had been fortunate enough to get into the hands of a director, it would not be helpful to make the director feel he or she was being told his or her job. If the screenplay is written well, the director will see the shots the writer had in mind but think that he or she (the director) thought of them.

If we return for a moment to Alan Ball's *American Beauty*, we see that he describes the shots he has in mind quite precisely:

```
INT. SUBURBAN HOUSE — DAY
```

In BLACK & WHITE: CLOSE on an ancient woman's paper HANDS as they button a cardigan sweater.

> LESTER (V.O.)
> Or my grandmother's hands, and the way
> her skin seemed like paper...

This is a powerful image and one that Ball has rendered economically and effectively, though we might ask whether he needed to use the phrase 'CLOSE on', and whether we would feel the vulnerability of her hands more without it.

Purging language of the extraneous, and especially things that call attention to artifice and take the reader out of the story, we believe, can only make the screenplay more vivid. Certainly, phrases like 'we see' are stale and overused, and continuing to use them does not make screenplays more compelling. The fact that they are widely used, even by highly successful screenwriters, does not mean they are effective, nor that screenplays could not be made more evocative without them. This is the language of the Hollywood pitch and to some extent the spec screenplay is expected to function as a sales tool. William Goldman, in his delicious book *Which Lie Did I Tell?*, distinguishes between different types of screenplays (2001: 308). Whereas Trottier uses the term 'spec', Goldman prefers 'selling version'. Further drafts, after the screenplay has been sold, for him become 'shooting versions'. The spec screenplay may very well be the selling version, but if it sounds like it is selling it is unlikely to be bought.

Conclusion

Sometimes, avoiding familiar, overused and distancing language has attendant benefits. The effort to observe a scene keenly enough in one's imagination, and to visualise precisely how that scene might unspool on film, may change what happens or appears in the scene, and may spark the finding of a telling detail that would otherwise not have appeared, a detail that might have great significance to the story as it develops, an 'unaccountable' addition.

Much has been written about the need for concision in screenplays; but much more could be written about the efficacy of the *mot juste*, and of the sounds of the lines of visual description. It may seem a field too far to speak of the sound of lines never meant to be sounded, but there is evidence that this, too, matters a great deal. Karin de Weille's essay, 'How We Are Changed by the Rhythms of Poetry', contains some provocative reporting of what happens in the body when we read silently.

> Even when we read a poem in silence, it is given voice. Sensors attached to the throat reveal that the musculature is stimulated as if the words were actually spoken. Thus, whether read aloud or not, poems are made of sound, and this sound manipulates us on the inside. We are – quite literally – moved.
>
> (2009: 58)

If this is true for poetry, why would it not be true for what should be the heightened and concise language of the screenplay's visual description? Let us consider these few lines near the beginning of the Coen brothers' 2000 screenplay, *O Brother, Where Art Thou?*

```
It is flat delta countryside; the straight-ruled road stretches
away to infinity. Mounted guards with shotguns saunter up and
down the line.

The chain-gang chant is regular and, it seems, timeless.
```

There is a weariness in the rhythm of these lines that brings to life both the landscape and the characters. Single-syllable phrases linked together – 'straight-ruled road' and 'chain-gang chant' – ring regular and insistent as song. The interplay of these single, emphatic syllables against multi-syllabic words like 'infinity' creates contrasts as stark as the options of those chained together labouring in the heat compared to the very concept of anything like infinity.

Ultimately, how writing of any kind reaches the highest level of art is a mystery; but in an industry where those who are charged with deciding which films get made freely admit they hate reading screenplays, any attention paid to making screenplays come alive on the page can only be beneficial. For the screenwriter, Wordsworth's 'the prison, unto which we doom/Ourselves, no prison is' (cited in Perkins, 1967: 290) can mean more than contentment to follow the rules of format: it can mean that we use them to concentrate, to crystallise, to open something new and entirely our own.

Note

1. The authors wish to thank dramaturge Jeanmarie Higgins for bringing this thought to their attention.

References

Anderson, W. and Coppola, R. (2011) *Moonrise Kingdom*, New York: Faber & Faber Film.

Ball, A. (1999) *American Beauty*, New York: Newmarket Press.

Batty, C. and Waldeback, Z. (2008) *Writing for the Screen: Creative and Critical Approaches*, Basingstoke: Palgrave Macmillan.

Coen, J. and Coen, E. (2000) *O Brother, Where Art Thou?* New York: Faber & Faber.

de Weille, K. (2009) 'How We Are Changed by the Rhythms of Poetry' in *The Writer's Chronicle*, 42(1), https://www.awpwriter.org/magazine_media/writers_chronicle_view/2009/how_we_are_changed_by_the_rhythms_of_poetry.

Field, S. (2006) *The Screenwriter's Workbook* (revd edn), New York: Bantam Dell.

Goldman, W. (2001) *Which Lie Did I Tell? More Adventures in the Screen Trade*, New York Vintage Books.

Holden, S. (2012) 'A Rowdy Tale, Told by Cellphone Cameras' in *The New York Times*, 29 November, available at http://www.nytimes.com/2012/11/30/movies/king-kelly-a-satire-of-lust-for-internet-fame.html?_r=0 [accessed 5 November, 2013].

Krasny, M. (ed.) (2004) *Toward the Open Field: Poets on the Art of Poetry, 1800–1950*, Middlewown, CT: Wesleyan University Press.

Longenbach, J. (2008) *The Art of the Poetic Line*, Minneapolis, MN: Graywolf Press.

Perkins, D. (ed.) (1967) *English Romantic Writers*, New York: Harcourt, Brace & World Inc.

Riley, C. (2009) *The Hollywood Standard: The Complete and Authoritative Guide to Script Format and Style* (2nd ed.), Studio City, CA: Michael Wiese Productions.

Scott, A.O. (2013) 'Twirling in Oklahoma, a Dervish for Love: Terrence Malick's *To the Wonder*, with Ben Affleck' in *The New York Times*, 11 April, available at http://www.nytimes.com/2013/04/12/movies/terrence-malicks-to-the-wonder-with-ben-affleck.html [accessed 5 November, 2013].

Shyamalan, M.N. (1997) *The Sixth Sense*, Berwyn, PA: Blinding Edge Pictures.

Stevens, W. (1957) *Opus Posthumous*, New York: Alfred A. Knopf.

Trottier, D. (2002) *Dr. Format Answers Your Questions*, Cedar Hills, UT: Applewood Arts.

2
Narrating Voices in the Screenplay Text: How the Writer Can Direct the Reader's Visualisations of the Potential Film

Ann Ingelstrom

Introduction

The field of screenplay research is divided into two different strands that can be separated through their points of focus. One of these strands focuses on the screenwriting process: that is, the process of writing and revising the screenplay text during a film's development stage. Researchers who follow this strand of research argue that a film does not solely originate from the screenplay text but rather from the film's development process, during which the screenplay is continuously being rewritten. Osip Brik, for example, finds that the screenplay format and its literary language are insufficient means to convey the film, and therefore the collaboration and the work on the screenplay during the film's development stage is far more important than the text itself (1974: 99).

The other strand of research focuses on the screenplay text as a text-type, arguing that despite the multiple drafts that exist, each draft can be examined in its own right as an 'enabling document' that is 'necessary for the production' of the film (Price, 2010: 113). The unifying purpose of all screenplay texts is to become a film. If a text does not want to become a film, then it cannot be regarded as a screenplay. Pier Paolo Pasolini finds that the main characteristic of the screenplay is its allusion to a potential cinematographic work, and that the reader needs to construct the potential film in his or her mind. He further finds that it is only if a screenplay successfully accomplishes this allusion that it can be defined as an autonomous work (1986: 54). In order for a screenplay to belong to the screenplay text-type and fulfil its purpose of becoming a film, it needs to successfully communicate such allusions to the potential film to the reader. If the writer fails to successfully communicate the allusions, then the reader will not be able to construct the film in his or her mind, which ultimately means that the screenplay has failed to fulfil its objective.

Marja-Riitta Koivumäki also emphasises the importance of a screenplay text's ability to communicate: 'choreographers, composers, dramatists or screenwriters all have to have a vision of the future performance, and the plan they create has to be in a format that communicates the vision to the director and performers' (2011: 28). It is worth highlighting here that both Pasolini and Koivumäki speak of a vision of the potential film, not the type of story that is being told. It is thus not what is being told that they emphasise, but how it is being told: how the telling allows the reader to visualise the potential film. This clearly indicates that the screenwriter needs to not only communicate the story of the potential film but also, more importantly, how it should be visualised on the screen.

Communication as the heart of the screenplay text is understandable if we consider that it is only through the writer's successful signalling of the potential film that the screenplay text can fulfil its purpose of actually becoming a film. Having a clear, all-encompassing purpose sets the screenplay apart from other text-types, such as novels and films themselves. A film's purpose can be to entertain, or, as David Bordwell states, to 'yield an emotional experience' for the spectator (2008: 124). A screenplay, however, even though it most definitely can entertain and move its reader, will always first and foremost exist in order to communicate the potential film.

The purpose of this chapter, then, is to explore how references to the potential film can appear in the screenplay through different narrating voices, and how the screenwriter can use these voices to direct the reader's visualisation of the potential film. It will relate theories from film and literature to the screenplay text and examine how understanding these theories can help the screenwriter gain more control over the telling of their story. Given its focus on how the screenwriter can actively alter the reader's visualisation of the envisaged film, and that only the screenplay text is at the screenwriter's disposal to achieve this, this chapter embraces the second strand of research as outlined above, focusing on the screenplay text itself which at a different time becomes part of the screenwriting process.

The 12 screenplay texts used as reference points for this chapter are published screenplay texts. As they are published, most of them are shooting scripts or drafts that stem from the later stages of the film's development process. This carries with it both a disadvantage and an advantage. As later drafts, members of the production team have revised them and it is not always clear when extra material has been added. For example, camera directions may have been a part of the writer's first draft but the director, when deciding in more detail how he or she wanted to film the scene, could also have added them. An advantage to using published texts, however, is that they have all undergone rewrites and can be identified as belonging to one specific text stage of screenplays: the published text stage. It is then possible to compare how the narration differs between a screenplay's different text stages; that is, to compare an early draft to the published draft. Such comparisons could be the focus of future screenplay research.

Who communicates to whom in a screenplay?

Having found that communication lies at the heart of every screenplay text, the obvious question that needs to be answered is, who communicates to whom? For the screenplay to fulfil its purpose it needs to make it to production and, as we know, not many screenplays do. Therefore, when writing the screenplay the only reader that the screenwriter should be concerned with is the one who has the power to recommend that it be put into development for future production, or production itself.

Claudia Sternberg distinguishes between three different types of screenplay readers: the property reader, the blueprint reader and the reading stage reader (1997: 47). The property reader is the potential buyer or investor in the screenplay, for example, one who has the power to green light the project, which could be a producer, a director, an actor or an external investor. The blueprint reader interacts with the screenplay text because they will carry out work that transfers the screenplay into a film. Examples of blueprint readers include the director, the producer, the actors, the cinematographer and the make-up artists. It is during its stage as a blueprint that Sternberg identifies the screenplay text to be in its most 'varied and artistically creative phase of reading' (1997: 50). The reading stage reader engages with the screenplay after the film is complete, and these include critics, scholars and the general public.

Even though it is only property readers that the writer needs to successfully communicate with in order for the screenplay text to be produced, it is the successful communication with blueprint readers that will ultimately determine the quality of the film. How the screenplay directs its readers to visualise the film is therefore of great importance, not only to move the screenplay into production, but to ensure that the readers who will transfer the text into a film have the same vision of how it is going to look. It should be emphasised, however, that a screenwriter can sometimes communicate directly with the production team during the development (blueprint) stage, but during the screenplay's property stage, the screenwriter can usually only communicate through the text itself. How that text manages to communicate the potential film is most important during the property stage, then, when the screenwriter submits the screenplay to potential buyers.

Though bound by the screenplay text to communicate the potential film, the screenwriter does indeed have tools at his or her disposal that can be used to direct the reader's visualisation of the potential film: different kinds of narrating voices. It is these voices and how the screenwriter can use them that will now be explored.

External and internal narrating voices

In order to examine the narrating voices available to the screenwriter, it is useful to look at both literary and film theories. Regarding a text as situated between a sender and a receiver (e.g. writer and reader) is a convention that most literary theorists follow.[1] In addition to the communication between the author and the reader that is expressed through the narrative text, however, literary theorists identify a second communication that takes place within the text itself: a communication of the story from a fictional narrator to a fictional narratee. A narrative text does not necessarily only consist of one intratextual narrating voice ('intra' referring to existing inside the text), but can contain multiple narrating voices. The French literary theorist Gérard Genette was amongst the first who discerned different kinds of fictional narrators depending on their relation to the story.[2] Susan Lanser, expanding on Genette's theories, identifies her narrating voices through relating them to the text, fiction, story, scene and action. Outside of the text is the historical author, inside the text but outside of the fiction is the extrafictional voice, and inside both the text and fiction is the public and the private narrator, as well as the characters (1981: 144).

Film theorist Edward Branigan, building on Lanser's theories, also identifies both extratextual and intratextual narrating voices, and similarly to Lanser puts them in relation to the text (e.g. the film), the fiction, the story, the scene and the action. Branigan further adds the levels of speech, perception and thought (1992: 87). It should be highlighted, however, that Branigan, in line with most film theorists, does not regard a film as an act of communication. Within film theory there is an argument that the film itself is the 'enunciating subject', the giver of the story, in which case both the concept of the fictional narrator and the real creators of the film are taken out of the communication situation. This allows film theoreticians to speak of the narration as stemming from the film itself instead of originating from its creators.[3]

Though providing a solid theoretical basis from which to understand narrating voices, this chapter will not go into further detail about the communication models from film and literary theory. Instead, it will focus on determining what narrating voices can be distinguished in the screenplay text and how these different extratextual and intratextual voices can be used. In other words, the focus is on how the screenwriter can use specific techniques of narration to communicate their film idea.

Narrating voices in the screenplay text

In order to separate the narrating voices that can be found in screenplay texts, it is necessary to identify what kind of information is communicated. To achieve this we can take the following example from the screenplay *(500) Days of Summer*:

```
A single number in parenthesis, exactly like so:
(488)

EXT. ANGELUS PLAZA — DOWNTOWN LOS ANGLES, CA — DAY

And we're looking at a MAN (20s) and a WOMAN (20s)
on a bench, high above the city of Los Angeles.
Their names are TOM and SUMMER and right now neither
one says a word.

CLOSE ON their HANDS, intertwined. Notice the
wedding ring on her finger. CLOSE ON Tom, looking at
Summer the way every woman wants to be looked at.
And then a DISTINGUISHED VOICE begins to speak to us.
```

```
                 NARRATOR
   This is a story of boy meets girl.
```
(Neustadter and Weber, 2009: 1)

In this example the reader of the screenplay is provided with information about how the potential film will look on three occasions: how the number 488 should appear on the screen, that Tom and Summer's intertwined hands should be shown through a close up, and that Tom's loving face also should be shown through a close up. Since this kind of information refers to the real world, where the screenplay will be made into a film, it will be identified as extrafictional information (the term 'extra' referring to being outside of the fiction). The extrafictional information is clearly directed to a reader from a production context. This example also provides the reader with information about the story: the characters' names and ages, their location, their relationship, and the kind of story this will be: boy meets girl. Since this kind of information refers to the fictional world, with its focus on the story being told, it will be identified as fictional information.

Both kinds of information can be seen as conveyed through two separate voices: an extrafictional voice and a fictional voice. It is thus the kind of information that a narrating voice provides the reader with that identifies the voice as being either extrafictional or fictional. In the example above, there are two different fictional voices that convey the fictional information: the scene text and the Narrator. A distinction between different fictional voices is therefore also necessary in understanding the text's communication of the film. First, however, the extrafictional voice will be examined in further detail.

The extrafictional voice

The extrafictional narrating voice can be identified as conveying information that is concerned with the extrafictional real world and thereby addressing the intended reader directly. Considering that the extrafictional voice can do this, it is the voice that most directly conveys the thoughts and directions of the screenwriter, and can therefore be regarded as the representation of the writer within the text. To further emphasise, the extrafictional voice is situated inside the text but outside of the fiction; that is, it does not belong to the fictional world of the story.

The most common information the extrafictional narrating voice provides the reader with is camera directions, as already seen from *(500)*

Days of Summer. Another example can be found in *The King's Speech*: 'HAND-HELD CAMERA, BERTIE'S POV' (Seidler, 2010: 3). The information given about what camera should be used and from whose perspective the scene is to be visualised clearly originates from outside of the fiction, and is directed to the production team of the real world.

The extrafictional voice does not, however, only provide information about which camera or angle should be used during production, which the following examples from *(500) Days of Summer, Fantastic Mr Fox* and *Hugo* demonstrate, respectively:

(PRODUCTION NOTE: Put Autumn somewhere subtle in the background)

(Neustadter and Weber, 2009: 46)

(NOTE: an alternate version of Mrs Fox will be used for this shot which can be literally lit from within)

(Anderson and Baumbach, 2009: 10)

[Or similar moment of comic frustration]

(Logan, 2011: 9)

The placement of these notes to the production team within a parenthesis further emphasises that it is not a case of the fictional narrator's communication, but a communication external to the fiction.

The King's Speech contains an interesting example of a bracketed note displaying a communication by the extrafictional voice that is not directed to the production team, but rather to a more general reader: '[For ease of reading, Bertie's stammer will not be indicated from this point in the script]' (Seidler, 2010: 4). Here, the extrafictional voice provides the reader with information about the look of the screenplay text and, just as with the previous example, is not concerned with the fictional story world but instead is directly addressing the reader in the real world.

Most direct allusions to a potential film, however, appear in the screenplay without a parenthesis or bracket, mainly addressing the production team and consisting primarily of camera directions. Such allusions often specify camera angles, as these examples from *The Kids Are All Right* display: 'Angle on Paul', 'NIC'S POV', and 'REVERSE ONTO NIC' (Cholodenko and Blumberg, 2010: 8, 80). Sometimes, though, the intent is not to specify a camera angle but to indicate a camera movement, as is the case in these two examples from *The Savages*: 'Still on the move, the CAMERA locates -', and 'AGITATED HAND-HELD as Wendy and Jon march down the path, their balloon in tow' (Jenkins, 2008: 1, 23).

The extrafictional voice is purposefully not being defined as a technical voice despite the fact that the information it provides is often of a technical nature. This is so as not to separate the voice from other parts of the screenplay text, meaning that although the extrafictional voice might be external to the fiction, it still forms part of the screenplay text's narration, and technical abbreviations and camera position are in the screenplay for their capacity to help the reader visualise the story in a particular way. They are thereby useful tools for the writer to direct the reader's perception of the potential film.

It should be highlighted, however, that many of the extrafictional voice's lines of communication could have been added during the film's development stage and not been a part of the writer's earlier versions. This is particularly likely in the case of bracketed notes to the production team, and most screenwriting manuals and how-to books especially advise against the use of camera directions. Syd Field, for instance, emphasises that the 'writer's job is to tell the director *what* to shoot, not *how* to shoot it' (Field, 2005: 218). Instead of using camera directions to indicate how the film should be visualised, most manuals encourage the writer to describe the scene visually. Dennis Martin Flinn, for example, urges the writer to '[s]ee your scene from the best angle. Without using camera talk, describe what you see' (Flinn, 1999: 111). If a writer describes a scene visually instead of providing camera directions, the writer uses the fictional voice instead of the extrafictional voice.

Before focusing on the fictional voice, however, the difference between how the extrafictional voice works in a screenplay text compared to how it works in a novel or a film needs to be mentioned. In film and literary theory, the extrafictional voice (referred to as implied author, extrafictional narrator or extrafictional voice) is seen to be responsible for forewords or acknowledgements, and the fictional story. Both Branigan and Lanser emphasise that the extrafictional voice in novels and produced films only exists through being implied by the reader or spectator. Lanser, for instance, finds that the extrafictional voice is 'a significant hidden presence' that stays with the reader 'throughout our reading of the fictional discourse' (1981: 131). In the case of the screenplay, however, the extrafictional voice exists throughout the telling of the story, through addressing the reader directly with information that is concerned with the extrafictional real world, involving both the production of the film and the reading of the text. Even screenplays that do not contain any camera directions or other addresses to the production team still address the reader directly through scene headings. It is only in screenplays that do not contain any scene headings that the extrafictional voice becomes less prominent and apparent. However, these screenplays are in a clear minority as most manuals prescribe the use of scene headings from the start, and screenwriting software (e.g. final draft, celtx, etc.) has scene headings as a standard setting. All scene headings (or sluglines) can be regarded as extrafictional since they contain technical abbreviations (EXT., INT.) directed at the production of the potential film in the real world. It is therefore, I suggest, almost impossible for the reader of the screenplay to forget that it is an artificial product created by a screenwriter, with the purpose that it will become a film. The direct communication of the extrafictional narrating voice to the reader is thus one of the most unique aspects of the screenplay text.

The fictional voice

Using the extrafictional voice to indicate camera positions is not the only way for a writer to direct the reader's visualisation. The same effect can be achieved through describing a scene's actions and objects in specific ways, which is clearly of specific interest to the screenwriter as they write and re-write their work. In addition, this is the way approved by manuals for a screenwriter to indicate how the film should look. The following examples of this in action are from *Cold Mountain, The Hours, Love Actually* and *Atonement,* respectively.

```
AN ARMY OF TINY CRABS scuttle across the sandy
march. A LARGE HAND grabs at a clutch of them.
Inman, starving, swills the crabs in a puddle then
proceeds to eat them.
```

(Minghella, 2003: 57)

```
At once a man's finger pressing the intercom.
```

(Hare, 2002: 61)

```
[A] man and his 11-year old step son in church —
with a crowd of 80 behind them, dressed in
black.
```

(Curtis, 2006: 223)

```
ROBBIE approaches the towering bulk of the
house, dragging his feet [...] Finally, he takes a
deep breath and tugs at the bell-pull.
```

(Hampton, 2007: 29)

The first two examples indicate close ups just as clearly as if they had used the extrafictional voice to state that a 'close up' shot of Inman and Louis's hands should be used. The third example also clearly indicates the size of the shot but in this case it is a wide shot, one that will allow all of the 80 people in church to be seen. This scene thereby clearly dictates how the reader should visualise the church, without the need to mention the camera or use any technical terms. In the first example from *Atonement*, two different angles on the scene are indicated: firstly, a wide shot that displays the 'towering bulk of the house', and secondly a closer shot of Robbie when he takes a deep breath and rings the bell. Once more, camera positions are alluded to without actual mention of the camera. The above examples do not use an extrafictional voice in order to direct the reader's visualisations. Instead, a fictional voice is used that only gives information about and through the fictional world of the story. It can be defined as being placed inside the fiction as well as inside the text, and only giving information that refers to the fictional world.

As previously mentioned, screenplays can contain more than one kind of fictional voice. This was seen in the example from *(500) Days of Summer*, where a voice called Narrator gives information about what kind of story will be told. Another example of this kind of fictional voice can be found in *Little Children*:

```
         As we PUSH IN on her — A NEW VOICE EMERGES. IT IS
         MALE, CALM, AND NON-JUDGMENTAL, IN SHORT, GROWN-UP.

                        VOICE
                   Smiling politely to mask a
                   familiar feeling of
                   desperation, Sarah reminded
                   herself to think like an
                   anthropologist. She was a
                   researcher studying the
                   behavior of typical suburban
                   women. She was not a typical
                   suburban woman herself.
                              (Field and Perrotta, 2006: 2)
```

The Voice here, giving information about Sarah's thoughts and feelings, is clearly separate from the fictional voice of the scene text: the text even introduces the Voice. The two types of fictional voices can be defined through how much the reader knows about them. In contrast to the fictional voice in the dialogue, the reader knows nothing about the fictional voice in the scene text. The fictional narrating voice of the dialogue can be defined as a personal fictional voice since the reader knows something about it, whereas the fictional voice of the scene text can be defined as impersonal.[4] The easiest way to separate these two fictional voices is that the personal narrating voice is always situated in the dialogue section of the screenplay text, and that the screenwriter can only direct the reader's visualisation through using the impersonal fictional voice to describe scenes in specific ways.

We-formulations

There is one more way for the writer to direct the reader's visualisation: the use of what I am calling we-formulations. We-formulations exist in many screenplays since they provide a way to direct the reader's visualisation as well as direct, or at least indicate, the reader's emotional response. The examples below are taken from *Burn After Reading, Traffic, Inglourious Basterds, The Constant Gardener* and *Billy Elliot*:

> HALLWAY
> We track at floor level, following a pair of
> well-shined shoes down a well-polished hallway.
>
> (Coen and Coen, 2008: 3)

> From the hallway we see Robert and Barbara and
> Caroline having dinner. A familiar tableau. We
> hear Barbara talking, the murmur of the days
> events.
>
> (Gaghan, 2001: 37)

> We don't move into them but keep observing them
> from a distance, like the farmer.
>
> (Tarantino, 2009: 2)

> Across the room Lorbeer has opened Wanza's
> cupboard and is now scooping into a bag what we
> assume to be her medicines: small blue boxes
> marked with a logo we can't clearly see.
>
> (Caine, 2006: 27)

> The music increasing in tension. BILLY, now in
> his early twenties, is looking on to the stage.
> We don't see his face but see the back of his
> head as the music is playing loudly in his ears.
> We feel the heart beating fast. The music wells
> up still further [...] The music gets louder and

```
louder. The anticipation cannot get any higher.
BILLY's heart is pounding. He leaps onto the
stage. Silence. As if we were inside Billy's
skull. The bright lights seem blinding.
```
(Hall, 2000: 96–97)

The first example indicates a very clear camera position but with the word 'we' substituting the word 'camera', the effect being that like a mention of the camera, we move in and observe freely the fictional world of the story. The examples from *Traffic* and *Inglourious Basterds* position the observer (i.e. us) firmly at a distance from the scene, keeping the action somewhat removed, which in *Traffic* emphasises the family as a unit and in *Inglourious Basterds* emphasises the approaching threat to the farmer. *The Constant Gardener* example not only positions the observer at a distance but also insinuates that there is important information the observer does not receive. Somewhat differently in the final example, the 'we' almost merges with the character's (Billy) experience, where the reader shares everything the character knows and feels.

The advantage for the screenwriter in using we-formulations over directions or descriptions by the impersonal fictional voice is that the reader can be given certain emotional responses; or, at least, the responses that the screenwriter wants from their reader and future spectator can be implied. In the *Billy Elliot* example, for instance, the reader is invited to experience the moment with the character, sharing his emotions and his racing heart. It is thus through we-formulations that the screenwriter can most clearly align or separate the reader emotionally from the characters in the scene, thereby creating particular responses. As described above, highlighting the importance of the family was the case in the example from *Traffic*.

Strictly speaking, the 'we' in screenplay texts belongs to the impersonal fictional voice since the 'we' is clearly positioned within the fiction and only relates information about the fictional story world. The 'we' might, however, be best understood as the impersonal fictional voice and the image of the reader it addresses put together and placed in a viewing situation of the potential film. The reactions, thoughts and feelings that the impersonal fictional voice indicates the 'we' to have are then the reactions the writer wishes from the reader and future spectator whilst reading or watching the screenplay or potential film.

Before moving on to discuss the different effects that extrafictional voices, impersonal fictional voices and we-formulations can have, it is worth noting that textual indications about how a scene should be filmed are not necessarily followed. Screenwriter Michael Arndt notes in the afterword to the screenplay *Little Miss Sunshine* that the production team followed none of the point-of-view shots he had indicated in the text (2006: 114). Therefore, allusions to how a film should be executed are not necessarily going to ensure that the production team follows them precisely, but rather work to bring the text to life for the reader and indicate how the writer intends the screenplay to be visualised. The extrafictional voice might thus be understood as the voice of a 'hidden director' who directs the film for the reader.[5]

Separating the impersonal fictional voice from the extrafictional voice

The above examples of how impersonal fictional and extrafictional voices can direct the reader's visualisation are easily separated from one another, but in most cases the two voices overlap in narrating the story. How the voices work together in order to direct the reader's visualisation, as well as garner an emotional response, can be seen in the following example from *(500) Days of Summer*:

> The sound slows down on the word 'friend' (which is an awful, awful word). THE IMAGE FREEZES AND WE ZOOM IN ON TOM'S STUNNED FACE
>
> (Neustadter and Weber, 2009: 8)

The extrafictional voice communicates to the production team that the sound should be slowed down and that the frame should be frozen. The impersonal fictional voice simultaneously indicates that 'we' should zoom in on Tom's stunned face, and that the word 'friend' in this case should be interpreted to be an 'awful, awful word'. That extrafictional and fictional voices overlap throughout the screenplay is another unique aspect of screenplay texts.

The effects of the different narrating voices

How, then, can the screenwriter use the different voices to create specific effects? As was seen in the example from *Inglourious Basterds*, different voices can indicate the distance between the reader/observer and the action in the scene. Depending on what voice is used, the writer can also affect the distance between the reader and the story. A writer using the extrafictional voice places the reader further away from the story than a writer using the impersonal fictional voice, due to the fact that any references to the real world remind the reader that the story is indeed fictional and has been constructed by a writer. The fewer references to the extrafictional world that the screenplay contains, arguably, the more intently the reader is able to focus on the story. Any mention of a camera puts an 'object' between the reader and the story, thus increasing the distance between them further since the reader is observing/visualising the story through a camera instead of seeing it directly in his or her mind.

The use of 'we', similarly to the use of the word 'camera', distances the reader from the story since it places the reader in a viewing situation. 'We' view the story, but not from inside; rather, we are a spectator 'watching' the potential film. Embedding the 'we' with particular responses and reactions can further distance the reader from the story if they do not agree with the emotion being encouraged.

Directing the reader's visualisation of the potential film through describing actions and objects creates the smallest distance between the reader and the story. Without any mentioning of a 'camera' or an observing 'we', the reader experiences the story directly in his or her mind. Due to the scene headings and the format of the screenplay, however, the reader is perhaps always aware of the text's purpose to become a film, which ultimately means the reader is never completely free to become immersed in the story.

Conclusion

Through regarding the screenplay text as a communication, it is possible to identify different narrating voices that not only communicate the story to the reader but also dictate how that story should be visualised as a film. Terminology from both film and literary theory can help identify these voices and thereby provide the researcher with a valuable tool to examine them. It is necessary, however, to slightly alter the terms in order for them to better suit the form of the screenplay text.

This chapter has identified three communicating voices that exist inside the text, which become available to the practising screenwriter: the extrafictional voice that communicates extrafictional information; the impersonal fictional voice that communicates information about the story and the characters in the scene text; and the personal fictional voice that communicates information about the story and the characters in the dialogue.

Considering that the purpose of the screenplay text is to become a film, the most important part of the writer's communication to the reader is how the text should be visualised. Through using the extrafictional and the fictional voice, the writer is able to direct the reader's visualisation and indicate an emotional response in the reader. It is important to remember that the communications of the voices exist simultaneously throughout the screenplay, and that they can be used interchangeably to create particular effects, distancing the reader closer or further away from the story and the characters, for example. The better the writer can understand this and put the available techniques into practice, the more likely it is that they will successfully communicate the potential film to their reader.

Notes

1. See, for instance, Seymour Chatman (1978), Susan Lanser (1981) and Shlomith Rimmon-Kenan (2002).
2. See Gérard Genette, 1980: 243–245.
3. See, for instance, Bordwell (1985), Metz (1974) and Branigan (1992). For film theorists who argue that film is an act of communication, see Laass (2008) and Kühn (2011).
4. The terms 'impersonal' and 'personal' are taken from Claudia Sternberg (1997: 133, 136), but her definitions of the terms differ slightly. For more details, see Igelström (2013: 49–50).
5. Claudia Sternberg referred to the screenwriter as a 'hidden director', since the screenwriter can anticipate the 'directorial input' through describing how the events should be presented in the film (1997: 231).

References

Anderson, W. and Baumbach, N. (2009) *Roald Dahl's Fantastic Mr Fox: The Official Screenplay*, London: Penguin Group.

Arndt, M. (2006) *Little Miss Sunshine*, New York: Newmarket Press.

Bordwell, D. (1985) *Narration in the Fiction Film*, London: Methuen Press.

Bordwell, D. (2008) *Poetics of Cinema*, New York: Routledge.

Branigan, E. (1992) *Narrative Comprehension and Film*, London: Routledge.

Brik, O. (1974) 'From the Theory and Practice of a Script Writer' in *Screen*, 15(3), 95–103.

Caine, J. (2006) *The Constant Gardener: The Shooting Script*, New York: Newmarket Press.

Chatman, S. (1978) *Story and Discourse: Narrative Structure in Fiction and Film*, Ithaca, London: Cornell University Press.

Cholodenko, L. and Blumberg, S. (2010) *The Kids are All Right*, New York: Newmarket Press.

Coen, E. and Coen, J. (2008) *Burn After Reading*, London: Faber and Faber.

Curtis, R. (2006) 'Love Actually' in *Six Weddings and Two Funerals: Three Screenplays by Richard Curtis*, London: Penguin Group, pp. 217–363.

Field, S. (2005) *Screenplay: The Foundations of Screenwriting: A Step-by-Step Guide from Concept to Finished Script* (rev. ed.), New York: Random House Publishing.

Field, T. and Perrotta, T. (2006) *Little Children*, New York: Newmarket Press.

Flinn, D.M. (1999) *How Not to Write a Screenplay: 101 Common Mistakes most Screenwriters Make*, Los Angeles: Lone Eagle.

Gaghan, S. (2001) *Traffic: Screenplay*, London: Faber and Faber.

Genette, G. (1980) *Narrative Discourse*, Ithaca: Cornell University Press.

Hall, L. (2000) *Billy Elliot: Screenplay*, London: Faber and Faber.

Hampton, C. (2007) *Atonement*, New York: Newmarket Press.

Hare, D. (2002) *The Hours*, London: Faber and Faber.

Igelström, A. (2013) 'Communication and the Various Voices of the Screenplay Text' in *Journal of Screenwriting*, 4(1), 43–56.

Jenkins, T. (2008) *The Savages: The Shooting Script*, New York: Newmarket Press.

Koivumäki, M.-R. (2011) 'The Aesthetic Independence of the Screenplay' in *Journal of Screenwriting*, 2(1), 25–40.

Kühn, M. (2011) *Filmnarratologie: Ein Erzähltheoretisches Analysemodell*, Berlin: Walter de Gruyter.

Laass, E. (2008) *Broken Taboos, Subjective Truths: Forms and Functions of Unreliable Narration in Contemporary American Cinema*, Trier: Wissenschaftlicher Verlag Trier.

Lanser, S.S. (1981) *The Narrative Act: Point of View in Prose Fiction*, Princeton: Princeton University Press.

Logan, J. (2011) *Hugo*, New York: Newmarket Press.

Metz, C. (1974) *Film Language: A Semiotics of the Cinema*, Chicago: The University of Chicago Press.

Minghella, A. (2003) *Cold Mountain*, London: Faber and Faber.

Neustadter, S. and Weber, M.H. (2009) *(500) Days of Summer*, New York: Newmarket Press.

Pasolini, P.P. (1986) 'The Screenplay as a "Structure that Wants to Be Another Structure" ' in *American Journal of Semiotics*, 4(1), 53–72.

Price, S. (2010) *The Screenplay: Authorship, Theory and Criticism*, Basingstoke: Palgrave Macmillan.

Rimmon-Kenan, S. (2002) *Narrative Fiction: Contemporary Poetics* (2nd ed.), London: Routledge.

Seidler, D. (2010) *The King's Speech*, London: Nick Hern Books.

Sternberg, C. (1997) *Written for the Screen: The American Motion-Picture Screenplay as Text*, Tübingen: Stauffenburg Verlag.

Tarantino, Q. (2009) *Inglourious Basterds: A Screenplay*, New York: Little, Brown and Company.

3
Horror Screenwriting: Blending Theory with Practice

Shaun Kimber

Introduction

Good ideas for horror screenplays originate from a range of sources. These inspirations could be personal, linked to the writer's life experiences, or cultural, reflecting wider socio-political concerns. Great horror storytelling, I want to argue, can be achieved through the linking of a well-researched knowledge of horror histories, industries and audiences, the creative application of craft skills and techniques, and the imaginative understanding of conceptual and theoretical approaches to horror. As such, the approach adopted in this chapter suggests that the creative intellect of horror screenwriters can be reanimated through the meaningful and constructive alignment of these intersecting practical and theoretical contexts. The ambition of the chapter, therefore, is to further promote the contemporary reinvigoration of horror screenwriting by blending theory with practice in a way that is meaningful for horror screenwriters.

The chapter examines seven intersecting themes linked to the creative use of theory within horror screenplay writing. Links are made to screenwriting processes and practices and examples of contemporary horror texts. The ideas outlined offer a flexible set of possibilities that screenwriters can work with and adapt in the development of horror screenplays. The blending of these theoretical and practical domains seeks to encourage horror screenwriters to generate effective ideas, fully develop their concepts and inject as much pre-production creativity as possible into their screenplays. Whilst the proposed theory-practice themes are presented in a rough chronology, they can – and perhaps should – be revisited at any stage in the development of a horror screenplay.

Producing chills and thrills

In relation to the development of concepts for horror screenplays, I propose six intersecting areas for screenwriters to consider. The first of these involves conducting research into screen horror. In recent years, despite the global recession, there has been a resurgence of horror within mainstream, independent and amateur production sectors. For example, there have been numerous innovative films and television series (*Cheap Thrills* (2013), *Hannibal* (2013–)), a host of sequels and prequels to established franchises (*Evil Dead* (2013), *Paranormal Activity 4* (2012)), and a plethora of remakes and re-imaginings of older properties (*Carrie* (2013), *Patrick,* (2013)). There have even been sequels to remakes and remakes of sequels (*I Spit on Your Grave 2* (2013), *Halloween 2* (2009)). It is essential for screenwriters to research a range of economic, industrial and institutional contexts to find out: which horror films and television series are in development, production and post-production; how these horror projects are being financed; which horror screenwriters are having their work made; which films and television series are making money; and which ones audiences are attracted to. This research will enable the screenwriter to establish a view of the bigger industrial picture and also help them to locate their particular project within current cycles of horror production, circulation and consumption.

The second consideration is about the medium or platform through which the story will be told. Horror screenwriters need to deliberate if their ideas are best suited to one medium, for example, film, television, online, mobile or game. They should also ponder which form aligns most closely with their concept, for example, short or feature film, television episode, mini-series or series. Increasingly, screenwriters need to contemplate if and how their horror world might support multiple characters and stories across several platforms, each story element making a distinct contribution to the overall narrative. For example, *The Blair Witch Project* (1999) unfolded online, in a television pseudo-documentary, through the film, comic books and a soundtrack (Jenkins, 2008).

The third consideration involves contemplation of the scale of the screenplay and the proposed budget for the project. The following breakdown is helpful when quantifying the project relative to recent horror films. No budget (£0–£50,000) usually incorporates amateur, self-financed or crowd-funded projects, such as *Death By VHS* (2013), made for $10,000 USD. Micro budget films (£50,000–£250,000) are independently financed projects, such as *The Demon's Rook* (2013), made for $75,000 USD. Low budget films (£250,000–£1,000,000) are usually independent and/or mainstream projects, such as *Stalled* (2013), made for £450,000, and bigger budget projects (£1,000,000–£60,000,000) are independent and/or mainstream, such as *The Purge* (2013), made for $3,000,000 USD. Big budget (£60,000,000+) equates to mainstream blockbusters, such as *World War Z* (2013), made for $170,000,000 USD.

The fourth consideration relates to the screenwriter's thoughts on the imagined audience for their screenplay. It is important to remember that the horror industry is increasingly audience-led, through the films people choose to pay to watch, buy and stream (Mancini, 2013). Screenwriters also need to appreciate that horror audiences bring very different expectations to the viewing experience when compared to mainstream audiences. Horror fans will often have different tastes, preferences and dispositions than mainstream audiences in relation to horror. They will undoubtedly be reading any horror text intertextually within the wider histories of horror culture. Moreover, horror fans will be expecting either intense sensations and/or to be challenged ethically or politically during their encounters with horror texts. Therefore, it is necessary to consider if a project is aimed at mainstream audiences or horror fans. Horror fans are very loyal to the genre, making it a good market to write for, but they are also often more experienced and knowledgeable than horror screenwriters. Horror fans will spot generic formulas and conventions from some distance, so it is important for horror screenwriters to know their audience in order to manipulate their expectations and to cue their surprise and dread, not their frustration and boredom.

The fifth consideration involves the screenwriter reflecting on their approach to the practice of horror screenwriting. Here an interesting deliberation is the degree to which the horror screenplay will orientate towards the known or unknown. For example, the screenwriter can interestingly contemplate how fully realised they want the screenplay to be, the degree of alignment between story world, theme, structure, character and dialogue, and if they wish to create gaps and spaces that can be explored by producers, directors and actors. For example, Ben Wheatley and writing partner Amy Jump structure their films using a screenplay and storyboards, but the texture of the film comes from the improvisation of cast and crew (Wheatley, 2013).

The final consideration is related to the various distinctions that can be made between *writing for* the project and *writing to support* the project. When writing for the project, it is useful for the screenwriter to differentiate between the writing that goes into the production of various drafts of the screenplay, the supporting development documents (sequence outlines, step outlines and treatments) and the selling documents (loglines, synopsis and treatments) (Batty, 2012). When writing to support the horror project, the idea of paratexts is helpful to the screenwriter (Grey, 2010). Here, it is useful to think how scripted texts such as Facebook pages, Twitter updates, trailers, virals and blogs can be employed to generate a positive impact on the reception and the meaning of the screenplay, both before and after it is read.

Understanding horror

It is crucial for all horror screenwriters to understand the nature of the genre as a way of getting to the sinister heart of the story they want to tell, and to ensure that terror has seeped into their story world and themes. Horror is fundamentally about fear. It engages directly (consciously) and indirectly (sub-consciously) with deep physical, psychological, social and cultural fears (Wells, 2000; Gledhill, 2007; Cherry, 2009; Kimber, 2011). These fears may be associated with death (infection, pain, illness), bodily vulnerability (injury, violence, trauma), insanity (transformation, mutation, possession), the unknown (evil, the other, insecurity), isolation (confinement, upheaval) and oppression (repression, subjugation). Horror also manipulates our anxieties, linked to our lack of control over these conditions and situations. Paradoxically, whilst creating negative affects such as unease, dread, terror, shock, disgust and repulsion (Blake and Bailey, 2013), horror simultaneously satisfies our desire to encounter fears, whilst testing our thresholds and boundaries (Hill, 1997). In doing so pleasure is created: the thrill and sensation of being scared. Horror screenwriting therefore provides a significant and powerful creative outlet for the dramatisation and pleasuring of our deepest fears and darkest desires.

Screenwriters can also cogitate on which form of horror best suits the fears and desires they plan to work with. For example, when developing a horror screenplay it can be useful for screenwriters to consider the differences between horror that confronts fears and horror that channels aggression. Confronting fears involves horror screenwriters engaging directly with the anxieties and desires of the day. These anxieties may be symptomatic of the political, social, cultural and economic moment, or they may be psychologically indicative of the unconscious, abject and uncanny manifesting in the fantasies and nightmares of the times.

Channelling aggression comprises of horror screenwriters directly confronting the status quo and the world around them. This may take the form of critiquing institutions, challenging authority figures, criticising social norms, questioning moral conditioning, violating taboos and transgressing boundaries of acceptability (Marriott, 2004). For example, *Srpski Film/A Serbian Film* (2010) concurrently channels the writer's aggression about Serbian society whilst localising a range of trans-cultural fears and taboos associated with sex, pornography, drugs, violence, sexual violence, paedophilia, incest, necrophilia, victimisation, degradation and children in sexualised and violent contexts (Kimber, 2014).

Another choice open to horror screenwriters is between constructing pure horror and developing a horror universe. Pure horror is pared to the bone: the horror just exists, with little or no justification or explanation, and the suspense can be relentless. By contrast, a horror universe offers elaborate mythologies, lore and backstories: the horror is explained, motivated socially or psychologically, and suspense is built up through the narrative. *Human Centipede II (Full Sequence)* (2011) offered little in the way of explanation for its horrors, but what it did offer parodied society's worst fears about the influence of horror films on audiences. This contributed to the film's initial banning in the UK by the British Board of Film Classification (BBFC, 2011).

Screenwriters can also contemplate the extent to which their work will display a utopian or dystopian worldview. Utopian horror engages with fears thus raising suspense, yet seeks to resolve its narrative with a high degree of clarity at the climax, potentially evoking emotional satisfaction and pleasure in the audience. Dystopian horror engages with fears raising suspense, but the resolution may be open-ended and characterised by a high degree of ambiguity, possibly denying satisfaction and evoking displeasure in the audience.

A more abstract deliberation for screenwriters to ponder is if their ideas could be read as being politically or ideologically progressive or regressive (Wood, 1986). Regressive horror maintains, reproduces and reconstructs the status quo by suppressing all threats, destroying monsters and presenting narrative closure. Progressive horror questions and deconstructs normality by not containing threats or vanquishing monsters, and by not offering reassuring closure. Whilst any evaluation of the progressive or regressive nature of a horror screenplay is open to interpretation and contestation, it is helpful for screenwriters to keep these categories in mind when reflecting upon the screenplay's world, themes, character relationships and, in particular, its ending.

When developing a screenplay, it can be extremely fruitful for screenwriters to muse the connections between a horror that makes you feel and a horror that makes you think. A horror that makes you feel affects audiences physiologically, emotionally and bodily, creating sensations and responses such as making their skin crawl, making them tense their muscles or look away, making their heart beat faster and possibly even turning their stomach (Barker, 2009). A horror that makes you think engages audiences ethically, politically and ideologically. This type of horror raises questions linked to fairness, morality, power and inequality; it can also test accepted norms and values and confront prejudices and taboos. All horror screenwriters can thus benefit from carefully thinking through how their screenplay will cue an audience's feelings and thoughts.

Working with horrific themes

There are recurring combinations of ideas, oppositions and allegories identifiable in horror texts that screenwriters can creatively draw on and seek inspiration from when developing horror screenplays. What is particularly interesting here is how screenwriters can re-work, augment and update these themes to help promote the innovativeness of their screenplay.

Horrific ideas that can be employed creatively in horror screenplays include: the monstrous and monstrous feminine (Creed, 1993); the grotesque and the carnivalesque (Bakhtin, 1984); the abject and abjection (Kristeva, 1982); the uncanny and the unconscious (Freud, 2003, 2005); and pollution and taboo (Douglas, 2002). It is interesting to think how many of these ideas are employed and re-worked in the television series *Hannibal*, such as the ways in which the series engages with a range of taboos linked to the dark side of eating without directly foregrounding the abject and grotesque elements often associated with the representation of cannibalism. A key question for the horror screenwriter to contend with here, and one that impacts on many of the ideas raised in this chapter, is the tension between generic classicism and generic revisionism. In other words, to what extent is the story best served by adopting a traditional understanding of horror ideas? And how can new twists be made to classical horror ideas to make them work for contemporary genre-literate audiences? The television series *True Blood* (2008–) is an interesting example of putting inventive new spins on classic horror tropes. For example, the series hybridises elements of the vampire sub-genre with a range of other supernatural forms (shape shifters, werewolves and fairies). Moreover, the characters within the series are used to explore the possibilities and challenges of co-existence between humans and non-humans, thus putting a contemporary twist on horror's conventional cultural work examining the boundaries and borders between the civilised and uncivilised, the human and monstrous, and alive and dead.

Horror screenwriters can also usefully think in terms of the cross-cultural exchange and localisation of horror ideas. The ways in which screenwriters can draw on fairy tales, folklore, myths and legends from around the world can help them develop their screenplays by an appropriation and re-imagining of these horrific viewpoints. An interesting example of this is the television series *Les Revenants/The Returned* (2012–), which takes the zombie genre, originating in the USA and developed across the globe, borrows several of its ideas but inventively localises them within contemporary French culture.

Binary oppositions such as good/evil, human/monster, human/animal, alive/dead, self/other, civilised/uncivilised, conscious/unconscious, inside/outside and solid/liquid are often employed in horror narratives. These oppositions are organised hierarchically and are underpinned by dominant value systems that tend to favour one term in the pairing more than the other. For example, good, human, alive, self, civilised and conscious might be favoured over evil, monster, animal, dead, other, uncivilised and unconscious. Binary oppositions help to establish clear borders, boundaries and thresholds in terms of social and cultural acceptability and taboo. A key and enduring feature of horror is that it actively seeks to transgress these binary oppositions and their implied borders, boundaries and thresholds as a way of reconfiguring them, drawing attention to their constructed nature and evoking fear through playful inversion and fusion. An interesting example here is the transgression of several of the binary distinctions listed above in the television series *Dexter* (2006–2013). For example, Dexter is a complex and ambiguous character whose motivations and actions vacillate between good/evil, human/monster and civilised/uncivilised. Moreover, his frequent narration in the form of a voice-over further collapses borders and boundaries between the conscious/unconscious, inside/outside and rational/irrational. It is useful therefore for horror screenwriters to ask themselves, how precisely does the screenplay work with binary oppositions in its narrative? And to what extent does the screenplay push at normative thresholds and borders?

Horror is also often thought of as operating metaphorically and allegorically (Gledhill, 2007). Horror screenplays can productively employ metaphor and allegory to say something about the world and the current state of affairs with respect to nation, society, politics, economics, culture and identity (i.e. class, gender, race, sexuality and disability). Influential modernist allegories and metaphors traditionally associated with horror include social alienation, crisis in evolutionary identity, the collapse of spiritual and moral order and the externalisation of the internal world (Wells, 2000: 3–6). Social alienation (influenced by the work of Karl Marx) critiques social and economic hierarchies. Here monsters transgress order revealing oppression in everyday life, such as in *Dawn of the Dead* (1978). Crisis in evolutionary identity (influenced by the ideas of Charles Darwin) deconstructs hierarchies linked to natural selection. Here the monstrousness and corruption of humans is explored, often linked to their attempts to control nature, such as in *Long Weekend* (1978) and its 2008 remake of the same name. The collapse of spiritual and moral order (influenced by the work of Friedrich Nietzsche) foregrounds a nihilistic worldview that questions reason and rationality. Here the world is characterised by conflict and uncertainty where human activity is a futile struggle to preserve order, such as in *Martyrs* (2008). Finally, the externalisation of the internal world (influenced by the work of Sigmund Freud) foregrounds the manifestation of latent subconscious and repressed desires and examines ideas linked to madness and psychosis, such as in *Maniac* (2012).

Here, then, it is particularly productive for screenwriters to reflect on the relationship between the real/literal and the imaginary/symbolic in their horror screenplays, and to carefully consider how accessible and comprehensible the screenplay's latent meanings and allegories are to potential audiences.

Engaging horror paradigms

There are several horror paradigms that screenwriters can inventively seek stimulus from when developing their screenplays. These paradigms work across mainstream, independent, art-house, exploitation and amateur modes of horror production. What is particularly enthusing about engaging horror paradigms is how screenwriters can enhance their screenplays by re-imagining, hybridising and adding twists to these macro blueprints.

A useful starting point is to establish if a realist or supernatural horror paradigm best suits the screenplay, or whether the screenplay will blend elements of both. Realist horror plays on the fear of the known and human monster. It exploits the everyday and may blend actual events or characters within its fictional narrative. Plots tend to be both rational and plausible and driven by cause and effect logic. Realist horrors often draw on formal procedures linked to directness and immediacy (i.e. realism and verisimilitude) and may play down overt aesthetic stylisation (i.e. soundtrack and montage). The influence of the realist paradigm can be seen in a range of horror sub-genres, including European extremism, found-footage, survival, torture porn/spectacle, serial killer and slashers. Recent film examples include *Big Bad Wolves (2013)*, *You're Next* (2013) and *The Bunny Game* (2010), which blends performance art and cinema.

Supernatural horror plays on the fear of the unknown. Narratives tend to focus on spiritual evil, monsters, fantasy and unusual psychic states, and whilst potentially rooted in the everyday, they take in more fantastical and surreal characteristics. Narratives tend to be irrational and implausible, where cause and effect may be loosened or abandoned in favour of imaginative leaps and gaps, and also of dream or nightmare logic. The influence of the supernatural paradigm can be seen in a range of horror sub-genres including ghost stories, gothic tales, monsters, the occult, haunted house and possession films. Recent film examples include *Haunter* (2013), *The Conjuring* (2013), *Mama* (2013) and *Insidious: Chapter 2* (2013).

Another paradigmatic choice useful for screenwriters to assess is between physical and psychological horror. Here, elements of both paradigms can be blended within horror screenplays. Physical horror places an emphasis on fear linked to bodily vulnerability and the depiction of graphic violence carried out against the body. Physical horror often examines the body as a site of struggle, exploiting fears linked to the monstrousness and uncontrollability of the body. Sub-genres working with physical horror include torture porn/spectacle horror, splatter/gore, exploitation and body horror, with examples including *Evil Dead*, *Antiviral* (2012) and *A L'interieur/Inside* (2007). Psychological horror places an emphasis on fear of the dangers and distortions that threaten normal life, located in the minds of deranged individuals. Psychological horror explores the inner tensions of the mind and its manifestations, including nightmares, psychosis, paranoia and doppelgängers. Sub-genres emphasising psychological horror include serial killers, ghost stories, supernatural, haunted house and possession films. Examples include *Chained* (2012), *Berberian Sound Studio* (2012) and *Sleep Tight* (2011).

A final paradigmatic option worthwhile deliberating is between serious and comedy horror. Similarly to the other horror paradigms, elements of serious and comedic horror can be synthesised. Serious horror tends to be dark and can be very grim. It can be confrontational, addressing uncomfortable issues that can be real or supernatural, physical or psychological. It is often narratively and tonally direct and immediate, and can potentially be very challenging and unsettling for audiences. Examples include *Antichrist* (2009), *Funny Games*

(2007) and *The Girl Next Door* (2007). Comedy horror, on the other hand, is often playful, satirical and fun, but can of course also be dark. Comedy is used to either diffuse or heighten horror and violence, and is often seen as being entertaining. Comedy horror takes many forms including parodies, slapstick, gross-out and black comedy. Examples include *Scary Movie 5* (2013), *Warm Bodies* (2013) and *Grabbers* (2012).

Playing with styles and sub-genre

According to McKee (1999: 80), the horror genre can be divided into three main sub-genres: the uncanny (where there is a scientific or rational explanation for the horror); the supernatural (where there is an irrational or spiritual reason for the horror); and the super-uncanny (where there is uncertainty as to whether the horror is uncanny or supernatural). For Duncan (2008: 110–134), there are four primary sub-genres for the screenwriter to work with: supernatural (ghost) fantasy; sci-fi horror-fantasy; neo-horror (slasher) fantasy; and neo-horror comedy fantasy. Whilst McKee and Duncan offer to screenwriters some useful starting points, they do not take us much beyond the paradigms outlined above. Rather, the analysis of Cherry (2009) is considered more useful to screenwriters who want to explore the depths of what horror has to offer, particularly as horror has a tendency to bleed into and out of a wide range of texts that may not always be thought of as horror by both screenwriters and audiences.

Cherry sees horror as characterised by diversity and fragmentation (2009: 2–51). Diversity can be seen in the historical range of transnational and transcultural horror film production, ranging from the 1920 German Expressionist horror and 1930s Universal horror films; the psychological, teen and sci-fi horrors produced in the USA during the 1940s and 1950s to the Hammer and European horror of the 1960s and the US New Horror of the late 1960s and 1970s; to the rise of Asian, European and Australian horror cinemas in the early years of the 21st century. Screenwriters may then research the horror film traditions, styles and national cinemas that most closely approximate their horror ideas. For example, for a writer developing a horror screenplay exploring the monstrous use of telekinetic powers, invaluable insights could be gleaned from analysing its treatment in films across various temporal, stylistic and cultural contexts, such as *The Village of the Damned* (1960), *Carrie* (1976, 2013), *Scanners* (1981), *Manhattan Baby* (1982), *Patrick* (1978, 2013) and *Kurosufaia/Crossfire* (2000).

Fragmentation can be observed in the wide range of horror sub-genres identifiable in industrial and academic discourses. Cherry lists sub-generic categories of cinematic horror as the gothic; supernatural, occult and ghost films; psychological horror; monster movies; slashers, body horror, splatter and gore films; and exploitation cinema, video nasties and explicitly violent films (2009: 5–6). For Blake and Bailey (2013: 21–40), horror can be divided into: the undead; monsters; psychological horror; demons, possession and child possession; the supernatural: ghosts, hauntings and poltergeists; witchcraft; werewolves and body horror, bad science; and slasher. Moreover, Marriott and Newman (2008) examine the history of a number of horror sub-genres and styles, including mad scientist, ghost, occult, eco-horror, giallo, urbanoia, slasher, cannibalism, serial killer and comedy horror. They also cite adaptations of the work of Edgar Allan Poe, H.P. Lovecraft and Steven King, along with comic book and television, as important horror variations.

Missing from these lists are recent sub-generic variations such as found-footage horror and torture porn/spectacle horror, and older traditions such as teen horror or the shockumentary. What is clear from this account is that whilst there is some clear consensus over horror sub-genres (e.g. supernatural and slasher), there is also a great deal of fluidity, variation, contestation and negotiation. The point here for screenwriters is that each of these horror sub-genres and styles has their own histories, traditions, codes and conventions that can be productively researched, studied, drawn upon and re-imagined within screenplays. It is precisely this flexibility and multiplicity of horror that attracts screenwriters to work with the genre or to use its generic elements in their work.

Another key feature of contemporary horror is the cross-generic play with themes and elements from two or more genres leading to new intersections and hybrid forms. Significant examples of generic hybrids combining with horror include: fantasy-horror *Byzantium* (2012); sci-fi horror *The Dyatlov Pass Incident/The Devils Pass* (2013); horror-pornography *Porn of the Dead* (2006); Western-horror *Cowboys and Vampires* (2010); horror-musical *Suck* (2009); comedy-horror *Tucker & Dale vs. Evil* (2010); and even the comedy-horror-musical *Highway to Hell* (2012). There are also examples of the hybridising of distinct franchises, such as *Aliens vs. Predator: Requiem* (2007) and *Freddy vs. Jason* (2003). Whilst often unpopular with fans and critics, there is industry interest in the economics of cross-generic play so it is relevant for screenwriters to be aware of this when developing their projects. This discussion aligns with the central paradox associated with genre writing, between reinvention and innovation and tradition and repetition.

Shaping horror characters

Characters and the relationships between them are a fundamental feature of horror screenplays, whether the project is character or action driven. Unforgettable characters such as Norman Bates, Regan MacNeil, Leatherface, Carrie White, Freddy Krueger, Asami Yamazaki and Jigsaw take time to develop, development that materialises through experimentation, refinement and alignment with theme, story world and narrative structure (Batty, 2012: 59–74).

According to McGlasson (2010), there are two main approaches to developing memorable characters within horror screenplays. The most common involves adapting and re-working existing character types and archetypes. For example, there have been hundreds of re-imaginings of Dracula (vampire), Dr Jekyll and Mr Hyde (shape shifter) and Frankenstein's monster (pseudo-human). According to McGlasson, this works because audiences recognise and respond to the history of fears, myths and representations associated with these character archetypes. The second approach involves innovation by creating original characters based on the screenwriter's imagination and research. Whilst challenging, given the range of horror narratives circulating within popular culture, there is always space to create new characters and character types that tap into contemporary fears and desires, or that examine untapped mythologies and folklores from around the world. For McGlasson, in practice many horror writers blend these methods by treading the line between originality and duplication. Taylor (2007: 137–140) suggests that the golden rule of modern monster making is to really know one's monster, which involves being knowledgeable of their generic history, clearly establishing the rules that govern them, fully characterising them and then working with, but also being prepared to bend, the rules governing the monster in order to engage knowing horror audiences.

A common criticism of horror screenplays is the lack of credibility and believability of their characters. Horror protagonists, and to a lesser extent monsters, can be seen as one-dimensional clichés with terrible decision-making skills and who add little to the narrative. Unless it is thematically motivated to have superficial characters, it is essential that screenwriters develop engaging and multifaceted horror characters that audiences will believe in and root for. This can be achieved,

I suggest, in three overlapping ways. First, it is useful to establish inner character by identifying the core needs, motivations and desires that drive a character's physical and emotional journey, and that align with the world, themes and structure of the screenplay. Second, working on outer character (characterisation) brings them to life through the visual and verbal transfiguration of inner character into their surroundings, clothing, actions, reactions and voice. Third, researching the role and function of various horror character archetypes, stereotypes and types, and the associated audience expectations of these categories of characters, is productive and can add dimensionality to a screenplay (Taylor, 2007; McGlasson, 2010; Batty, 2012).

Horror screenwriters are well advised to not only spend time working on credible and believable characters, but also to carefully develop them relationally within the overall cast of the screenplay. When developing relationships between main, secondary and minor horror characters, it is helpful for the screenwriter to reflect on the cultural work of the monstrous within their screenplay. It is helpful to remember that horror characters are productive and dynamic lenses through which the consequences of actions taken in relation to the fears and desires explored in the screenplay can be interrogated. In other words, the monstrous is not just a source of conflict, but when articulated through character and character relationships can be an insightful and revelatory allegory offering critical and radical insights into the world. For example, *Dark Tourist* (2012) uses its character study of grief tourist Jim Tahana, and his interactions with other characters, as a way of offering a critique of American mass consumption, its obsession with serial killers and its failure to fix the damage done to its citizens as a consequence of the violence and abuse they may have experienced.

A key relationship to consider when designing a horror cast is between the protagonists and the antagonists or monsters. Here, three interweaving types of relationship are useful to work with. The first is a relationship characterised by extremes, where characters are placed at opposing sides of a binary distinction, between, for example, good/evil, hero(ine)/villain and human/monster. Here the antagonist or monster is characterised as the monstrous 'other'; an antagonistic, threatening and transformative force that is simultaneously a site of fear/desire and disgust/attraction. Examples include *The Dead 2: India* (2013) and *I Spit on Your Grave 2*. The second, a variation on the first, is to reverse these distinctions and offer more complex and ambiguous characters and character relationships. Many contemporary horror screenplays feature monsters and antagonists that are increasingly humanised and sympathetic whilst other characters may be de-humanised and unsympathetic. Examples include *Cheap Thrills* and *We Are What We Are* (2013). The third is a relationship that reflects distorted similarities between characters. Here, different character relationships may offer insights into a single horror character or the horror theme. Horror has a long history of twins, lookalikes, doubles and doppelgängers: characters are twisted reflections of each other, where their fates are utterly entwined or may represent psychological manifestations of repressed guilt or desires. Examples include *The Banshee Chapter* (2013), *Dementamania* (2013) and *Stoker* (2013).

Constructing horror numbers

A key area of attention for screenwriters when fashioning a horror screenplay is the relationship between narrative and spectacle. A balance needs to be created between telling a good and well-crafted story that captures the imagination of an audience, and creating spectacular and stand-out moments that will linger in the imagination long after it has been seen or read.

Here, Freeland's notion of 'horror numbers' is interesting to consider (2000: 256–257). Horror numbers are scenes or sequences of heightened spectacle and emotion, often featuring monstrous behaviour and exaggerated violence, that deliver the thrills and sensations horror audiences want. Freeland argues that horror numbers have a similar function to dance numbers in musicals, in that they help to enhance and forward the plot rather than being interruptions within the flow of the narrative. When discussing the function of horror numbers in graphic spectacular horror, she suggests that they further the narrative and as such constitute a key part of a film's form and structure, produce the film's central emotional and cognitive effects (i.e. dread or fear), and provide aesthetic pleasures linked to an audience's awareness and knowledge of the genre. The point here for screenwriters is to carefully plan horror numbers to harness not only their narrative and affective power but also their appeal to audiences.

Kinder's idea of the 'narrative orchestration of violent attractions' (2001: 63–100) is also instructive here. She reflects on the use of screen violence as offering guideposts along a narrative journey. The invitation here is for screenwriters to contemplate how horror numbers can be used to structure the overall stylistic and narrative design of a screenplay, and not just configure a scene or sequence. For example, co-writer and director of *Sinister* (2012) Scott Derrickson, speaking at

Frightfest (2012), suggested that the film had been crafted so that the shocks were fully integrated into the narrative and carefully designed to heighten their effect as the story progressed. Screenwriters can thus cogitate on how horror numbers and the narrative orchestration of violent attractions might enrich themes and the horror world of their film by fully integrating them within the screenplay's communicative design.

Horror screenwriters should also think carefully about the strategies they draw on to organise the horror numbers in their narratives. Narratives that principally offer horror numbers without any motivation or justification, even when this is thematically the purpose of the story, tend to become overwhelming and potentially numbing, such as *August Underground* (2001) and *Slaughtered Vomit Dolls* (2006). This does not mean that horror screenplays should work rigidly within a standardised horror structure, such as a pre-credit sequence (mythology), first act (disruption), second act (all doomed), third act (utopian resolution) and/or a post-credit sequence (dystopian, open or sequel friendly ending). Rather, horror screenwriters can consider embracing alternative narrative structures including anthology horror, multi-act and multi-stranded narratives or more surrealist or avant-garde approaches to their screenplays. Horror screenwriters may therefore view narrative elements such as story and plot, temporality, spatiality, patterns of development, narration and story information as fluid and to be actively experimented with. Interesting examples here include *V/H/S/2* (2013) *The ABCs of Death* (2012), *Los Cronocrímenes/Timecrimes* (2007), *The Signal* (2007) and *Trick 'r Treat* (2007).

Another key feature in the development of horror numbers is the decision to 'go there' or not with the gore. Going there, as Marano (2007) points out, is to stare directly at the horror and violence; to have it fully visible on the page in all its wet, visceral and screaming detail. Violence that goes there should be direct, immediate, drawn out and made to hurt. It is violence that pushes audiences to their limits. Recent examples include *Evil Dead, No One Lives* (2012) and *Wither* (2012). Not going there is to look away from the horror and violence. It is to have action take place off the page or to be hidden and covert in the pages of the screenplay. The horror violence is either unseen or indirect and implied. Whilst it may be heard, it is often subtle, quiet and dry. Not going there can be very effective but the emphasis is on unsettling and unnerving the audience. Examples include *Låt den rätte komma in/Let the Right One In* (2008), *El orfanato/The Orphanage* (2007) and *The Others* (2001).

Screenwriters may elect to use a mixture of going there and not going there. The key point here is that when it comes to writing horror numbers, what is important is not just what we see/read (i.e. the violent content) but also the manipulation of how we are invited to see/read it (i.e. the design of the violence). As such, when crafting a horror screenplay it is important for screenwriters to reflect on how horror numbers can function as storytelling and not just description. In other words, how horror numbers can be productively employed to communicate something about the world, themes, ideas and characters of the screenplay.

Conclusion

It has been the intention of this chapter to offer screenwriters, screenwriting critics and those working in development a range of considerations that can be worked with and adapted during the production and critique of a horror screenplay. As has been argued, horror storytelling is enriched through an alignment of a well-researched knowledge of horror industries and audiences, the creative application of craft skills and techniques, and the imaginative understanding of conceptual and theoretical approaches to horror. This approach, blending theory with practice, has sought to move beyond trade articles and industrial information, the abstract nature of academic texts, and checklists for success found in some practical guides to horror writing. In doing so, it is hoped that the approach offered will inspire horror screenwriters to further re-animate horror storytelling through the creative blending of theory and practice. It is also hoped that screenwriters and screenwriting theorists will critique and augment these ideas to further enhance approaches that effectively blend theory into practice and practice into theory within horror screenwriting.

References

A L'interieur/Inside (2007) Wrs./Dirs. Alexandre Bustillo and Julien Maury, France, 82 mins.

Aliens vs. Predator: Requiem (2007) Wr. Shane Salerno, Dirs. Colin Strause and Greg Strause, USA, 102 mins. (unrated version).

Antichrist (2009) Wr./Dir. Lars von Trier, *Denmark/Germany/France/Sweden/ Italy/Poland*, 108 mins.

Antiviral (2012) Wr./Dir. Brandon Cronenberg, Canada, 108 mins.

August Underground (2001) (Video) Wrs. Allen Peters and Fred Vogel, Dir. Fred Vogel, USA, 70 mins.

Bakhtin, M. (1984) *Rabelais and His World*, Hoboken, JY: John Wiley & Sons.

Barker, J.M. (2009) *The Tactile Eye: Touch and The Cinematic Experience*, London: University of California Press.

Batty, C. (2012) *Screenplays: How To Write and Sell Them* (Creative Essentials), Harpenden: Kamera Books.

BBFC (2011) 'Human Centipede 2 (Full Sequence) Rejection Explanation'. Available from: British Board of Film Classification, http://www.bbfc.co.uk/releases/human-centipede-2-full-sequence (accessed 3 October 2013).

Berberian Sound Studio (2012) Wr./Dir. Peter Strickland, UK, 92 mins.

Big Bad Wolves (2013) Wrs./Dirs. Aharon Keshales and Navot Papushado, Israel, 110 mins.

Blake, M. and Bailey, S. (2013) *Writing the Horror Movie*, London: Bloomsbury.

Byzantium (2012) Wr. Moira Buffini, Dir. Neil Jordan, UK/USA/Ireland, 118 mins.

Carrie (1976) Wr. Lawrence D. Cohen, Dir. Brian De Palma, USA, 98 mins.

Carrie (2013) Wr. Roberto Aguirre-Sacasa, Dir. Kimberly Peirce, USA, 100 mins.

Chained (2012) Wr./Dir Jennifer Chambers Lynch, Canada, 94 mins.

Cheap Thrills (2013) Wrs. David Chirchirillo and Trent Haaga, Dir. E.L. Katz, USA 85 mins.

Cherry, B. (2009) *Horror (Routledge Film Guidebooks)*, London: Routledge.

Cowboys and Vampires (2010) Wr./Dir. Douglas Myers, USA, 94 mins.

Creed, B. (1993) *The Monstrous Feminine: Film, Feminism, Psychoanalysis* (Popular Fictions Seriese), London: Routledge.

Dark Tourist (2012) Wr. Frank John Hughes, Dir. Suri Krishnamma USA, 85 mins.

Dawn of the Dead (1978) Wr./Dir. George A. Romero, Italy/USA, 156 min. (Ultimate Final Cut).

Death By VHS (2013) Wrs. Scarlet Fry, Laurance Holloway, Jacob D. O'Neal, David Sabal, Brian Everet Smith and Richard Stoudt, Dirs. Scarlet Fry, Jscob D. O'Neal and David Sabal., USA, 75 mins.

Dementamania (2013) Wr. Anis Shlewet, Dir. Kit Ryan, UK, 83 mins.

Dexter (2006–2013) Wrs. Jeff Lindsay and James Mantos Jr. (96 episodes), Dirs. Various, USA. 60 mins.

Douglas, M. (2002) *Purity and Danger: An Analysis of Concept of Pollution and Taboo*, London: Routledge.

Duncan, S.V. (2008) *Genre Screenwriting: How To Write Popular Screenplays That Sell*, London: Continuum, pp. 110–134.

Evil Dead (2013) Wrs. Fede Alvarez and Rodo Sayagues, Dir. Fede Alvarez, USA, 91 mins.

Freddy vs. Jason (2003) Wrs. Damian Shannon and Mark Swift, Dir. Ronny Yu, Canada/USA/Italy, 97 mins.

Freeland, C.A. (2000) *The Naked and The Dead: Evil and The Appeal of Horror*, Oxford: West view Press.

Freud, S. (2003) *The Uncanny* (Penguin Modern Classics Translated Texts), London: Penguin Classics.

Freud, S. (2005) *The Unconscious* (Penguin Modern Classics Translated Texts), London: Penguin Classics.

Funny Games (2007) Wr./Dir. Michael Haneke, USA/France/UK/Austria/Germany/Italy, 111 mins.

Gledhill, C. (2007) 'The Horror Film' in Pam Cook (ed.) *The Cinema Book* (3rd ed.), London: British Film Institute, pp. 347–366.

Grabbers (2012) Wr. Kevin Lehane, Dir. Jon Wright, UK/Ireland, 94 mins.

Grey, J. (2010) *Show Sold Separately: Promos, Spoilers, and other Media Paratexts*, New York: New York University Press.

Halloween 2 (2009) Wr/Dir. Rob Zombie, USA, 105 mins.

Hannibal (2013–) Wrs. Bryan Fuller and Tomas Harris (14 episodes), Dir. Various, USA, 43 mins.

Haunter (2013) Wr. Brian King and Matthew Brian King, Dir. Vincenzo Natali, Canada/France, 97 mins.

Highway to Hell (2012) (Video) Wr./Dr. Richard Driscal, UK, 94 mins.

Hill, A. (1997) *Shocking Entertainment: Viewer Responses to Violent Movies*, Luton: John Libbey.

Human Centipede II (Full Sequence) (2011) Wr./Dir. Tom Six, USA, 91 mins. (uncut).

I Spit on Your Grave 2 (2013) Wrs. Neil Elman & Thomas Fenton, Dir. Steven R. Monroe, USA, 106 mins. (uncut).

Insidious: Chapter 2 (2013) Wr. Leigh Whannell, Dir James Wan, USA, 106 mins.

Jenkins, H. (2008) *Convergence Culture: Where Old and New Media Collide*, London: New York University Press.

Kimber, S. (2011) *Controversies: Henry Portrait of a Serial Killer*, Basingstoke: Palgrave Macmillan.

Kimber, S. (2014) 'Transgressive Edge Play and A Srpski Film/A Serbian Film' in *Horror Studies*, 5(1), 107–125.

Kinder, M. (2001) 'Violence American Style: The Narrative Orchestration of Violent Attractions' in David, J. Slocum (ed.) *Violence and American Cinema*, London: Routledge.

Kristeva, J. (1982) *Powers of Horror: An Essay on Abjection*, New York: Columbia University Press.

Kurosufaia/Crossfire (2000) Wrs. Kota Yamada, Masahiro Yokotani & Shûsuke Kaneko, Dir. Shûsuke Kaneko, Japan, 115 mins.

Les Revenants/The Returned (2012–) Wrs. Fabrice Gobert and Emmanuel Carrere, Dirs. Fabrice Gobert and Frédéric Mermoud, France, 52 mins.

Long Weekend (1978) Wr. Everett De Roche, Dir. Colin Eggleston, Australia, 92 mins.

Long Weekend (2008) Wr. Everett De Roche, Dir. Jamie Blanks, Australia, 88 mins.

Los cronocrímenes/*Timecrimes* (2007) Wr./Dir. Nacho Vigalondo, Spain, 92 mins.

Mama (2013) Wrs. Neil Cross, Andrés Muschietti & Barbara Muschietti, Dir. Andrés Muschietti, Spain/Canada, 100 mins.

Mancini, D. (2013) 'Directors Q&A *Curse of Chucky* (2013)' in *Frightfest*, London, 22 August 2013.

Manhattan Baby (1982) Wrs. Elisa Briganti and Dardano Sacchetti, Dir. Lucio Fulci, Italy, 89 mins.

Maniac (2012) Wrs. Alexandre Aja and Grégory Levasseur, Dir. Franck Khalfoun, France/USA, 89 mins.

Marano, M. (2007) 'Going There: Strategies for Writing the things that Scare You' in Mort Castle (ed.) *On Writing Horror: A Handbook by The Horror Writers Association*, Cincinnati: Writers Digest Books, pp. 53–57.

Marriott, J. (2004) *Horror Films*, London: Virgin Books.

Marriott, J. and Newman, K. (2008) *Horror: The Definitive Guide to the Cinema of Fear*, London: Andre Deutch.

Martyrs (2008) Wr./Dir. Pascal Laugier, France/Canada, 99 mins.

McGlasson (2010) 'Creating Memorable Horror Characters' Available from: ConstructingHorror.com, http://constructinghorror.com/index.php?id=124 (Accessed 4 October 2013).

McKee, R. (1999) *Story: Substance, Structure, Style and The Principles of Screenwriting*, London: Methuen.

No One Lives (2012) Wr. David Cohen, Dir. Ryûhei Kitamura, USA, 86 mins.

Patrick (1978) Wr. Everett de Rouche, Dir. Richard Franklin, Australia, 96 mins.

Patrick (2013) Wr. Justin King, Dir. Mike Hartley, Australia, 90 mins.

Paranormal Activity 4 (2012) Wr. Chrsitopher Landon, Dirs. Henry Joost and Ariel Schulman, USA, 88 mins.

Porn of the Dead (2006) (Video) Wr./Dir. Rob Rotten, USA, 100 mins.

Scanners (1981) Wr./Dir. David Cronenberg, Canada, 103 mins.

Scary Movie 5 (2013) Wrs. David Zucker and Pat Proft, Dir. Malcolm D. Lee, USA, 86 mins.

Sinister (2012) Wrs. Scott Derrickson & C. Robert Cargill, Dir. Scott Derrickson, USA/UK, 110 mins.

Slaughtered Vomit Dolls (2006) (Video) Wr./Dir. Lucifer Valentine, Canada/USA, 71 mins.

Sleep Tight (2011) Wr. Alberto Marini, Dir. Jaume Balagueró, Spain, 102 mins.

Srpski Film/A Serbian Film (2010) Wrs. Aleksandar Radivojevic and Srdjan Spasojevic, Dir. Srdjan Spasojevic, Serbia, 104 mins. (Uncut).

Stalled (2013) Wr. Dan Palmer, Dir. Christian James, UK, 84 mins.

Stoker (2013) Wr. Wentworth Miller, Dir. Chan-wook Park, UK/USA, 99 mins.

Suck (2009) Wr./Dir. Rob Stefaniuk, Canada, 91 mins.

Taylor, K.E. (2007) 'No More Silver Mirrors: The Monsters in Our Times' in Mort Castle (ed.) *On Writing Horror: A Handbook by The Horror Writers Association*, Cincinnati: Writers Digest Books, pp. 137–140.

The ABCs of Death (2012) Wrs. Various, Dirs. Various, USA/New Zealand, 123 mins.

The Banshee Chapter (2013) Wrs. Blair Erickson and Daniel J. Healy, Dir. Blair Erickson, Germany/USA, 87 mins.

The Blair Witch Project (1999) Wrs./Dirs. Daniel Myrick and Eduardo Sánchez, USA, 81 mins.

The Bunny Game (2010) Wrs. Rodleen Getsic and Adam Rehmeier, Dir. Adam Rehmeier USA, 76 mins.

The Conjuring (2013) Wrs. Chad Hayes and Carey Hayes, Dir. James Wan, USA, 112 mins.

The Dead 2: India (2013) Wrs./Dir. Howard J. Ford and Jonathan Ford, UK, 90 mins.

The Demon's Rook (2013) Wrs. James Sizemore and Akom Tidwell, Dir. James Sizemore, USA, 103 mins.

The Dyatlov Pass Incident/The Devils Pass (2013) Wr. Vikram Weet, Dir. Renny Harlin, USA/UK/Russia, 100 mins.

The Girl Next Door (2007) Wrs. Daniel Farrands and Philip Nutman, Dir. Gregory Wilson, USA, 91 mins.

The Purge (2013) Wr./Dir. James DeManco, USA/france, 85 mins.

The Signal (2007) Wrs./Dirs. David Bruckner, Jacob Gentry and Dan Bush, USA, 103 mins.

The Village of the Damned (1960) Wrs. Stirling Silliphant, Wolf Rilla and Ronald Kinnoch, Dir. Wolf Rilla, UK, 77 mins.

Trick 'r Treat (2007) Wr./Dir. Michael Dougherty, USA, 82 mins.

True Blood (2008–) Wrs. Alan Ball & Charlaine Harris (71 episodes), Dirs. Various. USA, 60 mins.

Tucker & Dale Vs Evil (2010) Wrs. Eli Craig & Morgan Jurgenson, Dir. Eli Craig, Canada/USA, 89 mins.

V/H/S/2 (2013) Anthology Concept Brad Miska, Wrs. Various, Dirs. Various, USA/Canada/Indonesia, 95 mins.

Warm Bodies (2013) Wr./Dir. Jonathan Levine, USA, 98 mins.

We Are What We Are (2013) Wrs.Nick Damici & Jim Mickle, Dir. Jim Mickle, USA, 105 mins.

Wells, P. (2000) *The Horror Genre: From Beelzebub to Blair Witch (Short Cuts)*, London: Wallflower.

Wheatley, B. (2013) 'Variety Spotlight: Ben Wheatley' in *Frightfest*, London, 23 August 2013.

Wither (2012) Wrs. Sonny Laguna, David Liljeblad and Tommy Wiklund, Dirs. Sonny Laguna and Tommy Wiklund, Sweden, 95 mins.

Wood, R. (1986) *Hollywood from Vietnam to Reagan...and Beyond*, New York: Columbia University Press.

World War Z (2013) Wrs. Matthew Michael Carnahan, Drew Goddard & Damon Lindelof, Dir. Marc Forester, USA/Malta, 116 mins.

You're Next (2013) Simon Barrett, Dir. Adam Wingard, USA, 94 mins.

4
Beyond the Screenplay: Memoir and Family Relations in Three Films by Gaylene Preston

Hester Joyce

Introduction

In 1992, emerging filmmaker Gaylene Preston recounted that as a child she was considered a 'very famous liar': 'I always preferred a story to reality. I am very interested in family stories, and I suppose being a storyteller this end of the twentieth century means you have to deal with the plastic. Stories are lies for good purpose' (Preston, 1992: 161). Her sentiment exemplifies the dilemmas facing biographical and auto-biographical screenwriters in a genre where the task is to choose from whole lives and weave stories that, whilst not necessarily *the* truth, do represent *a* truth. For such screenwriters and filmmakers, these dilemmas become even more conflicted when the truths belong to their own families, and when they are secrets. This chapter thus explores aspects of auto/biography and film memoir, and secrets, truth and family in particular, in three works by New Zealand filmmaker Gaylene Preston: *War Stories Our Mothers Never Told Us* (1995), *Perfect Strangers* (2003) and *Home By Christmas* (2010).

The last of these, *Home By Christmas*, is Preston's account of her father's experience as a soldier in Italy during World War II based on interviews she conducted with him late in 1991, not long before he died. Described by the filmmaker as a 'film memoir', the work blends fact and fiction to recount Ed Preston's war experiences and his four-year absence from his wife and newly born son. The film's complex narrative, built from reconstructed interviews, includes interwoven strands of voice-over narration, recollection, historical documentary and dramatisation, ultimately becoming Preston's own auto/biography of the secrets held between 'the before' and 'the after' of World War II for intersecting generations of her family.

War Stories, Perfect Strangers and *Home By Christmas* are here read as a trilogy, each film uncovering then building upon these family secrets. In *War Stories*, Preston's mother is interviewed about her wartime experiences in which she tells of having a romantic affair whilst her husband was away on active military service. Whilst *War Stories* is a documentary and *Home By Christmas* a memoir, *Perfect Strangers* is a fiction film, the story of a woman in a love triangle with two men, one of whom becomes a dead body hidden in a freezer. *Perfect Strangers'* figurative relationship to *Home By Christmas* provides a fruitful avenue of investigation into the tensions between private and public, and a way of reframing the ordinary and the heroic in the construction of film memoir. As such, it is useful for screenwriters in reflecting on the kaleidoscopic ways in which one story might be told, and ways in which biographical material might be mined for creative interpretation.

Backstory

Gaylene Preston's filmography is extensive, spanning a variety of forms including television and film, drama and documentary. Within these she has written, directed and produced across a number of genres including: fantasy thriller, *Mr. Wrong* (1985); historical biopic, *Bread and Roses* (1993); comedy, *Ruby and Rata* (1990); documentary, *Titless Wonders* (2001); and artists' portraits, *Hone Tuwhare* (1996), *Lovely Rita* (2007) and *Kai Purakau: Keri Hulme – Teller of Tales* (1987). The majority of Preston's[1] works are centred on women, and their stories are imbued with a feminist orthodoxy. Preston began her career in art therapy in New Zealand, then in drama therapy in the UK, returning home after seeing a London screening of *This is New Zealand* (Macdonald, 1970), a promotional tourism film produced for Expo '70. This anecdotal recollection, 'Oh, I have to go home. They can make films there!' (Wiles, 2010) is at the heart of Preston's screen storytelling and she is one of only a few internationally successful New Zealand filmmakers who remains in production 'at home'.

As her oeuvre attests, Preston's feminist sensibility is situated within a strong desire to explore personal issues against a background of New Zealand nationhood and national identity. Furthermore, the screenwriting, development and production in each case are determined by the subject matter, the characters, the nature of their stories and the film's industrial context. To say that Preston is a screenwriter and focus only on her screenwriting is to elide many of the facets that make her a consummate screen storyteller. Sam Neill describes her as a collaborator (*The Making of Perfect Strangers*, 2003), and Tony Barry recounts fondly, 'I think Gaylene is an alchemist, she can put together a white witches' brew that is going to be very nourishing to the spirit...' (*The Making of Home by Christmas*, 2010). By considering three aspects of her work – the 'voice,' the formal construction, and the production context – this investigation, through the unusual intimacy of the trilogy, explores the writing of audiovisual auto/biography and film memoir. The three films in question contest conventional notions of screenwriting, each using different processes and methods for building the film.

War Stories Our Mothers Never Told Us (1995)

> War Stories. I don't know when I started collecting them. I suppose I grew up in the shadow of the war. During the peace [...] Sitting under the table while the women talked above me. Never about the battles or the bombs. Always about the relationships. Dislocated or wrenched apart or sometimes worse, forced together again because of that time called 'during-the-war'.
>
> (Preston, 1995)

The story of these three films begins with secrets revealed in the first, *War Stories Our Mothers Never Told Us*. *War Stories* grew out of an oral history project in the early 1990s that collected interviews with over 60 'ordinary' New Zealand women remembering their experiences during World War II. One of these women was Preston's mother, Tui. From these interviews ideas for the film and a book developed, but the funding agency, the New Zealand Film Commission (NZFC), was reluctant to finance a film, Preston recalls, of 'seven old ladies talking about the war with a bit of archival footage thrown in' (Wiles, 2010). The NZFC, a government-funded film production agency, was at the time the primary source of film development and production finance for New Zealand filmmakers, and there was limited alternative private investment. Furthermore, local television broadcast was not providing the necessary opportunities for documentary production, and Preston 'held to the idea that in New Zealand it is cinema that remains the liberating social space' (Wiles, 2010). Confronted by the lack of support Preston began production, shooting (with cinematographer Alun Bollinger) interviews with five of the women and eventually convinced the NZFC that such a film would have cinematic value.

War Stories' aesthetic reflects its themes with the women, each seated alone against a dark background, speaking candidly about both the domestic minutiae and tragic turns of their lives. As they talk to us directly and share intimate details, their stories, intercut with personal photographs and archival wartime newsreel footage, are at once amusing, moving and heart-rending. In the telling, Preston maintains,

> my documentaries document the drama of people's lives and I let them speak, reveal themselves. Their stories reveal their own view of experience. My skill as a filmmaker is to not get in the way and to find a good structure to amplify the telling.
>
> (cited in Frances, 2005: 36)

Lawrence Simmons writes that *War Stories* is an example of 'video-testimony' that 'recuperates for us the function of story telling' (1996: 26). This is Preston's prime objective: to tell those New Zealand stories that no one else will (Frances, 2005: 36).

Carol Smart writes:

> Part of the pleasure in uncovering secrets is perhaps the way in which the discovery gives the lie to the idea of an idyllic past, when families are all supposed to be respectable, god-fearing and law-abiding. It may also be that recognizing human frailty in the past helps us to be more understanding of contemporary failings and mistakes.
>
> (2007: 109)

War Stories, demonstrates this cleaving of pasts, the publically shared and the privately known where Tui Preston recalls in a matter-a-fact way her early romance with her new husband Ed, his signing up for the infantry and his absence on active service in Italy. Her story is of being deeply in love and wretched at the thought of being separated from him, feelings amplified by her pregnancy. Ed's account in *Home by Christmas* is more larrikin, in which he insists he signed up for adventure and to earn some 'quick money' to set up his new family. His promise to return within months, by Christmas, becomes four years during which Tui gives birth to their first child. After receiving a telegram informing her that Ed was missing, Tui believed that Ed had died, and she recounts her falling in love and having a relationship with another man. On Ed's homecoming she returns to their marriage, motivated by the threat of losing their son 'to welfare'; a threat voiced by her mother and the small community she lives in.

Tui's recollection of the difficulties in the reunion was that both she and Ed were beset by severe depression that took them years to overcome. During the oral history project interviews, conducted by a third party in the mid-1990s, Tui revealed that she had had an extramarital affair whilst Ed was away. Preston only became a party to this information when she later made *War Stories*, however her curiosity had been stirred earlier during her father's interviews. His was an extensive account, 15 hours or so, of his experience as a soldier in Italy and Switzerland (Wiles, 2010). In the interviews, Preston presses Ed about the soldiers' sexual liaisons, but he diverts her. Perhaps quite believably, he at one point recalls, 'we didn't think about sex, we thought about food' (*Home by Christmas*). Similarly, regarding his reuniting with Tui and their young son whom he had never seen, not a lot is said. The remnants of her parents' different experiences stayed with Preston for several years whilst she continued to tell other screen stories. It was not until she made *Perfect Strangers*, a modern romantic fairy tale, that she became aware that she had returned to the preoccupation with the family secret, albeit in an allegorical form.

Perfect Strangers (2003)

> J.P. Sartre is nearer the truth when he says that autobiographers recollect their past passions in order to inter them in 'a calm cemetery'.
>
> (Pascal, 1960: 14)

Preston describes *Perfect Strangers* as her return to her own storytelling, for although she has screenwriting credits on the majority of her projects, this is the first that she solely authored: 'I don't think that I really, really, really arrived home until *Perfect Strangers*' (Frances, 2005: 37). *Perfect Strangers* tells the story of Melanie, an every woman living on the isolated south western coast of New Zealand, who meets The Man, 'the perfect man' to partner. This is a rugged, isolated place, beaten by raging seas and terrific weather. She sails to his island hut for the night only to realise that, fuelled by his own naive fantasy, he has taken her prisoner. During an altercation she stabs him, and after several attempts to save him fail, he dies. Having now fallen in love with him, she stores his body in the freezer and continues to live out both her own and his fantasies on the island. When former lover Bill, 'an every man', finds her alone on the island, he too becomes part of the twisted love triangle.

Preston describes *Perfect Strangers* as her most personal film, drawing from a subliminal consciousness, one that she 'had to get off her chest' (Frances, 2005: 37).

The film's auto/biographical aspects did not occur to the filmmaker until she was promoting it at the London Film Festival where she revealed:

> I realized as the questions came that I was born to make this film because I grew up in a marriage that had a third person in the metaphorical freezer. I was thinking, 'Yes my mother was in love with another man before my father came back from the war' [...] my mother was in love with a handsome stranger she had rejected to save the marriage. I hadn't realized until then that in the film I had unconsciously painted this portrait of the world I lived in as a three-year-old.
>
> (cited in Frances, 2005: 37)

Unlike *War Stories* and *Home by Christmas*, both of which were constructed from interviews, documentary footage and archival material, *Perfect Strangers* is a fictional story that underwent a more traditional development process, being one of eight films funded by the NZFC's Film Production Fund (FF1). The Fund was created as a result of a 'cultural recovery' package in 2000 and provided investment of between two and five million dollars to projects written and/or directed by experienced New Zealand filmmakers (Dunleavy and Joyce, 2011: 217). Projects financed by the FF1 were expected to find a further 40% offshore investment.[2] The Fund existed as a charitable trust independent of the NZFC, however it followed similar development practices, whereby screenplays for projects were submitted and read by independent readers including local and international script assessors and producers, before development or production financing was committed. Consequently *Perfect Strangers* began with a written screenplay.

What remains unconventional about the development process, however, is Preston's subversion of normalised genre conventions and the narrative structure of a romantic thriller. She argues that the three-act structure is as outdated as the notion of heroes and villains. Her characters are invested with a duality that plays out as predator and prey at various turns, defeating the familiar expectations of classical narrative. For example, Melanie, having assertively seduced The Man, sails on his yacht to an island, becoming his captive there. She initially rejects him, then lulls him into believing she accepts this submissive position and then turns on him, locking him out of his cabin. He tries to smoke her out but she retaliates, stabbing him as he forces his way in. She then falls in love with him in his incapacitated state, as if she is relieved to find a direction for her otherwise banal life. Preston intentionally avoids stereotypes of a female victim or *femme fatale*, instead landing on what she calls 'a real female predator' (Frances, 2005: 39). The characters' internal oscillations between 'good and bad' invest the storytelling with a fairy-tale sensibility. The Man is as habituated within the fairy tale as the woman, believing Melanie is as perfect for him as he is for her. The contestation of genre, exploration of gender and themes of fantasy and predation are recalled from Preston's earlier psychological thriller *Mr. Wrong*.

Perfect Strangers serves Preston's private and public purpose in that myth and fantasy lend themselves to other allegorical overlays. As she recalls, 'The mythological island [...] is actually a character in the story because it has such a strong effect on the characters, isolated in this beautiful place' (Frances, 2005: 40). Drawing on national tropes of 'man alone' and 'battling a hostile nature', the island metaphor stretches as far as the production design. As noted by designer Joe Bleakley (*The Making of Perfect Strangers*, 2003), The Man's domestic environment is imbued with isolated figures that serve to characterise him: a table, a chair, a work bench and cooking utensils each stand alone in his austere kitchen. Similarly, Preston draws a parallel here with the effect that living in New Zealand, on a remote group of islands at a distance from the rest of the world, has on the nation's psyche, an unease identified in the documentary film *Cinema of Unease: A Personal Journey by Sam Neill* (1995). National thematic elements of a woman alone, illusions of an island paradise and pioneering make-do are juxtaposed with preoccupations of sexual relations, romance and the nature of love, corroborating Preston's pursuit to reflect on larger social issues from a private sphere.

Home By Christmas (2010)

> I was born into a world where there were three times. There was before the war, after the war and a secret place that nobody talked about, during the war.
>
> (*Home By Christmas*, 2010)

> [This is] the mystery that I was born to try and solve. This is part of an investigation of a very long time.
>
> (*The Making of Home by Christmas*, 2010)

Home by Christmas is, in Preston's view, a densely constructed 'collage, a patchwork quilt of a film' (Wiles, 2010), an account of Ed Preston's wartime experiences between signing up for infantry service in 1940 and returning home in 1944. In the film, Ed recounts his memories of applying for infantry service and his naive assumption that he would be 'home by Christmas', just a few months away. His story is that of travelling by ship with his friends via Freemantle and Bombay to Alexandria, and beginning active service there in the Egyptian desert. Within weeks he is captured by Germans, transported to Italy and held in an Italian prisoner of war camp. His recollections are infused with wry 'Kiwi' humour, including accounts of amiable relationships with the guards where, at the New Zealand soldiers' request, there is a laying down of arms and the institution of 'smoko', ritualised morning and afternoon tea. When Italy surrenders he escapes across the Swiss border and spends two years in an internment camp with other New Zealand soldiers, waiting to 'get home'.

Roy Pascal argues that the line between autobiography and memoir or reminiscence is much harder to draw than, for example, that between autobiography and diary (1960: 5), but that memoirs 'have the sharpness due to a particular social slant, [where] the slant is taken for granted or at least not subjected to prolonged attention' (ibid.: 7). Preston describes *Home By Christmas* as a film memoir, blending fact, creative non-fiction, memories and imaginative reconstruction to recount Ed's four-year absence and what happened to him whilst away, interlaced with what happened to Tui back home. Built from audiotapes, the interviews with her father are reconstructed with the older Ed played by actor, Tony Barry. These are interspersed with fictionalised dramatic scenes in which Tui is played by Preston's own daughter, Chelsie Preston Crayford (thus playing her grandmother) and young Ed by Martin Henderson. Interwoven with this are sequences of archival ungraded military footage, family photographs and digitised military images, together forming the complex patchwork earlier referred to. The story slides seamlessly between archival family images and reconstructed fictional sequences reflecting the filmmaker's process of building the film from various sources informed by her experiences with oral history, memory and storytelling, where 'you get all the truths, and you add three and four and five and six people, and you start to get a story net' (Preston, 2009).

Within the field of literary studies 'auto/biography' is a newly formed term in which the inserted forward slash is 'used to denote the way autobiographical and biographical narratives are related and to suggest how the boundary between them is fluid' (Anderson, 2011: 140). Pascal also notes that there is a general difference in the direction of the author's attention 'in the autobiography proper, [where] attention is focused on the self. In the memoir or reminiscence [attention is focused] on others' (ibid.: 4). Further memoir concerns itself with public events rather than private relationships and 'penetration of the past by the present affects not only the shape of the autobiography, but also the mode of description, the style' (ibid.: 13). In her opening play with the voices within the film, Preston alerts us to questions about whose story is being told here, hers or her father's, and to how Ed's version is being mitigated through her own rendition. In her treatment of *Home by Christmas* Preston chooses a collage of forms that draws attention to 'kinds of truth' about this long-held family secret, teasing out her father's, her mother's and her own experiences, her close access to which situates her film as memoir (in Pascal's terms), rather than biopic or biography. Preston concurs, 'I have taken an imaginative leap with Tui's story and informed Ed's story with what she said' (Preston, 2009). Her use of a private family story to reflect on more universal experiences of New Zealand soldiers and their left-at-home wives and families confirms the characterisation as memoir.

In the context of the trilogy, *Home by Christmas* is both auto/ biographical and memoir, satisfying Preston's desire to redefine her present by understanding past family secrets. From the outset, Preston contests her position in relation to the material by centring herself as her father's interviewer, beginning with her own voice-over recounting her memories of the interviews, whilst also establishing herself as the film's director, introducing herself,

> This is Gaylene Preston and I am talking to my father about his experiences in World War II. I was often trying to get my father to tell me about his war but he resisted, refused, deflected, made it a joke. Then one summer he got sick, then he agreed to let me record his story on sound tape...

Here, the director plays herself and Tony Barry is her father. Barry, as Preston describes in *The Making of Home by Christmas*, 'is very like Ed' but is 20 or so years younger than Ed Preston was at the time of the interviews. Preston began the screenplay for *Home by Christmas* after completing *Perfect Strangers*:

> I realized that the war story that my father had told me was still sitting there in my computer; a series of interviews that had been

transcribed, with scenes I had worked on over the years [...] I like to follow my nose you know, follow what interests me.

(cited in Wiles, 2010)

Within the interview-centred screenplay Preston exploited the paradoxical space between spontaneity and storytelling by forbidding Barry from memorising Ed's responses as an actor normally would; instead, he listened to the original interview tapes and then improvised as Preston interviewed him directly on camera. The intention was that Barry, rather than appearing to remember lines, would seem to be recalling experiences, with an immediacy of self-discovery. For Barry, considering this process: 'I felt like I had been on that journey, I could see those characters [...] I was moved to be, rather than play Ed' (*The Making of Home By Christmas*, 2010).

Preston plays herself as interviewer for both financial and aesthetic reasons. As interviewer, she was able to write and edit the screenplay 'in action' as she drew recollections from the actor in the way that she remembered her father telling them to her. As she recalls, 'the way he told the story was about as interesting to me as what he was describing' (Wiles, 2010). The NZFC provided some financial assistance for the development of a screenplay, though Preston was reluctant to pursue the established screenplay assessment and redrafting process:

In that development proposal I mentioned that I felt it was not going to be possible just to develop the script in the usual way by writing and rewriting and getting assessments because I had to know whether a central reconstructed interview was going to work.

(cited in Wiles, 2010)

Contentiously, she used this limited investment to film the improvised interviews directly (again with Bollinger) effectively beginning the production with development finance in a bid to convince the NZFC (and herself) that such a writing process would serve the story. As with *War Stories*, this was enough to convince the NZFC to provide the necessary additional investments to complete the film (Wiles, 2010).

Beyond the screenplay

As described above, Preston's filmmaking practice in *War Stories* and *Home by Christmas* contests normal screenplay development as instituted by the NZFC. Rather than being dictated by a predetermined storytelling process, the distinctiveness of each project guides the process of its making. For example, a timeline depicting the collection of the Preston stories suggests a delicacy regarding the exposition of the material in the trilogy. In discussing life-writing, Claudia Mills asks whether 'one can value one's loved ones appropriately while also drawing on their lives as material for one's work', suggesting a tension between an inevitable 'betrayal of trust' and protection of a subject's posthumous interests. Employment of family secrets requires 'more than mere factual accuracy but a kind of fidelity to what *is*' (2004: 104). In Preston's work, Tui told her story for the oral history archive whilst Ed was sitting in a nearby room, but the content remained private until after he died; Ed told his story in 1991 shortly before his death; Tui's version, in which she fell in love with another man whilst Ed was at war, entered the public domain in 1995 when *War Stories* was released; Preston's allegorical version, *Perfect Strangers*, was released in 2003; and *Home by Christmas*, Ed's story as told by Preston, was released in 2010, two years after Tui's death. The timely public release of each version of this family's secret, whether intentional or not, appears to have taken into account the effect such personal information might have had on the players.

The flux between the conceived, written and produced work in *Home By Christmas* is evident within the range of the techniques used. The intimacies of the family are explored in the creative choices of the film's production. For example, the maternal legacy is strongly reinforced by Chelsie's performance as her own grandmother. Preston argues that Chelsie 'knows' Tui better than she does, not being so entwined in the mother/daughter relationship. Similarly, Chelsie confirms that she has close knowledge of her grandmother, 'I know her inside out,' having lived with her for several years as she grew up (*The Making of Home By Christmas*, 2010). As the dramatic re-enactments are often rendered with little or no dialogue, the emotional expression and interpretation between Chelsie and Henderson (playing young Ed) builds a romantic relationship between Tui and Ed that honours Preston's own memory of her parents' marriage. Such elements, I argue, are beyond the screenplay and make this film memoir unique; the familial embodiment has a curiously reinforcing effect when cutting from archival stills of Tui to close ups of Chelsie playing her. These visual connections are reinforced by attention to domestic details. For example, a floral print dress worn by Chelsie was remade from one of Tui's own that also, Preston recalls, became the cinematographic colour palate in the dramatised narrative arc (*The Making of Home by Christmas*, 2010).

Preston's exposition of her father's war story in *Home By Christmas* complements that of her mother's story expressed in *War Stories Our Mothers Never Told Us*. The intersection of private and public expression suggests that this is a eulogy of sorts to Ed Preston and to his marriage to Tui, the mystery around which the story is formed. Beyond the secret,

> My father's war story is not one that gets told in official versions. I [...] wanted to put something into the film catalogue that reflected an ordinary soldier's version of the war. Not only that but it's from a man who truly, truly is an anti-hero; he is otherwise invisible [...] the only nobility you have is of an ordinary man doing what he could to try and avoid being a part of this terrible thing he had got himself into.
>
> (Preston cited in Wiles, 2010)

Here the recognisable elements of national (Kiwi) family life are explored. The national ANZAC myth and ordinary women's lives are brought into relief through this un-heroic account, returning to Pascal's notion of memoir's intersection of past and present and the accessibility of the private as a recognisable public experience. Ed's stories tell of a reluctant antipodean soldier with the devil in details of his experience: the search for food; deteriorating health; relationships with his New Zealand West Coast mates; interactions with his prison guards. It is this sometimes banal and consistently prosaic recall that makes the private publically available. The stories are bound together by historical footage sourced from New Zealand war recordings, material from the Australian War Museum, L'Istituto Luce Museum in Italy and from the UK. Amateur footage includes material taken by soldiers who were on the same ship as Ed. The public and private become further enmeshed when digitally altered stills of Ed, using the face of the young Ed (Martin Henderson), are interspersed with archival footage and voices of the young contemporary actors blended into the soundscape. Each of the elements arises out of a production strategy that builds the film from a variety of found and sourced materials that shape this version of the story rather than being predetermined by a completed screenplay.

Conclusion

Memoir's sources, then, are in the ways in which ordinary people represent their lives: in spontaneous, unique oral narratives; in anecdotes that are not only told but retold as signature stories; in personal stories that may be passed down as family or institutional lore.

(Anderson, 2011: 140)

As Linda Anderson reminds us, memoir is often drawn from intimate experience, whether it be remembered, hidden or recovered, told and retold. Pascal further suggests that memoir is 'an interplay, a collusion, between past and present; its significance is indeed more the revelation of the present situation than the uncovering of the past' (1960: 11). For Preston, in exploring mysteries from her family's past, the screenwriting is never finished. Talking about an earlier film, she asserts her belief that 'it's a mistake to think that the writing is over when the final draft of the script is there, I think certainly in my experience, all sorts of things [can] happen' (1997). Consideration of Preston as a screenwriter cannot be limited to her screenplays or her screenwriting practice: her collaborative working methods and extensive experience of oral history and screen storytelling (as screenwriter, director and producer) lend her work to a more complex analysis. The trilogy exemplifies both the focused pursuit of a tapestry of family stories that uncovers a truth and a careful management of how that truth might be revealed. Each film shows ways in which private memories can be turned to public expression, fulfilling the demands of auto/biography and film memoir.

On the one hand, *War Stories Our Mothers Never Told Us*, *Perfect Strangers* and *Home By Christmas* demonstrate an auto/biographical journey in the expression of a hidden family secret. Yet, on the other hand, these private matters in her possession are a memoir that reflects on public lore, as she reasons here:

> Because we have personal memories and how those personal memories get expressed is part of our communal oral history. There's the way we choose to tell it, and there's the way that we actually remember it.

(cited in Wiles, 2010)

Notes

1. In this chapter 'Preston' identifies Gaylene Preston, the filmmaker. As there are several other family members being referred to, given names will be used.
2. In the case of *Perfect Strangers*, the FF1 controversially chose to waive this requirement and underwrote the production through an international bank and sales agent. See Wakefield, 2002, for a fuller discussion.

References

Anderson, L. (2011) *Autobiography* (2nd ed.), Oxford: Routledge.

Dunleavy, T. and Joyce, H. (2011) *New Zealand Film and Television: Institution, Industry and Cultural Change*, Bristol: Intellect.

Frances, H. (2005) 'Facts, Fairytales and the Politics of Storytelling: An Interview with Gaylene Preston' in *Cineaste*, Fall, 36–41.

Home by Christmas (2010) Wr./Dir. Gaylene Preston, New Zealand, 90 mins.

Mills, C. (2004) 'Friendship, Fiction, and Memoir: Trust and Betrayal in Writing from One's Own Life' in P.J. Eakin (ed.) *The Ethics of Life-Writing*, London: Ithica, pp. 101–120.

Pascal, R. (1960) *Design and Truth in Autobiography*, Cambridge, MA: Harvard University Press.

Perfect Strangers (2003) Wr./Dir. Gaylene Preston, New Zealand, 96 mins.

Preston, G. (1992) 'Reflecting Reality: Gaylene Preston an interview' in J. Dennis and J. Beiringa (eds.) *Film in Aotearoa New Zealand*, Wellington: Victoria UP, pp. 161–172.

Preston, G. (1995) 'War Stories', http://www.gaylenepreston.com/Writings_WarStories.html [accessed 10 May 2013].

Preston, G. (1997) Interview with Hester Joyce, 4 September.

Preston, G. (2009) 'Using Oral History as a Primary Source' in *National Oral History of New Zealand Conference*, Wellington, 31 October–1 November, http://www.oralhistory.org.nz/conference.html [accessed 10 May 2013].

Simmons, L. (1996) 'Guardians of an Absent Meaning' in *Illusions*, 25, 26–29.

Smart, C. (2007) *Personal Life*, Cambridge: Polity.

The Making of Perfect Strangers (2003) Dir. Gaylene Preston, New Zealand, 56 mins.

The Making of Home by Christmas (2010) Dir. Nigel Hutchinson, New Zealand, 56 mins.

This is New Zealand (1970) Dir. Hugh Macdonald, New Zealand.

Wakefield, P. (2002) 'Film Fund favouritism' in *Onfilm*, July, 1–3.

War Stories Our Mothers Never Told Us (1995) Dir. Gaylene Preston, New Zealand, 95 mins.

Wiles, M. (2010) 'A Gentle Voice in a Noisy Room: An interview with New Zealand Filmmaker Gaylene Preston' in *Senses of Cinema*, 56, available at http://www.sensesofcinema.com/issue/56/ [accessed 20 June 2011].

5

Costume as Character Arc: How Emotional Transformation is Written into the Dressed Body

Craig Batty

Introduction

A screenplay represents a moment in time. It captures the essence of the human condition and the everyday lived experience, connecting character and audience on a subliminal yet highly powerful level. As Grodal asserts, the screenplay paves the way for an eventual psychosomatic experience: in a film, body and mind are connected as one as 'our eyes and ears pick up and analyze image and sound, our minds apprehend the story, which resonates on our memory; furthermore, our stomach, heart, and skin are activated in empathy with the story situations and the protagonists' ability to cope' (1997: 1). A screenplay also represents a transformation, capturing the shift in a protagonist from problem to resolution; from wounding to healing; from dramatic need to dramatic fulfilment. Characters are propelled into territories unknown, overcoming progressive obstacles and life challenging battles in order to attain physical and emotional achievement. The transformation of the protagonist represents the essence of a screenplay. It captures the story lurking beneath the action, and only when transformation is complete can the theme be understood by an audience, bestowing resonance. Character transformation thus lies at the emotional core of a form that is, by its visual nature, framed by action.

The costumed body on screen is a visual symbol of such character transformation. As Stella Bruzzi writes, 'Clothes, through evocative and complex signifiers, are a means of understanding the body or character who wears them' (1997: xiv). For Marit Allen, costume designer for the film *Brokeback Mountain* (2005), 'Hopefully you don't notice the clothing, but you feel the emotions that the clothes convey' (cited in Australian Centre for the Moving Image, 2013). The visual and the physical (the act of wearing and of dressing up) are thus understood in direct relation to the emotional (the character him or herself), where clothes worn, accessories carried and make-up applied create a visual discourse that illustrates how a character both feels and fares in a given story situation.

Furthermore, the way in which the performative space of costume changes throughout a narrative, either by choice or by force, can be seen to symbolise how a character transforms; or, to use screenwriting terminology, how a character grows, develops or arcs. Piers Britton, writing on the television series *Dr Who* (1963–), has noted that the role of costume design in narrative has been excluded from academic study, yet in fact it occupies an important position in the process of authorship (1999: 324). For Britton, the costume designer can be seen as a 're-writer' or an 'over-writer', using their skills to re-articulate, and sometimes advance, what has been suggested in the script. He argues that such designers should be accorded with as much authorial status as the screenwriter, 'for costume constitutes a visual "text" which is often at least as potent as the screenplay' (1999: 324). This echoes the idea behind the recent Hollywood Costume exhibition, which premiered in London (2012) and then went on to Melbourne (2013), where 'the integrity of the story takes precedence over glamour' and 'When clothing is authentic, the audience believes in the story' (cited in Australian Centre for the Moving Image, 2013).

The intention of this chapter, then, is not to discuss the role of the costume designer per se, but rather to discuss costume and its close relationship to the narrative of a screenplay. By investigating this specifically from the point of view of screenwriting practice, I aim to articulate how the physical iconography of the costumed body can be seen to represent the character-driven emotional transformation that lies at the heart of a screenplay. Or, in the words of Christina Hamlett, how the screenwriter possesses a powerful accessory for use in a screenplay: 'the secret decoder ring that can communicate characters' emotions, ambitions, and anxieties to everyone who will one day meet them for the first time' (2011: 9).

Screenwriting, storytelling and costume

Stories are inherent in everything we do. From dressing in the morning to relaxing at night, and from decorating a living room to cooking a meal, we play out small but important narratives that, when pieced together, tell the bigger story that is our life: small cells of a bigger picture. Films and television dramas offer a way of representing this fascination for what I would like to call a *storied world*, in that they transport audiences on an audio-visual journey of humanity; a journey of what it is like to live, breathe and feel in this world. Robert McKee writes:

> A storyteller is a life poet, an artist who transforms day-to-day living, inner life and outer life, dream and actuality into a poem whose rhyme scheme is events rather than words – a two-hour metaphor that says: Life is like *this!*

> (1999: 25)

The screenwriter's insistence upon telling stories with emotional depth possesses a power and magnitude akin to that of the poet; but the crucial difference is that screen audiences can be transported on a journey not only through sound and imagination but also through sight. This journey, understood in basic terms as a motivation plus an opportunity, leading to an affirmation of the motivation and a new opportunity, has an archetypal appeal that works to 'represent the universal need to develop, change, and grow through the archetypal themes of rebirth and transformation' (Indick, 2004: 133).

I propose that this journey, for both the character and the audience, is made up of two narrative components: the physical journey and the emotional journey, that work together across a narrative in a symbiotic relationship (Batty, 2011). The physical journey represents the plot (action), pulling the protagonist along and forcing him or her to make decisions that will have an effect on his or her emotional arc. It represents every step taken and every action undertaken: everything that the protagonist physically does. The emotional journey represents the inner desire of the protagonist that propels him or her to make these decisions, drawing on feelings stirred from his or her psychology. How the protagonist fares when the journey comes to an end is the essence of the emotional journey, providing the underlying universal theme that we understand as the real story. A careful interweaving of the physical journey and the emotional journey creates a complete story experience. They are identified as separate components, but function together for the same narrative.

How, then, does this relate to the costumed body and screenwriting? As will become clear, it is my assertion that the use of costume on screen can be compared to the physical journey; the narrative component demonstrated visibly through the clothing, apparel and make-up of a character. The character's emotional arc is both symbolised and emphasised by this physical appearance, and especially how it changes. As Adam Ganz outlines when discussing how an audience constructs a story from what they see,

> Indeed one might describe the process, not as the screenwriter telling a story, but as the audience assembling the story from the clues and traces they find. The story is created through the audience's active speculation about the meaning of those traces. The task of the screenwriter is therefore not to write the story, but to give the audience the tools to imagine the story for themselves.
>
> (2011: 127)

What this tells us is that an audience plays an active role in the construction of meaning when watching a film or television drama, and therefore it is the role of the screenwriter to help that construction by providing 'clues' and 'traces'. With costume in mind, I would like to suggest that deciding what a character should wear, not from a costume design vantage point (specific fabrics and colours, designer names, etc.) but from a narrative need (what general apparel they wear, when they change into something else, etc.), can offer strong emotional subtext that an audience will understand in relation to what they are seeing. Costume thus becomes a valued object (Batty and Waldeback, 2008: 52–53) that possesses meaning beyond functionality, especially as it travels through a narrative.

The understanding of costume as character is not entirely new academic territory. Drake Stutesman, for example, writes that 'Film clothes disclose who someone is [...] how that person feels [and] where s/he's going [...] in ways that will fill out a non-expositional script' (2005: 28). This is as much a visual studies approach as it is a film studies approach, and like most, Stutesman's general observation here is just that. It is perhaps a given that screen costumes depict screen characters, and much of the research in this area tends to focus either on *mise-en-scène* and costume's relationship with specific moments in a film or television drama, or on costume's significance in relation to culture, gender, sexuality and specific fashion designers.

What lies at the heart of this chapter is an examination of costume in relation to dressing up, and dressing up as revealing story. It is about the assimilation of character onto clothing, and vice versa.

If, as Bruzzi argues, screen costumes can represent 'the liberation and performative potential of clothes and the fluidities of identity' (1997: xv), then what will be examined here is how the transformation of a character's emotional identity can be traced through the physical performance of costume on the body. From scene to scene and from act to act, skirts, trousers, t-shirts, dresses, shoes, sunglasses and handbags are all viewed as surface components of a 'unique, culture-specific expression' of plot (McKee, 1999: 4) that visually symbolises the protagonist's emotional journey.

I will concentrate here on 'dressing up' narratives, which might be identified as films and television dramas that have a specific focus on the act of choosing, wearing and talking about clothing in relation to plot; and, moreover, that locate emotional character transformation within such artefacts. *Legally Blonde* (2001) and *The Devil Wears Prada* (2006) are examples of such films because of the importance of dressing up and fashion advice in their narratives. In both films, female characters that work in and have knowledge of the fashion industry assert a strong sense of how dressing the body has the potential to transform the inner person, and the potential downfalls for not 'conforming' to the rules of fashion. This notion is also very evident in disguise-driven dressing up films, such as *Tootsie* (1982), *Sister Act* (1992) and *Mrs Doubtfire* (1993). In these films, characters that are physically hiding under clothing are forced to learn emotional lessons and experience strong character arcs. Television series such as *Sex and the City* (1998–2004) and *Ugly Betty* (2006–2010) also employ strong notions of how clothing possesses cultural and social meaning for the human wearer, where dressing up is not incidental, but narratively crucial.

Mapping the protagonist's journey

Gilbert Adrian, MGM's Head of Costume between 1928 and 1942, believed in costume's power of storytelling. He is quoted to have said, 'One could line up all the gowns and tell the screen story' (cited by Stutesman, 2005: 27). As well as having a general potency about the power of costume, Adrian's acknowledgement that gowns – plural – need to be lined up to make sense of the story is highly suggestive of a visual transformation. The gowns promise a narrative journey in and of themselves, and it is this journey that first needs to be investigated. Although there are numerous ways of analysing the narrative structure of a screenplay, the model that will underpin the argument here is that of the Hero's Journey, as written about by Christopher

Vogler in his book *The Writer's Journey: Mythic Structure for Storytellers and Screenwriters* (1999). Vogler's model offers a contemporary variation of what Joseph Campbell proposed in his seminal book *The Hero with a Thousand Faces* (1949, 1993), an archetypal story structure or 'monomyth' that is universal in both its appeal and its approach to storytelling:

> A hero ventures forth from the world of common day into a region of supernatural wonder: fabulous forces are there encountered and a decisive victory is won: the hero comes back from this mysterious adventure with the power to bestow boons on his fellow man.
>
> (Campbell, 1993: 30)

Key to this monomyth, and to the work of Campbell more generally, is a sense of duality: that narratives work on two levels, incorporating both physical and emotional aspects. Vogler's interpreted model, intended primarily as a guide for screenwriters and story consultants, thus presents 12 narrative stages of the archetypal Hero's Journey that together build a framework for telling and understanding a screen story. These stages are:

1. *Ordinary World*, where a protagonist lives in normality but experiences some kind of dramatic problem.
2. *Call to Adventure*, the disturbance to the normality that calls into question the problem and sets a challenge to be undertaken.
3. *Refusal of the Call*, where the protagonist deliberates between undertaking the challenge or remaining where he is.
4. *Meeting with the Mentor*, a moment of confirmation where guidance, advice and sometimes tools are given to the protagonist in order to undertake the challenge.
5. *Crossing the First Threshold*, where the protagonist begins his journey to resolve the challenge and fully commits to the new world.
6. *Tests, Allies, Enemies*, which are the people, places and problems encountered, overcome and appropriated along the way, posing progressively difficult obstacles and forcing new choices to be made.
7. *Approach to the Inmost Cave*, the dark moment where the protagonist nears the end of his quest but is haunted by fear and the possibility of defeat.
8. *Supreme Ordeal*, where the greatest fear is encountered and it seems that the protagonist may not succeed.

9. *Reward*, where the protagonist finally achieves what he came look-
    ing for and has overcome the seemingly insurmountable.
10. *The Road Back*, where the Ordinary World has to be reached again
    but not before a final test for the protagonist.
11. *Resurrection*, the final challenge that tests the protagonist's under-
    standing of the journey he has undertaken and the lessons he has
    learned.
12. *Return with Elixir*, where the protagonist can go back to where he
    came from but he has learned enough to see it differently; it is not
    the end, but a new beginning.

As a way of dealing with the notion of duality, underpinning each of
the general narrative stages is an emotional 'beat' that helps to map the
protagonist's emotional arc (Vogler, 1999: 212). These are:

1. limited awareness of a problem
2. increased awareness
3. reluctance to change
4. committing to change
5. overcoming reluctance
6. experimenting with first change
7. preparing for big change
8. attempting big change
9. consequences of the attempt (improvements and setbacks)
10. re-dedication to change
11. final attempt at big change
12. final mastery of the problem.

The model of the Hero's Journey is particularly useful for exploring
costume as character not only because of its emphasis on the journey
travelled by a protagonist, but also because it highlights the physical
conflicts required to make a story work. The result of this is that a
protagonist's emotional transformation can be traced within the frame
of a physical environment. In direct relation to costume, the visual
discourse of clothing, apparel and make-up provides a physical frame
within which a character arc can be traced. More specifically, we can use
the model to discover how screenwriter-plotted moments of physical
dressing up symbolise the emotional landscape of a protagonist.

In order to make these ideas more tangible, I will now offer an analysis of a film that I feel represents this argument well. In one sense,
any film might offer the possibility of being read through the lens of

costume as character arc; indeed, as evidenced by the recent Hollywood Costume exhibition, the specifics of costume play an integral part of all films, from *Vertigo* (1958) to *The Bourne Ultimatum* (2007) to *The Big Lebowski* (1998) (cited in Australian Centre for the Moving Image, 2013). However, it is these 'specifics' that are limiting when the concern is to understand the character arc: a focus on coats, sunglasses, boots, etc. can represent a mere narrative moment, not necessarily the complete narrative itself.

Therefore, the film I will use to present my argument is the US feature *Connie and Carla* (2004), written by and starring Nia Vardalos, about two young women who begin to understand and 'improve' themselves by dressing up in a variety of ways along what is a chaotic journey. Set against the backdrop of a Los Angeles drag club, where costumes and gender bending are aplenty, the analysis will demonstrate that costume is far from an incidental component of the screenwriter's toolkit. Rather, costume assumes the identity of a performative stage upon or underneath which another distinctive narrative is told.

Costume as character arc in *Connie and Carla*

Costume is highlighted as an integral part of the film's narrative from the very outset. The film opens in the past with the eponymous protagonists at school, dressed as cowgirls in the canteen and performing a song from *Oklahoma!* to their less than impressed peers. Connie and Carla are set up as the laughing stock of the school, making visual and verbal fools of themselves. However, for Connie and Carla this is their dream: all they want to do is perform. The song is then spliced into a scene set in the present, about 15 years later, where Connie and Carla sing the same song but this time in front of delayed passengers at Chicago's O'Hare airport.

This opening sequence provides the audience with crucial backstory about the pair's hopes and dreams of a career, and the use of costume to do so depicts this plight effectively. Throughout the present-day musical medley, Connie and Carla literally strip away layers of 'stock' costumes used to represent the songs they are singing. We see them physically undressing and adjusting outfits for *Oklahoma!*, *Jesus Christ, Superstar* and *Cats*. This undressing/re-dressing routine is important because it represents how they currently accept themselves performing as others, thus far possessing no individual identity. Part of their dramatic problem in this Ordinary World is that they have no sense of who they are and how they can define themselves confidently. As such, they rely on excessive physical representations of others that act as a mask. In this way, their bodies are confined by the rules of others (albeit through stereotypes) and it is suggested through emotional subtext that only when the body can break free and create its own identity can Connie and Carla find a resolution to their dramatic problem.

The Call to the Adventure comes when Connie and Carla witness the murder of airport bar manager Frank. Just prior to the murder, Frank is seen hiding a package of cocaine in Connie and Carla's 'show bag', which is another important use of costume because it is precisely this bag that the murderers are hunting down throughout the film. Having to deal with the two witnesses is one obvious element of the chase that ensues, but in actual fact, the central narrative drive of the murderers is to retrieve the high-value drugs from the bag. In story terms, the inciting incident of the whole narrative resides in a carried accessory: the cocaine was hidden in the bag, and for now Connie and Carla are carrying it unwittingly.

Now that this normality has been disturbed, Connie and Carla are forced on a journey to escape possible death; though, as a comedy, we as the audience realise that this will highly unlikely to happen. The pair quickly pack their bags and load up their car, hiding behind a layer of wigs, sunglasses and make-up. This 'over dressing' is not only credible in story terms – a disguise to help them escape – but it is also symbolic of Connie and Carla's desire to escape from what they see as their real selves, and foreshadows what they will become once they enter the Special World.

Connie and Carla find themselves in Los Angeles. After some initial fun and sightseeing, which functions as the Refusal of the Call, to delay not only the story's action but also their need to transform, they realise that they need jobs; and where better but than a beauty salon? Although only a brief sequence because they are fired, this job reinforces Connie and Carla's appreciation of costume and 'the look' to reflect one's identity, which helps to set up the central theme of 'dressing how you feel'. They help Mrs Morse, a middle-aged woman who desperately wants the 'Californian look'. They radically change her hair and make-up, much to her delight, but at the same time they themselves are confined to the tight, white beautician outfits that belong to the salon. The costumed body operates on two levels here. Firstly, Connie and Carla are once again restrained in their appearance by the rules of others and are thus forced to assume another identity, which is yet another marker of their central dramatic problem. Secondly, and perhaps more importantly, via an association with the minor character of Mrs Morse, we are given important story information that suggests Connie and Carla possess the ability to redefine identity and improve the emotional self by undertaking work on the body's physical appearance. This becomes a significant feature of the film, and of Connie and Carla's character arcs.

A turning point sequence in the film, incorporating both Meeting with the Mentor and Crossing the First Threshold, comes when Connie and Carla stumble upon *The Handle Bar*, a financially struggling drag club. Auditions are taking place for a new drag act that will help manager Stanley out of financial ruin, and before they know it the pair find themselves auditioning. At first they are nervous about being caught out as real women, but they soon realise that this could be the perfect opportunity: it is a paid job, it allows them to perform, and because of the disguise they are highly unlikely to be found by the murderers. Excited by this opportunity, Connie and Carla strut into the bar wearing leopard skin, black mesh body stockings, wigs and excessive make-up. They are quintessential drag queens, with their over-dressed and made-up bodies providing visual confirmation of the departure from the Ordinary World to the Special World. After some initial confusion, where the other 'wannabe' drag queens cannot work out if they were lip-synching or not, there is rapturous applause and they are signed up immediately.

The initiation into their new world sees Connie and Carla sing more songs, gain more fans, and, crucially, adorn more costumes. From leather bodices to feathered headbands to fake eyelashes to padded bras, they display what can be viewed as an excessive femininity that for them serves the purpose of convincing everyone that they are drag queens. As such, not only do they cross the threshold into another world here, but they also meet with their mentors: their alter egos in the form of their drag personas, who function to guide and teach them throughout their experience of the Special World. The importance of this visual transformation is at the core of their emotional journeys: Connie and Carla are physically encountering a world that is dominated by dressing the body; and each time they themselves 'over perform' their own femininity by wearing drag, covering up their real bodies so they are not found out to be real women, they are learning about themselves. They physically, bodily journey through a world as other people, and all the whilst their own identities are in transit too. The fluidity of the inner self shifts as a result of the transforming, costumed body, where physical encounters facilitate emotional growth, testing the protagonists' inner strengths and abilities. The costumed body is as much an obstacle that has to be overcome as it is a magical tool that will help them along their journey. The success of their show not only helps Stanley to save his business and gives inspiration to the wannabe drag queens, it also validates Connie and Carla's worth and their place in the world. In a stark contrast to the drought of the Ordinary World, where Al calls them 'dreamers,' they are giving pleasure to people and finally feeling that their dreams are being fulfilled.

Screenwriting thrives on conflict, and so for narrative purposes Connie and Carla require moments of danger to remind them that they are in a temporary world that must eventually be left behind, albeit with gained knowledge and emotional growth. In structural terms, they now have many Allies but also need Tests and Enemies. Many of these moments are best exemplified in the scenes set in Connie and Carla's apartment. Now that they have become local 'stars,' they are prone to unannounced visitors who either offer support or require advice. Each time this happens, Connie and Carla must quickly 'dress down' with dressing gowns, face packs and shower caps so that they are not caught out as real women. The quick costume switches we see are symbolic of the dilemma that the pair have found themselves in: the frantic pulling on of comedy clothing represents the cracks in their emotional arcs, stuck in a place between wounded and healed. Not only do the pair have to hide under a façade of clothing, they have to do so in their personal environment, which suggests that unless they reveal and come to terms with their true identities, they will never be able to escape the confines of costume: they will be trapped in the special but false world.

An important scene to highlight this dilemma comes when Connie literally bumps into Jeff outside her and Carla's apartment. Connie has fallen in love with Jeff, the straight brother of their transvestite friend Robert/Peaches, but because he thinks she is a drag queen – a man – the feelings are not reciprocated. This leaves Connie in a strange place, where on the one hand she wants to reveal herself and share her feelings, but on the other hand she knows this could ruin her and Carla's career and jeopardise their safety from the murderers. This dilemma, which is at the heart of Connie's emotional drive at this point in the film, is once again represented effectively by symbolism through costume. When Connie and Jeff bump into each other, Connie's handbag upturns and its contents are spilled. An array of cosmetics, the very things used to hide her identity, are now strewn all over the sidewalk. Amongst the cosmetics is a tampon, which clearly threatens to reveal her identity as a woman. However, she pretends that it is a 'cotton absorb' and quickly dabs it on her mouth, a 'false accessory' being used to hide under. This is a moment representative of the Approach to the Inmost Cave, visually signifying the danger in the performance of 'excess femininity' and suggesting that potential hazards lie ahead if Connie's real identity is not revealed. Connie bluffs her way out of the awkward situation, but it is clear to us that she longs to be herself, and wishes she could dispose of the figurative and sometimes literal mask that she is wearing. Ironically, when Jeff asks her why 'he' dresses as a 'she', she says that sometimes dressing is like how you feel inside. Although initially framed as a response from the position of someone covering up the truth about who she really is, this line of dialogue is perhaps a moment of realisation for Connie, who now understands the significance that dressing the body can have on one's life. In this sense, Connie has now also entered the cave and is about to experience the Supreme Ordeal, where it seems that there might be no way out of her and Carla's situation.

The true validation of a character's emotional growth is often found in the climax of a film: the moment of Reward where protagonists physically get what they want and emotionally achieve what they need. In *Connie and Carla*, this moment is visualised and therefore amplified by somewhat obvious yet narratively credible uses of costume, in a sequence that mirrors yet contrasts with the opening of the film. By now, Connie and Carla are a success: the dinner theatre, which they helped to transform from a lowly bar, is full, and even Debbie Reynolds has come to visit. The pair has total control of their audience, unlike when they were performing at the school canteen and at the airport bar, and perform with style and confidence. This is physically symbolised by the range of costumes that Connie and Carla are not only comfortable in, but which they command. From the clichéd mock musical outfits at the start of the film, they have graduated to a higher level of expensive and elaborate costumes. Furthermore, they have also helped the wannabe drag queens to achieve their own artistic dreams by becoming part of the show as well. The Belles of the Ball, as they are now known, also wear glamorous, well-made costumes, and dance with precision and vigour, a visual marker of their character development.

As the energy of the show escalates, so does the danger. Connie and Carla soon become aware that the murderers are in the audience; they have been discovered as a result of their local fame. What is important here, in an understanding of costume as character arc, is the way in which Connie and Carla actually overcome their antagonists by the very use of an item of costume. When the pair are caught by the murderers, a true moment of Supreme Ordeal, two waistcoats that have earlier been planted in the narrative come into shot. Previously, these waistcoats have been deemed an unimportant prop, but in hindsight we see that they are crucial because of the set-up that has taken place: that the waistcoat beads come off very easily. In what thus becomes the Reward, just as Connie and Carla are faced with a gun, the waistcoats are reintroduced as a vital weapon. In an instant, the pair grab the waistcoats and shake them hard. The beads shed, the murderers are confused and drop their guard, and Connie and Carla escape. In costume terms, this is an integral moment that represents Connie and Carla's ability to dispose of the excess apparel they have been hiding under and experience an emotional climax. From this point on, they no longer have to hide under a physical guise and can finally be who they have discovered they are.

The film subsequently draws to a close where Connie and Carla both reveal their true identities. Again, in relation to costume as character arc, this is achieved when they open their blouses and 'reveal all'. The show's audience, the Belles of the Ball and Stanley are all shocked, but they soon give their support back to the pair when Mrs Morse, who is in the audience, stands up and reveals that Connie and Carla made her feel beautiful when what she wanted (the 'Californian look') was not what she needed. Connie and Carla finally rip off their wigs and, for the first time, are happy with an appearance that they have chosen. They are no longer confined to wearing a costume enforced by others (or, indeed, by their repressed selves), and sing us to the credits in slinky dresses that show off all of their female glory.

Conclusion

Clearly, the screenwriter has only a very limited influence on the costume design of a film, and in almost every case will have nothing to do with the production once the screenplay has been green lit. Nevertheless, and to refer back to Hamlett, understanding how costume has the ability to work on the level of character symbolism can be very potent for the screenwriter. They might use this knowledge in the development of characters, whether for developing scene-level metaphors, or, as has been the focus of this chapter, for developing emotional arcs that require physical manifestations.

If 'costume embodies the psychological, social and emotional condition of the character at a particular moment in the story' (cited in Australian Centre for the Moving Image, 2013), then the screenwriter can be encouraged to consider how they might visualise their characters. They might not be designing and making the costumes, but they can certainly allude to them in the screen directions that they write. The power of clothes worn, accessories carried and make-up applied should not be underestimated by he or she who is ultimately orchestrating the story. Where would we be, for example, without the wedding dress in *Muriel's Wedding* (1994), the necklace in *Titanic* (1997), Richard's bandaged arm in *Me and You and Everyone We Know* (2005), and the Louis Vuitton suitcase in *Leap Year* (2010)?

Drake Stutesman posits that costume has the ability to become 'a stage in itself' (2005: 37), a metaphor for the idea that costuming the body can possess significance far beyond its functional credibility. In *Connie and Carla*, the transformations undertaken by the protagonists are not only visualised by costume, but in fact costume itself functions to shape the transformations. Physical dress informs emotional growth, and emotional growth shapes physical dress. They represent an intricate interweaving of story and plot. Ruth Myers' work as costume designer on the film gives a visual narrative that moves from schoolgirl fancy dress to full blown drag, each costume change, big or small, externalising character transformations. As can be seen in probably all dressing-up films, Connie and Carla are what they wear, and they wear what they are. Only through a decorating of the body with costume are they able to discover who they are. As Connie says herself, 'It's like dressing how you feel inside'.

References

Australian Centre for the Moving Image (2013) *Hollywood Costume* [Exhibition held at the Australian Centre for the Moving Image, 24 April–18 August 2013].

Batty, C. (2011) *Movies That Move Us: Screenwriting and the Power of the Protagonist's Journey*, Basingstoke: Palgrave Macmillan.

Batty, C. and Waldeback, Z. (2008) *Writing for the Screen: Creative and Critical Approaches*, Basingstoke: Palgrave Macmillan.

Britton, P.D.G. (1999) 'Dress and the Fabric of the Television Series: The Costume Designer as Author in *Dr. Who*' in *Journal of Design History*, 14(2), 345–356.

Brokeback Mountain (2005) Wrs. Larry McMurty and Diana Ossana, Dir. Ang Lee, USA/Canada, 134 mins.

Bruzzi, S. (1997) *Undressing Cinema: Clothing and Identity in the Movies*, London: Routledge.

Campbell, J. (1949, 1993) *The Hero with a Thousand Faces*, London: Fontana.

Connie and Carla (2004) Wr. Nia Vardalos, Dir. Michael Lembeck, USA, 98 mins.

Dr Who (1963–) Cr. Sydney Newman, Wrs. Various, Dirs. Various, UK.

Ganz, A. (2011) 'Let the Audience Add Up Two Plus Two. They'll Love You Forever: The Screenplay as a Self-Teaching System' in Jill Nelmes (ed.) *Analysing the Screenplay*, London: Routledge, 127–141.

Grodal, T. (1997) *Moving Pictures: A New Theory of Film Genres, Feelings, and Cognition*, Oxford: Oxford University Press.

Hamlett, C. (2011) 'Dressing the Part: Defining Your Characters Through Costuming' in *Writers' Journal*, 32(5), 7–9.

Indick, W. (2004) *Psychology for Screenwriters: Building Conflict in Your Script*, California: Michael Weise.

Leap Year (2010) Wrs. Deborah Kaplan and Harry Elfont, Dir. Anand Tucker, USA/Ireland, 100 mins.

Legally Blonde (2001) Wrs. Karen McCullah and Kirsten Smith, Dir. Robert Luketic, USA, 96 mins.

McKee, R. (1999) *Story: Substance, Structure, Style and the Principles of Storytelling*, London: Methuen.

Me and You and Everyone We Know (2005) Wr/Dir. Miranda July, USA/UK, 91 mins.

Mrs Doubtfire (1993) Wrs. Randi Mayem Singer and Leslie Dixon, Dir. Chris Columbus, USA, 125 mins.

Muriel's Wedding (1994) Wr./Dir. P. J Hogan, Australia/France, 125 mins.

Sex and the City (1998–2004) Cr. Darren Star, Wrs. Various, Dirs. Various, USA.

Sister Act (1992) Wr. Joseph Howard, Dir. Emile Ardolino, USA, 100 mins.

Stutesman, D. (2005) 'Storytelling: Marlene Dietrich's Face and John Frederics' Hats' in Rachel Moseley (ed.) *Fashioning Film Stars: Dress, Culture, Identity*, London: BFI.

The Big Lebowski (1998) Wrs. Ethan Coen and Joel Coen, Dirs. Joel Coen and Ethan Coen, USA/UK, 117 mins.

The Bourne Ultimatum (2007) Wrs. Tony Gilory, Scott Z. Burns and George Nolfi, Dir. Paul Greengrass, USA/Germany, 115 mins.

The Devil Wears Prada (2006) Wr. Aline Brosh McKenna, Dir. David Frankel, USA, 109 mins.

Titanic (1997) Wr./Dir. James Cameron, USA, 194 mins.

Tootsie (1982) Wrs. Larry Gelbart and Murray Schisgal, Dir. Sydney Pollack, USA, 116 mins.

Ugly Betty (2006–2010) Cr. Silvio Horta, Wrs. Various, Dirs. Various, USA.

Vertigo (1958) Wrs. Alec Coppel and Samuel A. Taylor, Dir. Alfred Hitchcock, USA, 128 mins.

Vogler, C. (1999) *The Writer's Journey: Mythic Structure for Storytellers and Screenwriters*, Basingstoke: Pan Macmillan.

Part II

Screenwriting and the Development Process

6
Developing the Screenplay: Stepping into the Unknown

Margot Nash

Introduction

The world is littered with an ever-increasing pile of screenwriting text-books, script development workshops, script gurus and script doctors all promising certainty in a volatile and uncertain industry. Like the search for El Dorado, many have searched for the winning script formula, but like El Dorado no one has ever found it. How-to books inevitably become the grail for aspiring screenwriters, yet those who dutifully follow the rules all too often produce formulaic screenplays that fail to ignite the imagination. The screenplay rules and structural paradigms may well provide useful tools during the script development process, but the gold always lies elsewhere. I suggest a more exploratory approach is needed, and in order to discuss this I wish to reflect on my own practice.

As a screenwriter and a film director I tend to work primarily from my instincts, learning new skills on the job through getting my hands dirty rather than following the rule books. My early-stage script development always involves engaging with ideas: reading, thinking, dreaming and debating with others; exploring the known world first and then heading out into the unknown to hunt and gather images, sounds and ideas. The next step is to surround myself with pictures and quotations gleaned from my outward explorations. Then a mysterious, alchemical process starts to occur and ideas that have been fermenting begin to take shape and express themselves cinematically. Rather than following

An earlier version of this article was published in the Journal of Screenwriting (4.2, 2013) under the title 'Unknown Spaces and Uncertainty in Film Development'.

a predetermined shape, I try to let structure emerge out of the material and be a response to the ideas. The ubiquitous three-act structure is held up today as a paradigm to be adhered to, even in the very early stages of development, but I strongly suggest that the mysterious and often messy process where ideas need time to ferment should be valued; and that the formulas and rules with their neat answers, held up as the secret to success, should be questioned, particularly during the initial creative process.

In his essay 'The Storyteller', German philosopher Walter Benjamin argued that it is in the nature of every real story to contain something useful; that in every case the storyteller is someone who has counsel for the reader; and that the purpose of storytelling, as it used to be, was the conveyance of something of value, of use, of wisdom (Benjamin, 1970a: 86). In this chapter, I venture out into the unknown and consider two areas often neglected within screenwriting pedagogy. The first is the uncertain nature of early-stage creative development, where ideas of value are struggling to find form. The second is an investigation into the latter stages of development, where the screenwriter must refine the gaps or spaces within a screenplay that then activate a creative response in others.

The uncertain nature of the creative process

> Ring the bells that can still ring. Forget your perfect offering. There is a crack in everything. That's how the light gets in.
>
> (*Anthem*, 1992)

In her article 'Inspiring Creativity', Australian novelist and creative writing teacher Glenda Adams argues that

> Writers don't really know what to do or how to do it. They are uncertain. Writing a work of fiction can be called a journey toward uncertainty. Henry James wrote that when he begins a novel he does not know and does not care how it will end. Joan Didion says she writes in order to find out what she thinks – if she knew already, there would be no need to write.
>
> (2007: 8)

Australian visual artist Susan Norrie states: 'The idea and reality of being in unsafe territory, as well as the intuitive, play a large part in my work. I like the idea of free falling into an unknown space' (2007). Uncertainty, risk and entering unsafe territory all have negative connotations for those whose business it is to return money to investors, but for artists like Norrie this process is thrilling, for it leads to the new. Norrie is not alone in engaging in a process like this. Creative development in less expensive art forms often has an exploratory phase where artists are funded to spend time developing ideas, but this is rare in the film industry. The pressure to follow a market-driven development process has led many aspiring screenwriters to embrace the script rules and structural templates without question, rather than embrace a discovery-driven uncertain process, in search of originality, story and meaning.

The creative process inevitably involves uncertainty and those brave enough to enter this space must prepare themselves for both frustration and the possibility of failure. Yet film investors often have a poor tolerance for experimentation and risk, and especially any failure that might come as a result. The quest for certainty, so prevalent within the film industry, I suggest ignores the positive role of a temporary frustration or failure and sees only the negative. Yet it is through taking risks, and at times failing, that we learn 'what we do not know'. Failures test us and teach us, and embracing possible failure helps us endure the inevitable setbacks that are part of developing a screenplay and trying to get it made.

A discovery-driven script development process

Apart from notable exceptions like *Le Film Qu'on Ne Voit Pas/The Secret Language of Film* (Carrière, 1994), most books about screenwriting use conventional Hollywood films as models for analysis, and work backwards. They avoid both the difficult terrain of early development and the challenges of films that do not fit the neat paradigms. In a 1983 interview with Jason Weiss, French screenwriter Carrière argued that

> if you rely consciously on your experience to say 'I did it like that before, so I know how to do it', you run the biggest chance of going wrong. [...] This sort of uncertainty is only acquired after a long series of set backs, of choices made [...] It takes a lot of time, a lot of patience, and a lot of humility to arrive at this uncertainty.
>
> (cited by Weiss, 1983: 8)

Entering the world of a film and searching for the key that might unlock its mysteries is part of the uncertain and often solitary detective work of the screenwriter. It involves intuition and experimentation as well as the difficult job of becoming the internal critic, or analyst, of the work when things go wrong (Jones, 2011). However, if a screenplay is fortunate enough to be transformed into a film, it is inevitably left in the hands of others anyway. Australian screenwriters and script editors Barbara Masel and Cory Taylor suggest that

> Collaborators, often with the best intentions, may value the notion of mastering technique over surrendering to process. This is because the dogged application of technique can sometimes be soothing: neatening up the untidy trail of authentic creative investigation [...] Fixing a script can seem like a welcome alternative to the difficult job of searching for authority inside the material.
>
> (2011: 119–120)

Correcting screenplay format is something screenwriting teachers and script editors often resort to, but this is a diversion from the real work of encouraging 'ideas of value' to be explored. Like trying to fix a script, it focuses on mistakes. Instead of opening up a conversation, these strategies thus run the risk of sending enquiring minds off in search of formulas, rather than actively encouraging them to take risks and enter the unknown spaces of their own creativity.

Brazilian literacy teacher Paulo Freire argues for respecting students' life experiences rather than constructing them as lacking. He advocates involving each student in an active process of finding solutions to problems themselves, rather than what he calls the banking approach to teaching and learning, where the student is constructed as empty and the teacher's work is to fill them up with knowledge, thus creating a structure of power where the teacher has authority and the passive student is disempowered (1984: 58). His influential thoughts on pedagogy continue to inspire teachers around the world to activate students to participate in problem solving: to find creative solutions themselves.

Teaching screenwriting classes about character and structure, for example, are crucial, but encouraging students to enter a discovery-driven process that quickens their pulses and fuels their creativity has the potential to produce screenwriters whose 'felt' experience will give them the confidence, and the desire, to jump headlong into that unknown, uncertain space again. If screenwriting students are to develop new and exciting works, they need a safe space to take risks; but they also need to be inspired to imagine different ways of doing things. A recent experience in teaching a seemingly unrelated class has inspired me to draw lessons about the nature of the creative process, and consequently about screenwriting development and pedagogy.

Australian underground and oppositional film history: A pedagogical experience

Since 2011, I have been teaching an Australian film history subject devoted entirely to the study of the neglected and the unknown; in particular, underground and oppositional Australian films. The final assignment is a creative response to a film or group of films studied in class. It is a risky, open-ended assignment where students can choose the form of their response. Some choose to write screenplays, whilst others make short films, write short stories, create blogs or photographic essays, or write critical essays. The subject, 'Australian Film', is part of an under-graduate sub-major called 'Reading Australia'. In developing this subject I decided to 'read' Australia through the study of the lost and forgotten, to look for 'cracks' in the narrative of the conventional mainstream, and to try to let the light in.

In his 'Thesis on the Philosophy of History', Benjamin argues that history is written by those who win the battles and this inevitably means the repression of dissenting voices; and that the task of the historical materialist is to 'brush history against the grain' by challenging this 'universal' history that 'has no theoretical armature. Its method is additive; it musters a mass of data to fill the homogenous empty time' (1970b: 259, 264). In its place he advocates a materialist historiography where

> Thinking involves not only a flow of thoughts but their arrest as well [...] Where thinking suddenly stops in a configuration pregnant with tensions [...] A historical materialist recognizes the sign of a Messianic cessation of happening, or put differently, a revolutionary chance to fight for oppressed past.
>
> (1970b: 264–265)

Approaching the historical subject of Australian Film from this perspective necessitated researching work largely ignored in the history books: films and film movements often too marginal to warrant close attention. Of particular interest was the period from 1940 to 1970 when the Australian feature film industry went into decline and, according to the history books, nothing much happened until its renaissance in the 1970s. It was a 'cessation of happening' ripe for reappraisal. In placing this period in its historical context, it became obvious that students had no idea of Australia's remarkably prolific and successful early film industry; that the first full-length film thought to be made in the world was Australia's *The Story Of the Kelly Gang* (1906); or that the Hollywood juggernaut almost destroyed the local Australian feature film industry in the 1940s.

The research uncovered a rich history that includes the Realist Film Group and the Waterside Workers Film Unit from the 1950s, who were inspired by the works of Russian filmmakers Eisenstein and Pudovkin; Giorgio Mangiamele, who brought Italian neo-realism to Australia in the 1950s and whose experimental feature *Clay* (1965) screened in Cannes; and the Sydney Ubu Film Group from the 1960s, whose experimental films were inspired by the American and European avant-garde, and LSD. Further research has included the Carlton/Godard movement in the late 1960s, which produced 16 mm black and white urban dramas that flouted both Hollywood and the censorship restrictions of the time; the work of second-wave feminist filmmakers in the 1970s, who challenged both male power and the male gaze; and the pioneering work of the Aboriginal Black Film Unit which, in the spirit of the Russian agit-prop trains, in the late 1970s put 'black' films in the back of a car with a projector and took them out to Aboriginal communities living on the fringes of the cities and country towns.

As part of the lecture on second-wave feminist filmmaking, I decided to show extracts from my first film: a provocative experimental short called *We Aim to Please* (1976), made collaboratively with performer Robin Laurie. This is not a film I would show in a screenwriting class because the script, as such, consisted of overflowing shoeboxes full of images, poems, quotations and scribbled ideas that had been fermenting in our cupboards for years. *We Aim to Please* had an exploratory development process, and its structure in fact emerged in the editing room. Yet it has become an Australian feminist classic and is now represented in a permanent exhibition, 'Screen Worlds: A History of the Moving Image in Australia', at the Australian Centre for the Moving Image (ACMI). In screenwriting pedagogy and professional training, the argument that you have to know the rules in order to break them is persuasive; but in making *We Aim to Please*, we knew none of these rules. Such is the power of 'orthodox screenwriting wisdom' that to advocate a development process like this, clearly intent on creating something unconventional, would 'seem feeble even quaint' in a serious screenwriting class (Masel and Taylor, 2011: 119). The Australian Film class is free of this dilemma. For their final creative response assignment, students are not required to engage in a structured development process the way screenwriting students are. Some class time is devoted to discussing ideas, but students are then left to choose what they want to do and how they want to do it, largely without input from the tutor. The results have been unprecedented in my experience as a teacher, the engagement of the students and the creativity of their responses both surprising and inspiring.

In 2011, for example, a student wrote a manifesto as a tribute to the underground canon of Australian film. It was in response to an avant-garde short film about the Vorticist's 1914 Blast manifesto, made in 1971 by Australian experimental filmmakers Arthur and Corinne Cantrill. Another student embroidered an evening purse as a tribute to the McDonagh sisters, silent film pioneers in Australia in the 1920s. The manifesto and the purse have since been acquired by the National Film and Sound Archive (NFSA) as part of their collection of film documents and artefacts.

In 2012, a student made a silent film in which she 'interviewed' audiences leaving a cinema about their knowledge of Australian film history. It is both delightful and revealing about the gaps and spaces in contemporary knowledge of Australian film history. Another student made a wickedly funny rag doll in response to early feminist filmmaking. The doll has what Barbie lacked, namely nipples and a vagina. It comes with a baby, floating with its umbilical cord still attached, and a set of clothes representing both women's oppression and liberation.

In trying to analyse what prompted this creative outpouring, I identified a number of factors that may be useful to consider when investigating both the nature of the creative process in general, and the pedagogy and professional development of screenwriting in particular. It was a discovery-driven process for students and teachers alike: showing unconventional work seemed to open up creative possibilities, rather than shutting them down the way conventional models often seem to. The students were given clear boundaries (in so far as they were required to respond to work discussed in class), but they were also given licence to convey their ideas in different ways: to take risks and discover their own solutions. This process seemed to activate them to enter the unknown and risky spaces of creativity, and the discovery of a hidden history of rebellion and resistance to convention gave them a sense of belonging, which they then embraced.

In advocating a screenwriting pedagogy that is discovery driven, I would argue for introducing students – and professional screenwriters, for that matter – to new ideas through the use of unconventional models as well as conventional ones, for a critical and historical approach to the study of both conventional and unconventional models, and for an exploratory rather than a formula-driven approach to script development. Valuing the unconventional may seem counterproductive to those wishing to make a living by giving the market what it wants, but surely what the market wants is distinctive new works that capture the public imagination. The dilemma inherent in market-driven strategies is the all-pervasive quest for certainty in an uncertain business that ultimately relies on a lively creative process to continue to stimulate new ideas.

Unknown spaces within a screenplay

The quest for certainty at script stage is understandably pervasive. A screenplay has a critical role when decisions about investment are being made, but a screenplay is not a film. Until it is interpreted and actualised by others it remains the 'promise' of a film, destined to undergo a number of changes as it transforms into a film. As the legendary French film director Robert Bresson famously observed,

> My movie is first born in my head, and dies on paper: is resuscitated by the living persons and real objects I use, which are killed on film but, placed in a certain order and projected on to a screen, come to life again like flowers in water.
>
> (1997:13)

Carrière also writes about this metamorphosis, arguing that the screenplay itself vanishes, often left discarded in the studio rubbish bin at the end of the shoot (1994: 150). Whilst the emphasis is always on getting the screenplay right before financing can be approved, a screenplay must be read as a transitional object, not an end in itself. No matter how well structured, how well defined its characters' goals, or how clear the premise or genre, a screenplay cannot promise certainty and must be read as part of a dynamic and creative process that continues until and including the moment when the audience receives the film imaginatively. It is not a blueprint, which is by definition a technical drawing created in order to be reproduced with scientific accuracy; it is more a recipe where the results will vary according to the availability of ingredients and the inventiveness of the cook and those who work in the kitchen.

Developing a screenplay involves finding the right words to evoke the images and sounds that unfold the story. However, there is also the work of removing some of those words in order to create gaps, or spaces within the text so that others might respond imaginatively. Hemingway said that 'if you take something OUT of a piece of writing it always shows' (Clapp, 1997: 42) and it is within these spectral traces that the unspoken and the unnamed leave hints as to their existence. Something does not quite make sense, does not fit. There is a crack in the narrative. This is what Australian screenwriter Laura Jones calls 'the elisions where the shadow narrative is built' (2009). I asked Jones to elaborate on this idea just after she had emerged from writing a draft for a screenplay based on the book *Runaway* (Alice Munro, 2004) for Jane Campion. Before this she had been unwilling to talk, explaining that the creative process requires a different way of thinking to the process of theorising. She was quick to say that building a shadow narrative

> is not something you do. It is something that happens through struc-ture but you only see it after you have written it. You have to see if the elisions and gaps mean what you want to say. It is how you make the steps – and the bits that are left out make the leap thrilling.
>
> (Jones, 2011)

An elision can create a sense of lack, as if something is missing. This lack in turn creates the desire to fill in the gap. It activates people to question, to imagine. A screenplay that micro-manages every detail can irritate and dull those who engage with it. It is a screenplay without spaces to respond to, hypothesise about, make suggestions for and participate in. In a more concrete way, I encourage valuing the white space on the page, to break action up into shots down the page, so that those who engage creatively with the text might be inspired to play within these spaces.

The last film I directed, *Call Me Mum* (2005), was a feature-length series of highly theatrical monologues where five characters share their inner-most thoughts with the audience, as they rehearse what they might say to each other when they meet. It was based on the true story of a white woman who fostered a little boy from the Torres Strait Islands and, when he was a teenager, decided to reunite him with his black mother. As they travel towards this reunion, we meet the black mother struggling with the truth. We also meet the white foster mother's racist parents who are plotting a very different kind of reunion. It was a dense and challeng-ing screenplay and I encouraged the writer to break the monologues up on the page, partly to create rhythmical spaces, but also to create white spaces for the actors and the other key creative crew to dream in. In a monologue where a character is alone, the mask slips and subtext, nor-mally buried, becomes text. In this case the task of the director and the actors is to search for the repressed material lying even deeper within the unconscious of character.

At the end of the shoot, I retrieved two 'vanishing' script pages from the studio rubbish bin where one of the actors had used the white spaces to sketch pictures of her character and to write various ideas for her performance (Figures 6.1 and 6.2).

There is one word squashed inside one of the white spaces that just says 'vomit'. It is a brief moment in the finished film where the repressed revulsion the mother feels towards her daughter, who is a lesbian, is fleetingly embodied. These visceral moments are what actors thrive on. Actors want to know what is happening under the surface in order to discover how to enter a character's body and bring them to life on the screen. This is why actors can be so stimulating in script development workshops: they ask questions screenwriters often forget to ask. What does this character want? What do they do to get what they want? Some actors call it 'the thought script', some 'the internal monologue'. They play the subtext we do not see: yet we do see it for its traces are

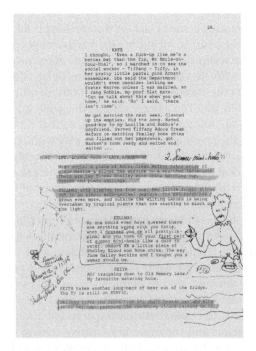

Figure 6.1   Call Me Mum script, p. 28. Drawings by Lynette Curran

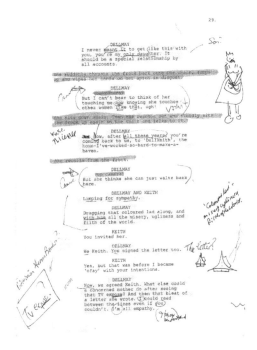

Figure 6.2 Call Me Mum script, p. 29. Drawings by Lynette Curran

written on the body. This work is often invisible, speaking directly to the unconscious rather than the conscious mind.

Just as the role of actors during film development is often underrated, so is the role of the script editor. 'The usual assumption is that script editing is about removing material that does not work [...] when in fact it is about re-writing, replacement, review and is always engaged with problem solving and resolution' (Wells, 2011). Like the work of the actor in trying to understand unspoken desires, the work of the script editor is often invisible, yet it too speaks to the unconscious process by which a film is received by an audience.

Mysteries and secrets and the unconscious

If text is the 'conscious' of a screenplay, then subtext is its 'unconscious' and the unconscious always speaks in a different language to the conscious. It is the language of repressed desire and it hides itself the way images in dreams disguise their true meaning in order to protect unconscious wishes from detection. It shows itself in the language of the body, and in slips of the tongue. It shows itself in what people do when no one is looking, and in the lies they tell. It creates mysteries, riddles and puzzles to be solved. To create subtext is to delve deep into the unconscious desires and needs of character:

> And desire is the important term here, because desire springs from that which we do not know about ourselves. This makes the realm of desire a privileged terrain when it comes to visionary creative work.
>
> (Sainsbury, 2004: 75)

It is the unspoken and often unconscious desires of character that are the fuel driving the story forward. The plot unfolds because of them and it is our desire to close or fill in the gaps that makes us, the audience, active as we piece together motivation, desire and need. Like Jake, the detective protagonist in *Chinatown* (1974), we do not know what is going on, but we are driven by the desire to find out, to uncover the hidden along with him. Nothing is as it seems in *Chinatown*: the main plot unfolds under the surface as a shadow narrative driven entirely by subtext, with the unspoken eventually finding voice in a riddle. Jake, driven by his unconscious desire to re-write history and emerge the hero, must finally, along with us, suffer the film's 'outrage ending' which defies the neat closure of the hero's journey.

Inspired by the hidden history of a massacre of Algerian demonstrators by the French police in 1961, Michael Haneke's film *Caché/Hidden* (2005) uncovers repressed racism through the creation of shots that create new and therefore unknown spaces. The opening use of video footage, which is then replayed, shows the protagonist walking straight past where the camera operator must have been in order to create the shot, yet he sees nothing. This puzzle works as a metaphor for racism: the white man who does not see the black man even when he is standing straight in front of him. This film, with its impossible camera angles and puzzles within the frame, challenged and infuriated audiences who were used to the literal and unused to having to work so hard to create meaning. Yet Haneke is recalcitrant about his work:

> My films are intended as polemical statements against the American 'barrel down' cinema and its dis-empowerment of the spectator. They are an appeal for a cinema of insistent questions instead of false (because too quick) answers, for clarifying distance in place of violating closeness, for provocation and dialogue instead of consumption and consensus.
>
> (1992: 89)

Like in many of his films, the provocation in *Caché* lies in its power to implicate us, the audience. Like the protagonist, it is not necessarily what we see that is so powerful, it is what we do not see. In animation it is the spaces between the frames that are crucial to the movement we see on the screen. These spaces are not seen but the length and rhythm of them determines the movement that we do see. Pioneering Canadian animator Norman McLaren declared that the art of animation lay not in the frames that are drawn, but between the frames. Animation, he argued, 'is not the art of drawings-that-move, but rather the art of movements-that-are-drawn. What happens between each frame is more important than what happens on each frame' (cited by Solomon, 1987:11).

In his essay 'Hearing the notes that aren't played', David Mamet reveals a 'priceless tip' from record producer Joel Silver: 'Leave out the third – we hear it anyway'. Mamet argues that all forms of drama 'build on the revelation that omission is a form of creation – that we hear the third anyway – that the audience will supply the plot' (2002).

Carrière writes about the early days of cinema when people were confused by different shots being placed next to each other, and a man called an explicator would stand out the front and point to the screen with a long stick in order to explain what was happening to the audience (1994: 7). We no longer need this kind of direction, because a more sophisticated cinematic language has evolved over time. This is what Carrière calls the 'secret' language of film. A literal translation of his book title *Le Film Qu'on Ne Voit Pas/The Secret Language of Film* (1994) is The Film That One Does Not See.

It is this unseen and unspoken language that 'speaks' within the gaps and spaces that lie ready to activate us into participating imaginatively in the final realisation of the work. This language is what screenwriters need to fully comprehend, for the art of screenwriting lies not just in the images and sounds that are written, nor in the story that unfolds, nor in the veracity of the dialogue; but in the unknown spaces, hidden between the lines that lead to the active and imaginative participation of others.

Haneke's *Amour* (2012) tackles ageing and the inevitability of death, revealing the death of one of the main characters in the first few shots. Having got this out of the way, Haneke then invites us to participate in the imaginative space of the other main character as he negotiates the decline and death of his love. Haneke masterfully makes us work as he confronts us with the shadow narrative of our own, and our loved ones' decrepitude and inevitable death, as well as the unspoken shadow narrative that leads up to the decision the character finally makes. In the final shots he creates mystery and magic, refusing narrative closure and setting us free to imagine what might have happened next. As Meyerhold (1969: 26–27) reminds us,

> 'A work of art can influence only through the imagination. Therefore it must constantly stir the imagination' (Schopenhauer). But it must really stir it, not leave it inactive through trying to show everything. To stir the imagination is 'the essential condition of aesthetic activity as well as the basic law of the fine arts. Whence it follows that a work of art must not give everything to our senses but only as much as is necessary to direct our imagination on the right track, letting it have the last word' (Schopenhauer).
>
> (Meyerhold, 1907: 26–27)

Conclusion

A great screenplay and a great film may well activate our desire to participate, to fill in the gaps, to create meaning; but

> There are some mysteries you don't try to analyze, like the hessian bag and the lace in *Cet obscur objet du désir/That Obscure Object of Desire* (1977) or the box in *Belle de Jour* (1967) for logic can kill, and these mysteries are gifts.
>
> (Jones, 2011)

Followers of orthodox screenwriting wisdom continue to seek both logic and revelation through conventional paradigms, rarely entering the intuitive and passionate spaces of creativity where ideas are fluid and in a shifting process of constant change. The alchemical space where ideas are dismembered and allowed to ferment is full of putrescence, darkness and fear. It is a space that those who engage in creative practice know well, for it is a space where the repressed return; where our most forbidden and destructive desires are given space to break down and re-form; where new connections and patterns are discovered. It is from this dark place that new ideas emerge fully formed and enter the light of day. They do not come from the world of logic, but must be seized by the conscious mind and forged into something altogether more concrete. Then we will be 'in the presence of the triumph of what is no longer seen. It is like those years of stubborn practice that pave the way for the athlete's few simple moves when the day of the competition arrives' (Carrière, 1994: 170).

Figure 6.3   The gap

For it is within this interplay of discipline and spontaneity; of the known and the unknown; of logic and intuition; of passion and reason, that creativity lies. And it is within these gaps and spaces that we can learn to play (Figure 6.3).

References

Adams, G. (2007) 'Inspiring Creativity' in *Australian Author*, 39(3), 6–10.
Amour/Love (2012) Wr./Dir. Michael Haneke, France, Austria, Germany, 125 mins.
Anthem (1992) Wr. Leonard Cohen, Stranger Music Inc., USA.
Belle de Jour (1967) Wr. Jean Claude Carrière, Dir. Luis Buñuel, France, 105 mins.
Benjamin, W. (1970a) 'The Storyteller' in Hannah Arendt (ed.) *Illuminations*, trans. Harry Zohn, London: Jonathan Cape, p. 86.
Benjamin, W. (1970b) 'Thesis on the Philosophy of History' in Hannah Arendt (ed.) Illuminations, trans. Harry Zohn, London: Jonathan Cape, pp. 259–265.
Blast (1971) Wrs./Dirs. Arthur Cantrill and Corinne Cantrill, Australia, 6 mins.
Bresson, R. (1997) *Notes sur le cinématographe/Notes on the Cinematographer*, trans. Jonathan Griffen, Copenhagen: Green Integer, p. 13.
Caché/Hidden (2005) Wr./Dir. Michael Haneke, France, Austria, 117 mins.
Call Me Mum (2005) Wr. Kathleen Mary Fallon, Dir. Margot Nash, Australia, 76 mins.
Carrière, J.C. (1994) *Le Film Qu'on Ne Voit Pas/The Secret Language of Film*, trans. Jeremy Legatt, New York: Pantheon Books, pp. 7, 150, 170.
Cet obscur objet du désir/That Obscure Object of Desire (1977) Wr. Jean Claude Carrière, Dir. Luis Buñuel, France, 102 mins.
Chinatown (1974) Wr. Robert Towne, Dir. Roman Polanski, USA, 130 mins.
Clapp, S. (1997) *With Chatwin Portrait of a Writer*, London: Jonathan Cape.
Clay (1965) Wr./Dir. Giorgio Mangiameli, Australia, 84 mins.
Freire, P. (1984) *The Pedagogy of the Oppressed*, New York: Continuum.
Haneke, M. (1992) 'Film als Katharsis' in Francesco Bono (ed.) *felix: zum österreichischem film der 80er Jahre/felix: on the Austrian film of the 80s*, Graz: Blimp, p. 89.
Jones, L. (2009, 2011) Personal Communication, Tuesday 24 March 2009, Sydney and Friday 29 July 2011, Sydney.
Mamet, D. (2002) 'Hearing the Notes that aren't Played: Writers on writing' in *The New York Times*, 15 July, http://www.nytimes.com/2002/07/15/arts/writers-on-writing-hearing-the-notes-that-aren-t-played.html [accessed July 2012].

Masel, B. and Taylor, C. (2011) 'Unscripted: The True Life of Screenplays' in *Lumina*, 7, 119–120.

Meyerhold, V. (1969) 'The Naturalistic Theatre and the Theatre of Mood' in Edward Braun (ed.) *Meyerhold on Theatre*, London: Eyre Methuen, pp. 26–27.

Munro, A. (2004) *Runaway*, New York: Vintage.

Norrie, S. (2007) Artist Statement, HAVOC, room sheet n/p, Fondazione Levi, Venice Biennale.

Sainsbury, P. (2004) ' "Visions, Illusions and Delusions": Australian Screen Directors' Association Conference, September 2002'in *Critical Quarterly*, 46(1), 73–92.

Solomon, C. (1987) 'Animation: Notes on a Definition' in Charles Solomon (ed.) *The Art of the Animated Image: An Anthology*, Los Angeles, CA: AFI, p. 11.

The Story of the Kelly Gang (1906) Wr./Dir. Charles Tait, Australia, 60 mins.

We Aim to Please (1976) Wrs./Dirs. Robin Laurie and Margot Nash, Australia, 13 mins.

Weiss, J. (1983) 'The Power to Imagine: An Interview with Jean Claude Carrière' in *Cineaste*, 13(1), 6–11.

Wells, P. (2011) 'Sorry Blondie, I Don't Do Backstory' conference presentation, Beyond Boundaries: Screenwriting Across Media, Brussels, 8–11 September, 2011.

7

The Irish Film Board: Gatekeeper or Facilitator? The Experience of the Irish Screenwriter

Díóg O'Connell

Introduction

> Producers in Europe spend too little on development, screenwriters are underpaid and scripts underwritten.
>
> *David Kavanagh, Board Member, Scriptwriters Federation in Europe and former Director, European Script Fund.*
>
> (cited by Flynn, 1995)

This chapter explores the global and local influences on the working relationship between Irish screenwriters and the Irish Film Board (Bord Scannán na hÉireann), through scrutinising the balance of power and authority between the institution and the writer. In examining this topic, key questions are identified, teased out and framed against the backdrop of ongoing research into cultural policy and the Irish Film Board (IFB) (e.g. O'Connell (2010) and O'Connell (2012)). Through a survey of support systems for the script development process at the IFB and how these policies were changed, developed and enacted in the past decade, the chapter seeks to establish to what extent the IFB has a 'writer-friendly' institutional approach, serving the needs of the screenwriter in particular.

For example, can it be suggested that the IFB's approach to script development focuses on nurturing the screenwriter's career, or instead emphasises the process of writing a screenplay and narrative development? This discussion addresses whether the focus on development schemes as put in place by the IFB streamlines the approach to screenwriting as a means to an end, to satisfy the demands of a mainstream market and its needs, rather than the individual careers of screenwriters themselves. The impact on the national film industry as a consequence of the policy direction of the IFB is clearly crucial to its place in a wider global sphere; as such, this chapter explores national cinema in the context of increasing globalisation.

Answering these questions is framed within the broader theoretical discourse of the relationship between 'institution and writer', and with regard to the collaborative nature of the film development process. Particular to this is the growing occurrence of collaboration between screenwriters, producers and directors, something explored by Bloore (2012: 69–91) in his work on managing creativity in the script development process. The screenwriter, it can be argued, is contextualised very differently to writers working in other forms, such as the poet, the novelist or the short story writer. Arguably more closely aligned to the playwright, the screenwriter is part of a complex process that starts with the work of the writer but has a life well after the work is complete, increasingly in a collaborative way. This position is supported by Susan Rogers' study of the British screenwriter, which asserts that

> working relationships formed through the collaboration between a screenwriter and any of the film's executives, producers and directors involved in the screenplay's development can be close and unlike those in any other creative fields, such as novelists, fine artists and composers, where the work is generally solitary.
>
> (2010: 378)

Similarly, Michael Coutanche's 2012 study on the Canadian film industry establishes the importance of networking and mentoring for the screenwriter and their career, and is explored as a premise for the Irish film industry in this chapter.

Social capital/working life

Central to understanding the relationship of the screenwriter to the institution is framing it through the concept of 'social capital' and the role it plays in the screenwriting process. Through the prism of social capital, the working life of the screenwriter is examined in terms of an alternative currency, principally in terms of mentors, networks and contacts. This approach looks beyond funding mechanisms, film policy and direct supports within the film industry for the screenwriter and towards other connections between the screenwriter and the industry shaping their working life. This paper explores how relationships are constructed between the screenwriter and the institution, and among screenwriters themselves, as an example of social capital. The role of screenwriting as part of a larger process of social capital is interesting on two fronts. Firstly, writing is often perceived as a solitary activity, the image of the writer in the garret being iconic; yet, screenwriting is a stage in the process of a highly collaborative art form where production involves many different stages of collaboration and many different and diverse inputs. Secondly, screenwriting itself is also a collaborative process: either through a team writing approach, and/or taking the process through various stages of development that might involve the writer, the script editor, the 'script doctor' and the script consultant. Understanding the nature of screenwriting as a collaborative activity and setting it aside from other forms of writing is aided through the concept of social capital.

Social capital is generally understood, in simple terms, as social relations that generate productive benefits. Social capital is about the value of social networks, bringing people of shared interest and activity together in a mutually beneficial relationship. Social capital is fundamentally about how people interact with each other, and it refers to a system that explains how the interaction people have with groups and individuals can bring about economic benefits in terms of work and industry. It explains a form of advancement not based on meritocracy but connected to social intelligence, making certain social interactions highly productive (e.g. Coleman (1988); Lesser (2000); Dekker and Uslaner (2001)).

Pierre Bourdieu described social capital as 'the aggregate of the actual or potential resources which are linked to possession of a durable network of more or less institutionalized relationships of mutual acquaintance or recognition' (1986: 248). Social capital is not about casual relationships or ad hoc acquaintances, but rather structured encounters through networks that facilitate individuals of a shared interest or activity. Social capital is constructed of 'social obligations ('connections'), which are convertible, in certain conditions, into economic capital and may be institutionalised in the form of a title of nobility' (Bourdieu, 1986: 243). Therefore, social capital refers to what happens when an individual or group convene in some way to share by way of networking. This network becomes 'durable' and 'institutional', in a conscious or unconscious way, to benefit the members.

Social capital, therefore, is a very useful concept to explore the working life of the screenwriter in Ireland, and more specifically how the IFB, through its policy development facilitates, nurtures and creates these relationships. Understanding the IFB in this context will shed light on the nature of the working life of the screenwriter and begin to define to what extent social capital plays a role. According to Coleman,

> social capital is defined by its function. It is not a single entity, but a variety of different entities having two characteristics in common: they all consist of some aspect of social structure, and they facilitate certain actions of individuals who are within the structure.
>
> (1990: 302)

This helps us in an understanding of the relationship between institution and screenwriter, and also how the access to social capital supports or hinders the working life of the writer. This is particularly interesting when we examine more specific aspects of the screenwriter's milieu, connected particularly to issues of gender and regionality. These connections can appear, at face value, to be informal and casual. However, they are often much more structured and therefore pivotal to the mechanism of the relationship: it is not simply about film and media being a contact industry or networking being a vital component of career activity. Through the framework of social capital, then, our understanding of the unconscious barriers and/or gateways to this industry can be better understood.

In Rogers' 2010 study, 'Who Writes British Films?' the principle of social capital is identified as playing a significant role in the working life of British screenwriters. In her survey of British screenwriters, 50% of those responding had a previous working relationship, and many had a personal relationship with the producer, director or production company responsible for hiring them at the start of the project: 'not only did the employer know the screenwriter's previous work in advance of the project, but also quite often they had worked together previously' (Rogers, 2010: 378). In Coutanche's report on the Canadian film industry, he notes that 'along with formal education and additional training, mentorship is an important factor in the Canadian screenwriting occupation' (Coutanche and Davis, 2013: 18). In fact, his research found that nearly half of all screenwriters reported having a mentor. The nature of social capital is therefore reported as significantly important to the screenwriter, as is their relationship with the institutional structure that frames their art/craft on an economic level.

It could also be suggested that the screenplay itself forms part of the structure of social capital. Unlike the novel, poem or short story, the screenplay is never a stand-alone document enjoyed for pleasure: it is a blueprint for something else, principally the finished screened production, or part of the process thereof. Whilst this is not to take away from the value of the screenplay as a literary and narrative document, screenplays are part of a larger machine, or at least aspire to a larger process of development, production, distribution and exhibition. In this sense, they form part of a structure involving phases and stages with many forces conspiring in the building and completion of this structure: political, cultural, economic, etc. In the context of this chapter, the role that social capital plays in establishing and developing relationships between writer and institution is how I seek to understand and illuminate such a process.

Bringing the screenwriter in from the cold...

Policy changes and developments at the IFB have been successful in bringing the screenwriter more centrally into the film-financing process. By tracking institutional changes at the IFB since the mid-1990s, and developments and evolutions from 1994 to 2009 in particular, the policy shifts are identified as part of a design process rather than an accidental side effect, particularly those affecting the writer and the process of script development (O'Connell, 2012). These changes in policy, which include the appointment of a development executive to the IFB, a script editor to each script and schemes allowing writers apply for funding alone, were implemented in distinct phases and have led to a characteristic shift in the way that films are scripted and subsequently produced as features in Ireland. The initiatives introduced during this period, particularly at the level of script development, have helped to shape Irish film, culminating in an identifiable pattern of narrative style since 2000 (O'Connell, 2012).

Criticisms made in various industry reports in the late 1990s prompted increased resources and focus on the script development phase, and brought to the surface discussions about storytelling technique, narrative and the writing process. This all served to highlight a need for change in Irish film policy. At the same time, there was a wider international context for this development. English-speaking Europe witnessed the arrival of the Robert McKee 'roadshow' and the proliferation of screenwriting and story manuals from Vogler (1999), McKee (1997) et al., all of whom contributed to the growing and widespread interest in script development and the normalising of the process within film pre-production (O'Connell, 2010).

The emergence of the script development process in Ireland reflected a wider European trend, which included the support mechanisms put in place by the MEDIA initiative, funded by the European Union, particularly through the Arista and Sagas programmes in the 1990s, programmes that focused particularly on script-editing skills development. This was responded to nationally through programmes by Screen Training Ireland, a subsidiary of the state-supported national training agency, FÁS (now SOLAS). The concentration on script development, script editing and the growth in screenwriting courses in Irish higher education, methods of institutionalising the activity of the screenwriting profession, craft and skill throughout the 1990s and into the new millennium, was not an approach unique to Ireland but reflected the growing globalisation of film production where Hollywood practices merged with European traditions (O'Connell, 2010).

Rogers describes feature film script development as 'an intensely creative, technical and interpretive endeavor' and also states that for a 'screenplay to progress to a polished draft upon which a film can be based, as many as fifteen drafts, sometimes more, may be written' (2010: 375). The practical changes made at the IFB in the late 1990s, including the appointment of a development manager to oversee script development and an allocation of funds to cover development loans for individual projects or company applications, proved necessary to a national industry in gestation. In the early 2000s, two new schemes were also introduced, both enabling individuals and companies to develop a range of different script projects. This expanded the sphere of pre-production and shifted the emphasis to include more structural supports for the writing process. Under these new procedures, and in addition to the increased development budget, all scripts supported by the IFB were assigned a script editor. This change was welcomed by the film production community, yet at the same time it exposed a skills shortage in the area of script editing and consulting.

The fruits of this activity can be viewed in the 2000–2005 period when changes in approach to scripts and screenwriting surfaced. This period saw the emergence of a diversity and eclecticism in screen stories and narratives alongside a popular genre approach, both of which appear to have been favourable with Irish audiences, for example *About Adam* (2000), *When Brendan Met Trudy* (2000), *Adam & Paul* (2004) and *Goldfish Memory* (2003). Whilst the shift towards script development and a more significant role for the script editor may have accounted partly for improved exhibition rates, due in many respects to a more commercial focus on the stories being told, increased distribution opportunities need also to be acknowledged. More Irish films had box office releases and there was higher DVD/video distribution than ever before (Barton, 2004: 191–192).

This focus on script development was further consolidated in 2007 when the IFB changed its approach to encourage 'writer only' projects, involving an application for funding as early as possible in a project's development. Prior to this, most projects came to the IFB having been developed to at least 'treatment' stage, meaning that screenwriters had to work with producers early on to have their screenplays at a certain level before even applying for funding. This funding change thus allowed screenwriters to apply for development funding at initial idea or outline stage, and to be able to apply as a sole applicant or as part of an emerging production team. Once funding on this basis was approved, a script editor was assigned to the project or the screenwriter was facilitated in procuring the services of a script editor. This approach provided an infrastructure for the activities of the screenwriter at the nascent stage of a project, a key development for the writer and their practice: not only could they be part of the collaborative process from early on, the script could now be developed significantly in advance of collaboration. This placed the screenwriter much more centrally within the script development process, bringing them in from the periphery – on paper at least. The thinking behind this policy development might be that a screenwriter need not work in a vacuum or in isolation, suggesting that the work environment of the writer is subject not only to the influences of social capital but also to political and economic factors.

At this time, the IFB divided script development funding in two ways: first draft loans (now known as screenplay development) and fiction development loans. These schemes can change from time to time, in name and in structure, but what is significant is that their existence suggests a solidifying of the development process as a way of making the screenwriter a central part of the production infrastructure. Both schemes allow a certain level of independence to remain with the screenwriter. First draft loans have been provided to writers who have yet to acquire a producer or production company, which is one of the ways that screenwriters can maintain their autonomy and independence, at least for the first stage of writing, and be supported for it. In terms of social capital, those new to the field and uninitiated in the film production business are thus able to gain a foothold in the process by applying as a sole agent.

This policy change also means that funding goes directly to the screenwriter, and is not funnelled through a production company or a producer at this early stage. As well as providing income for the writer, the IFB can take on a mentoring role by matching the writer with a producer and/or production company, in preparation for applying to the next scheme. In fact, the writer must be connected with a company if they are to be awarded further funding for their screenplay. For a screenwriter starting out, who does not already have an established network in the film industry, this scheme can productively aid and facilitate their efforts at entry level.

The second scheme, the fiction development loan, also allows for the writer to remain independent. When looking at the way that teams/individuals are funded through this scheme, there is a marked emphasis on the screenwriter, whether alone or in collaboration, which we might suggest is another positive development in the IFB's recent history. The stepping stone approach therefore, from being the sole applicant to a collaborative arrangement, involves networking and mentoring so that the writer who starts out alone can become connected to potential collaborators as their project develops. Networking and mentoring are highlighted as important factors also for Canadian screenwriters. According to Coutanche and Davis, 'the high degree of formal and informal mentorships in the screenwriting industry is evidence of the importance of networking and the forging of professional relationships in an unstructured work environment' (2013: 34).

Policy and practice/working life

The approach to policy development and implementation in this period is linked to a number of factors: the reception of indigenous feature films at the box office; a response to critical and commercial acclaim; responses to a range of industry-commissioned reports; and a developing industry reacting to external factors.[1] As an institution charged with public policy, the IFB aligned itself with a mainstream approach to popular filmmaking and guided scripts towards a more streamlined approach, particularly in the early 2000s, witnessing a slight shift in the direction of *auteurist* cinema and personal films in recent years. Contextually, it can be seen to be part of a wider European and American approach to script development that has developed over the past 20 years, encouraged by trends in mainstream screenwriting, what might be called the 'Robert McKee roadshow' and European MEDIA policy for script development, under the umbrella of Sources 2, an advanced training programme for European film professionals working in the field of script and story development (www.sources2.de).

This chapter is interested in the impact these policies have on the screenwriters directly affected by it, asking, how is the relationship between the institution and the writer constructed in light of such policy shifts? The research thus shifts away from a political and economic approach to the institution towards the direct, personal and professional experiences of the screenwriter within the infrastructure. This is seen from a number of perspectives, but principally by those involved in the screenwriting process directly: how policy impacts on the ground, so to speak. Clearly, the work of the IFB and that of the screenwriter are closely entwined: both share the same objective of seeing the screenplay produced. Therefore, the experience of the writer and how it has changed as a result of policy shifts is important. In this way, the approach to policy becomes a way of addressing the micro experience of the screenwriter and/or the macro experience of the industry, thus impacting on the national industry.

Particular to this project is the growing occurrence of collaboration between screenwriters, producers and directors in Irish film, a process that has developed in the past 15 years as a result of changes to the funding mechanisms at the IFB. Whereas in 1993 when the IFB was re-activated and there was a tendency for directors to write their own screenplays, there has been a shift, particularly since 2004, towards a more collaborative approach between screenwriter and director. This dynamic, or working relationship, between screenwriter/director and institution (in this case, the IFB), can partly be revealed through an analysis of policy development but it also requires uncovering the underlying ideological motivation of the institution, as it carves out an infrastructure for a cultural industry. The needs and responsibility of the institution is different to the writer; one is answerable to the 'public purse' whilst the other has a professional responsibility. Thus, the challenge facing the screenwriter is balancing their own independence and self-expression once they become involved at institutional level, whilst also playing by the rules. Their working 'space' needs to be protected by the IFB whilst also guarding the institution's responsibility to public policy and accountability. Through interviews undertaken with key IFB personnel, Andrew Meehan, Development Executive in August 2011 and Sarah Dillon, Production & Development Co-coordinator in October 2013, and two questionnaires (2011 and 2013) distributed to screenwriters funded through these policies, a picture of the dynamic between the institution and writer begins to emerge, explored later in the chapter.[2]

The role of development executive at the IFB is viewed internally as someone who works with screenwriter/producer teams in a collaborative and supportive way whilst also nurturing the careers of screenwriters and directors. The role of development at the IFB has evolved in the past five years. The writer is now considered important not just in the script development stage, but also when the script goes into production, a notable shift in policy. This approach can be viewed as pro-active and interventionist as a way of managing and structuring the industry. The thinking behind this corresponds to the way the IFB sees itself as pivotal to the construction and development of an indigenous industry, whilst at the same time safeguarding the notion of the cultural industries. The institutional approach can be defined in terms of priority, not so much for first-time screenwriters getting a break, but for second and subsequent project realisation. The IFB's objective in recent years has been to emphasise having a slate of scripts in the development phase and reaching completion for a collaborative team, rather than achieving just one signature production for a screenwriter.

When the IFB was re-activated in 1993, it was maintained that getting the first feature to completion, which often takes four or five years, was not as big a challenge as getting the second feature written and into production (O'Connell, 2010). The IFB addressed this with the introduction of micro- and low-budget schemes, particularly in 2007 with its Catalyst scheme (*Rewind* (2010), *One Hundred Mornings* (2009) and *Eamon* (2009)). This scheme was deemed successful at the time, by getting these three films through the production process and to completion in a shorter time frame and on a smaller budget than other Irish productions, and with positive critical acclaim. However, the scheme was allowed to lapse and only recently re-activated in 2013, now with an emphasis on training, low-budget filmmaking and mentoring.

In facilitating a quicker advance from first to second feature, we might ask, is the role of the IFB one of mentor, adviser or gatekeeper? In recent times the IFB has explored alternative ways of finding screenwriters, and has adopted a proactive approach to doing so. In addition to writers submitting screenplays by way of the producer route or on their own, an initiative involving 'scouting' for new writers, such as at comedy festivals and theatre productions, has emerged. In this instance, key IFB personnel might approach writers and/or performers and suggest that they submit a script. Whilst this might not yield a critical mass in screenplay production, it does reveal a shift in the IFB's institutional approach: away from a central funding organisation to a commissioner/producer, more akin to the national broadcaster, RTÉ (Radio Telefís Éireann). This raises certain ideological questions and alters the relationship between the screenwriter and institution, arguably quite a significant shift. It also suggests that the role played by social capital is more central to the process, something that screenwriters and commissioners need to be keenly aware of.

Another way the IFB is interested in the careers of screenwriters, particularly in helping them to sustain their livelihoods between writing projects, includes keeping some writers on a retainer for reading projects and undertaking script editing. Whilst giving a certain degree of financial security to the writers, it goes some way in bridging the skills shortfall in areas such as script editing and script doctoring. Laudable in intent, Andrew Meehan, former Development Executive at the IFB, states that it is still very difficult, almost impossible, to make a living as a screenwriter in Ireland. Similarly in Canada, 'most Canadian English-language screenwriters do not earn a living entirely from screenwriting' (Coutanche and Davis, 2013: 5–7) and generally have to supplement income in other ways.

These findings, which result from close analysis of changes to policy and speaking with IFB personnel, suggest that the IFB involves itself much more proactively in creating and nurturing an industry and an infrastructure for the screenwriter than it did ten years ago. Just like the Canadian Film Centre is central to the career of Canadian screenwriters, screenwriters in Ireland are much more central to a funding infrastructure than they were 20 years ago. Despite economic recession since 2008, this system is set to continue, revealing a longer-term view of the film industry and the individual player in it. The screenwriter cannot afford to remain outside.

However, many questions still need to be addressed when considering these developments, principally around freedom and independence for the screenwriter, and institutional autonomy. There is always a danger of institutionalising the process, the product and the person, and creating a system of patronage. Screenwriters might feel obliged to fulfil the needs of the institution at the expense of their own autonomous role and individual creativity. Whilst the IFB is part of a wider globalisation project from which it cannot remain immune, to what extent these practices dilute indigenous and cultural specificity in screen stories in order to satisfy a global market needs to be considered. As such, what role does the screenwriter play in this process?

What the screenwriters say ...

This research seeks to illuminate the position the screenwriter holds within the broader structures of the Irish film industry, and particularly whether there is a more positive and productive experience as a result of the establishment of a support infrastructure for them. A key question arising from this is, does the screenwriter actually still remain on the periphery of the process or are they more centrally placed? Answering this question might be possible in a number of ways:

- by looking at how screenwriters work: in collaboration or alone
- by exploring the types of stories writers are creating, and whether they serve an industry need or are more autonomous, individual personal expressions
- by examining whether writers are developing a range of screenplays and performing other screenwriting-related functions to sustain a living.

Analysing changes to policy and speaking with IFB personnel suggests that the IFB involves itself proactively in creating and nurturing an industry and an infrastructure for the screenwriter, much more than they did ten years ago. This reveals how similar many of the key issues and concerns of the Irish screenwriter are to those working and living in other territories. On one level, this suggests that in spite of local agreements and practices, the writer works and lives in a wider globalised frame. Screenwriters often refer to 'development hell': the slowness of the development process; drafts being prolonged in development; feedback and decision making taking a long time; the priority given to producers; and the lack of control and ownership over a screenplay as the project advances. These observations came from Irish screenwriters in response to questionnaires, but are also echoed in other territories, notably in the British and Canadian reports already cited.

The IFB is central to the work of any Irish screenwriter, and therefore closer scrutiny of their activities and assessment of their impacts is important. Writers who responded to the first questionnaire (sent out in August 2011 to 29 Irish screenwriters who had received funding from the IFB in the previous three years, yielding a 33% response) tended to be satisfied with the support structures offered by the IFB, and more than half agreed with the improvements made to procedures and processes in the previous five years, seeing them as helping to build a support structure for them. Two thirds of respondents agreed that they maintained sufficient independence within the IFB's structure, with just over half agreeing that schemes directed at writers promoted innovation. Two thirds of respondents had initiated their screenplays by themselves, whereas one third had been commissioned by a producer. Just under half had applied alone to the funding schemes whilst the remainder was in collaboration with a producer.

One area consistently referred to by all those taking part in this research involved the role of the producer. Screenwriters appear divided on the priority afforded to the producer by the IFB. Those who were critical perceived a privileged status for producers in the development of scripts, and on overly commercial emphasis placed on the process by them. On the other hand, those who welcomed the collaborative approach of writer and producer did so for reasons of completion: the producer enabled the project to work through the system in the direction of actual production. The gap between these two positions may be bridged by actively encouraging what we might call 'creative producers'. Sarah Dillon, Production and Development Co-coordinator, suggested that the IFB should encourage and facilitate more creative producers, a system she has witnessed working well elsewhere. In Ireland producers place greater emphasis on the production phase of a screenplay, but good practice in other European countries suggests that creative producers can play a central role in enabling a project through the development phase. This is one area the IFB sees as enhancing and developing the infrastructure for the writer.

In summary, the results from the two questionnaires I used to undertake the research suggest that screenwriters' dealings with the IFB are satisfactory. This is qualified on two levels: firstly, it is noted that the respondents had been successfully funded by the IFB and therefore one may assume hold a positive disposition towards the Board. Secondly, Ireland is a small country (population four million) and thus there can be a tendency not to 'bite the hand that feeds'. It can be difficult to get criticism of the Board on record with respondents keen to ensure confidentiality. However, there were some notable examples of dissatisfaction. There was a stark gender divide in satisfaction levels. Thirty per cent of respondents were female and in all cases where high levels of dissatisfaction were expressed, this was by female screenwriters, principally in the area of getting female-centred stories supported through the process.

Similarly, Coutanche and Davis found that 'there are nearly twice as many men as women writers in the Canadian screenwriting profession' and in the aggregate, 'men have an advantage in attaining positions that allow for control over the overall creative and production aspects of screen-based writing in Canada. Female writers attain a lower degree of creative control than that enjoyed by their male counterparts' (2013: 20–21). Roger's study found an under-representation of female screenwriters in the British film industry, with women employed to write fewer genres than men. She states that the 'low proportion of female to male screenwriters is nowhere close to parity. Women writers on the selected films wrote in fewer genres than their male counterparts, writing only in animation, comedy, fantasy and drama' (2010: 380).

Ireland has similar levels of under-representation and, although this study was not primarily focused on gender, it surfaced in notes from respondents and is thus impossible to ignore. For example, women write around 10% of films funded by the IFB. The genre-based approach to funding Irish film sees an emphasis on comedy, gangster and road movies, genres that are heavily dominated by male writers. Where women screenwriters were awarded development funding, their films rarely made it to the next phase of production.[3] The low representation of women in Irish film is not unique to Ireland, but runs much deeper within the systems established globally. Nevertheless, it is worth highlighting here as something that requires further investigation. In the Canadian survey, it was revealed that women make more use of the value of social capital and that twice as many women as men take specialised courses in screenwriting (Coutanche and Davis, 2013: 16). The study revealed that more women use the mentoring system than men, and that 'notably, women report valuing mentorship more than men: 52% vs. 40%' (Coutanche and Davis, 2013: 19). These statistics clearly raise gender issues in the working life of the screenwriter, and suggest an area for further research. For example, we might ask, to what extent is social capital harnessed to overcome some of the barriers and gender inequalities for female screenwriters at a local level?

Conclusion

The Irish film industry is playing a game of catch up. For most of the 20th century, the Irish official response to film was either to control it for propaganda purposes or to censor as a way of protecting the audience from outside influences (Gibbons et al., 1988). It is only since the early 1990s that there has been a consistent, if small, level of institutional support for film production. It is no surprise, therefore, that support mechanisms for Irish screenwriters fall short of those of its European neighbours. At the same time, however, it is clear that the Irish film industry has much in common with other territories, evident from the studies carried out in Britain (Rogers, 2010) and Canada (Coutanche and Davis, 2013). This is particularly the case in terms of income, gender representation and geographical bias. What this chapter has attempted to do is shine a light on the nature of the working life of the Irish screenwriter as a local activity operating within a global experience. Very early on in the emergence of film production in Ireland, it was revealed that Irish screenwriters could not rely on Ireland's international reputation in the literary world for automatic success in the screen world. Following 15 years of developing and adapting schemes, it can be argued that a screenwriter can now emerge as a writer for the screen rather than having to apply their skills in other media. However, this is not easy: whereas in Britain informal apprentice schemes exist in the form of writers' rooms, often followed by television commissions that can lead to experience in film production, in Ireland the outlets are very limited. That said, national boundaries should no longer be limiting and just as Canadian screenwriters experience Los Angeles as another region of work, Irish screenwriters have easy geographical access to other European territories.

The value of social capital is important on a number of levels. In developing skills and honing craft, being connected to the wider community of film development is important. Because it is almost impossible to make a living as a full-time screenwriter in Ireland (as it is elsewhere), working in other areas of development (script reading and editing, etc.) and in other media (soap opera, radio drama, etc.) is important and indeed harnessed more easily through processes of social capital. Networking, mentoring and making facilitated connections through IFB personnel is important for emerging screenwriters. Public bodies, however, should to be aware of unconscious bias, particularly regarding gender, in the systems that they implement.

In some respects, this chapter raises more questions than it answers, and suggests areas for future research. Whilst localised studies are important to reveal the idiosyncrasies of national territories, comparative approaches suggest that many issues are more global than local. Much can be learned from other experiences and, if used wisely by an industry still very much in gestation, pitfalls might be avoided and areas of bias addressed. Ultimately, this will lead to a deeper and more solid structure for the emerging screenwriter.

Notes

1. The following reports were consulted in the course of this research: 'New Procedures & Principles: Multiple Project Development', The Irish Film Board. www.filmboard.ie (accessed 2 September 2013); 'Adapting to the Changing Competitive Dynamics of the International Film Industry', report to the Department of Arts, Sport & Tourism, November 2005 (accessed 2 September

2013); The Economic Impact of Film Production in Ireland, 1995, IBEC: A Report by the Irish Business and Employers' Confederation.
2. An early part of this research was presented in 'The Future of Screenwriting: Impact of Globalization on Screenwriting' by Dr. Díóg O'Connell, panel presentation at Screenwriting Research Network, Brussels, September 2011.
3. Depuis, Nicola. 'Celluloid Suppression: A Study of Irish Female Screenwriters and their Position in the Irish Film Industry' Post-graduate thesis, University College Cork, paper presented at the Sibeal Postgraduate Conference 2010 (unpublished).

References

About Adam (2000) Wr./Dir. Gerard Stembridge, Ireland/UK/USA, 97 mins.
Adam and Paul (2004) Wr. Mark O'Halloran, Dir. Lenny Abrahamson, Ireland, 83 mins.
'Adapting to the Changing Competitive Dynamics of the International Film Industry: A Report to the Department of Arts, Sport & Tourism', November 2005 (accessed 2 September 2013).
Barton, R. (2004) *Irish National Cinema*, London: Routledge.
Bloore, P. (2012) *The Screenplay Business: Managing Creativity and Script Development in the Film Industry*, Abingdon: Routledge.
Bourdieu, P. (1986) 'The Forms of Capital' in John G. Richardson (ed.) *Handbook of Theory and Research for the Sociology of Education*, New York: Greenwood Press, pp. 241–258.
Coleman, J. (1988) 'Social Capital is the Creation of Human Capital' in *American Journal of Sociology*, 94, 95–120.
Coleman, J. (1990) *Foundations of Social Theory*, Cambridge: Harvard University Press.
Coutanche, M. and Davis, C. (2013) '2012 Report on Canadian Screenwriters', RTA School of Media, Ryerson University, Toronto.
Eamon (2009) Wr./Dir. Margaret Corkery, Ireland, 86 mins.
Flynn, R. (1995) 'Our Man in Nirvana: Interview with David Kavanagh, Board Member, Scriptwriters Federation in Europe and former Director, European Script Fund' in *Film Ireland*, June/July.
Gibbons, L., Rockett, K. and Hill, J. (1988) *Cinema and Ireland*, London: Routledge.
Goldfish Memory (2003) Wr./Dir. Elizabeth Gill, Ireland, 85 mins.
Lesser, E.L. (2000) *Knowledge and Social Capital*, Waltham, MA: Butterworth-Heinemann.
McKee, R. (1997) *Story: Substance, Structure, Style and the Principles of Screenwriting*, New York: Harper Collins.
'New Procedures & Principles: Multiple Project Development', The Irish Film Board, available at www.filmboard.ie [accessed 2 September 2013].
O'Connell, D. (2010) *New Irish Storytellers: Narrative Strategies in Film*, Bristol: Intellect.
O'Connell, D. (2012) 'Irish Cinema 1994–2009: The Trajectory of Script Development Policy at the Irish Film Board' in *Journal of Screenwriting*, 3(1), 61–71.
One Hundred Mornings (2009) Wr./Dir. Conor Horgan, Ireland, 85 mins.

Rewind (2010) Wrs. Ronan Carr, P. J. Dillon and Roger Karshan, Dir. P. J Dillon, Ireland, 80 mins.

Rogers, S. (2010) 'Who Writes British Films? A Summary on the UKFC Report and a Call for Further Research' in *Journal of Screenwriting*, 1(2), 375–383.

'The Economic Impact of Film Production in Ireland, IBEC: A Report by the Irish Business and Employers' Confederation, 1995.

Dekker, P. and Uslanner, E. M. (eds) (2001) *Social Capital and Participation in Everyday Life*, London: Routledge.

Vogler, C. (1999) *The Writer's Journey*, London: Pan Books.

When Brendan Met Trudy (2000) Wr. Roddy Doyle, Dir. Kieron J. Walsh, UK/Ireland, 94 mins.

8

First Impressions: Debut Features by Irish Screenwriters

Susan Liddy

Introduction

Emerging writers often lament the difficulty in getting a first feature film into production; and, indeed, it can be a mammoth task. The writer first needs an original idea that will excite development executives, producers and funding bodies. The treatment and/or script must be crafted in such a way that it stands head and shoulders above the rest. The project needs to attach a director who, ideally, shares the writer's vision. As well as having creative strengths, the writer must exhibit tenacity and industry know-how. Networking and peer support are crucial to understanding the field and, hence, maximising the possibility of success. We often ask ourselves, what is it about *that* writer or *that* project that made the difference. Is there anything we could have done differently to stack the odds in our favour? Hopefully, this chapter will go some way to answering those questions.

A series of personal interviews critically examines the writing practices and strategies of a group of Irish screenwriters who have succeeded in getting their first feature film produced. It has often been said that screenwriting is a craft that can be nurtured and developed. Indeed, research psychologists studying creativity suggest that the notion of the 'natural born artist' is largely a myth. Contrary to popular perception, 'creativity is not an elite activity' but a set of behaviours that can be enhanced 'through conscious effort' (Carson, 2010: 10). Indeed, it has been argued that creativity is close to 80% 'learned and acquired' (Gregersen, cited in Sawyer, 2013: 5). To heighten our creativity Csikszentmihalyi stresses the need to 'internalize the system' and learn the rules and context of the domain in which one wishes to excel (1999: 332). By modelling the skills that have given these screenwriters 'the edge' and facilitated their first, crucial, breakthrough into production, it is hoped that other screenwriters may find encouragement, support and, ultimately, success.

The debut features under discussion in this chapter are written across a range of genres including horror, satire, dramatic comedy and black comedy. However, there are many similarities in the mindset and habits exhibited by this group of successful screenwriters which may go some way to explaining how they 'made it'. The following screenwriters will share their views on creativity, overcoming obstacles, their writing practice and the all-important breakthrough into production: Lauren Mackenzie (*The Daisy Chain*, 2008); Margaret Corkery (*Eamon*, 2010); Terry McMahon (*Charlie Casanova*, 2011); Ian Power (*The Runway*, 2011); Ciarán Foy (*Citadel*, 2011) and Ailbhe Keogan (*Run and Jump*, 2013, co-written with director, Steph Green).

With the exception of Keogan and Mackenzie, all the writers interviewed here direct their own work. The greater number of writer–directors in this group is in line with a more general trend observable in films financially supported by the Irish Film Board (IFB) from 2009 to 2012, as outlined in their 2013 Production Catalogue (IFB, 2013). More than half of all supported films had a writer–director at the helm and nearly three quarters acknowledge the director in the writing credits (IFB, 2013: 110–119).

Indeed, Lauren Mackenzie reflects that writers who do not direct themselves may be at some disadvantage:

> It is always hard to hand over your work for someone else to direct. Some scenes can be dramatized better than you ever imagined and other not so. You can only hope the balance remains equitable. These days I do believe the hyphenate writer-director is a much easier sell. I have had several scripts languish while we looked for directors to attach.

Writers and writing

The six writers interviewed here do not subscribe fully to the notion that great writers are, in some way, born 'special', a breed apart. In line with research by Csikszentmihalyi, Carson, Sawyer and others, there is support for the importance of craft. As Sawyer suggests, 'in a creative life, you're constantly learning, practicing, mastering, becoming an expert' (2013: 5). To what extent successful writers have something extra, an inbuilt talent, which a proficiency in screenwriting craft can further nurture, is a matter of debate among these screenwriters. Margaret Corkery believes hard work and craft are 95% of the endeavour. Indeed, Ailbhe Keogan believes that 'everyone has stories to tell. Everyone. It's just that it's kinda hard to find time to express them artistically. So unless you really feel it, it's not going to happen.' Similarly, Mackenzie insists:

> I don't believe the ability to write is some magical talent. Observational skills, empathy, a good ear, eye for detail or eye for the extraordinary, a love of words, rhythm, a curiosity, or righteous anger, the desire to make someone laugh, are all elements, not exclusive to writers, which can make writing great. The combination of some or all of these elements is what gives a writer their unique voice.

For Terry McMahon and Ciarán Foy, writers are both born and made; a combination of nature and nurture. McMahon argues that 'you can teach writing but you can't teach talent and personality', thereby distinguishing between an in-built aptitude and a craft that can be learned. Indeed, as Foy observes, 'if writing could be one hundred per cent taught, then there would be highly successful writers strutting out of college every year like computing or engineering graduates. Art is different.' Yet, whilst Ian Power also points to the importance of 'natural ability', he is clear where the weighting lies between talent and application: 'Lots of talent and no craft will result in a worse writer than lots of craft and a small amount of talent. But you need to be able to tell a story and have an instinct for story.'

Significantly, then, all six writers are passionate about the necessity of mastering the craft of screenwriting. This is not to deny the existence or importance of talent, but to stress that individuals can do a lot to develop themselves as screenwriters. All this begs the question: where did these screenwriters acquire and hone their own craft?

Four of the six writers have studied screenwriting formally and at an advanced level, whether as university undergraduates or postgraduates. Additionally, Power, Foy and Mackenzie have attended screenwriting master classes with such names as Linda Seger, Babette Buster, Beth Serlin, Laurie Hutzler and Linda Aronson. All of the writers stress the importance of watching and analysing film; all of them have read a variety of screenwriting books, even if only to ultimately dismiss them. Keogan admits that when she was commissioned to write her first screenplay, she was 'clueless' and had no idea how to go about it. Robert

McKee's *Story* gave her 'the language of screenplays' and was useful in providing a shared frame of reference with her script editor.

Margaret Corkery also initially relied on McKee and Syd Field to introduce her to the specifics of the craft. 'Yes, I read all the manuals. You must read them to study the form.' Corkery has also drawn upon online resources such as *The Script Lab and Wordplay* and adapts what works for her. 'You deviate fifty per cent of the time but, before you do that, you need to educate yourself.' Even a more experienced writer like Mackenzie has read, and continues to read, books on screenwriting craft admitting that 'some have been revelatory, others, uncomfortably mechanical. I utilise tools from various books at different periods of writing and rewriting.' Mackenzie makes specific mention of the work of Christopher Vogler, Howard Mabley and Ken Dancyner and Jeff Rush. Interestingly, Viki King's 21-day writing plan has, at times, also been useful to Mackensie, 'by emphasising forward movement and avoiding the critic'.

McMahon is more caustic about screenwriting manuals, despite being a graduate of an MA programme in screenwriting; for him, the greater education is to be found in the autobiographies of directors such as John Huston, Elia Kazan and Sidney Lumet. However, he insists, 'the best movie school in the world is in your DVD store. Watch movies. Then watch them again. Study them. Learn from practitioners rather than self-appointed screenwriting gurus who, in truth, have written fuck-all movies.' Whilst acknowledging he has 'read all the books', Ian Power shares some of McMahon's scepticism. 'Screenwriting books are useful', Power admits, 'but ultimately dangerous because people treat them as prescriptions for films when they are only deconstructed observations of films.' Nonetheless, Power references Linda Seger (*Making a Good Script Great*), William Goldman (*Adventures in the Screen Trade*) and Stephen King (*On Writing*) because 'you read them and you understand that writing is difficult even for the most successful writers and they're full of passion and encouragement and craft'. Indeed, Power insists, he has learned more about the craft of writing from editing films: 'In many ways, Walter Murch's *In the Blink of an Eye'* is a better book for a writer than many of the screenwriting manuals.'

Overcoming obstacles

Despite having their first feature film screenplays produced, all these writers admit to facing continual struggles and obstacles in their writing life. These include creative blocks, procrastination, self-doubt and the pressing, and ever-present, need to earn a living in this most precarious of careers. However, their commitment to finding solutions to creative problems, rather than giving up or resorting to self-blame and despair, is what sets them apart from novice writers. Here, then, are some of the common obstacles experienced by the writers interviewed, and their approaches to overcoming them.

Creative blocks

Some writers experience blocks and have devised strategies to deal with them. Mackenzie reflects:

> I have suffered blocks mostly because the project I'm working on has stumped me, or I'm fighting the situation around it, or I'd far rather be writing something else. True despair doesn't happen in the writing, it happens when I face too much rejection and can see no way of doing things differently.

The only real cure, for Mackensie, is to write and find the flow again.

Foy's response to creative block is a combination of perseverance and distraction. He notes:

> You just have to ride it out. I watch movies or take a bus journey, listening to music related to the type of scene or genre I'm writing about. Eventually, when you're not looking, the solution presents itself.

For Corkery, that solution took time to manifest. During the months she was writing *Eamon*, she suffered severe creative block; but a steely determination to complete the screenplay drove her back to the page three weeks before her deadline, and she wrote her way through it: 'Now, I see certain pitfalls; I see them coming. So I can move around them; find a way through.' With the clarity of hindsight, she now believes that the reason she experienced a block lay in misguided creative choices; she was forcing characters into stories in which they did not belong.

Procrastination

Whilst Keogan loves 'giving life' to her characters, like a lot of writers, she often delays the writing process. She admits:

> If you asked me do I enjoy writing, it would not be an equivocal 'yes'. I procrastinate a lot. A LOT! Sometimes, I positively hate it. But on a good writing day, I feel like the universe is perfectly aligned.

For Mackenzie and Foy, the most difficult part of the writing process is beginning. 'I had "just do it" as my sleep screen for some years!' Mackenzie admits. However, whilst McMahon empathises with 'the frustration of the blank page', he refuses to feed procrastination and creative block:

> I find it bizarre when writers talk about suddenly feeling 'blocked.' I'm blocked every fucking time I sit down to write, but isn't that what writing is: transforming our human weakness into aesthetic strengths?

Self-doubt

All of the writers speak of their struggle through arid patches in their writing lives. Mackenzie's recalls those periods when a writer's back is against the wall on a number of projects:

> I've had months where I've waited for news on several projects and then had rejections on all of them at once, leaving me with a terrifyingly blank period ahead. There's many a time I've wanted to pack it in but the universe, being what it is, always sends a little hope just in time. I often feel like a gambler, accumulating losses but forever hopeful the next project will be the one to cross the line.

Similarly, Foy considers walking away from writing on a daily basis, and acknowledges the many setbacks he has experienced and the sacrifices he has made to forge a career in writing:

> I pretty much sacrificed my twenties to get to where I am. I've suffered economic knockbacks, as well as the kind that take a beating on your spirit. What keeps me going is a belligerent belief that I'm good at this, that I'm meant to do it, as well as the love and support of those closest to me. When I'm creating I feel alive. I'm doing what gives me the best sense of purpose. That's worth fighting for. Life isn't easy for anyone. As the character Rocky wisely said, 'It aint how hard you hit. It's about how hard you can get hit and keep moving forward.'

Self-doubt has also plagued McMahon from an early age. He explains:

> I came from an incestuously parochial little Irish town that prided itself on Gaelic Football and the gift of the gab. I was athletically incompetent, had a bad stammer and, due to a problematic birth, my

legs were fucked. So I acquired that writer's sense of disenfranchised self-doubt early; however, it would be a long time before it would manifest as words on a page.

Does he ever feel like 'packing it in'? 'Halfway through this sentence I will. And, again, halfway through the next sentence.'

The joy of writing is tempered by an internal struggle for Keogan. On the one hand, writers are burning with a desire to communicate but, on the other, they question the validity of what it is they long to say. As she highlights:

> It takes great discipline to sit down and write everyday with the belief that what you have to say is worthwhile. That belief, in my case, is very fragile so I have quite a shrill, over-reaching confidence that barely disguises the fact I think my writing is total shit. A lot of writers I talk to feel the same. I guess it's only from hard work and an honest humility to your craft that a lovely rich, *quiet* confidence, emerges. It's what I'm trying to work towards.

Financial constraints

For the most part, writing is a poorly paid and unreliable occupation. Irish screenwriters can apply for the Screenplay Development Loan Scheme from the IFB 'to enable the writing of first draft and/or revised draft feature film screenplays' (IFB). This is the first step taken by most Irish screenwriters – five of the six writers interviewed here applied to the IFB for development funding; four were successful. Such funding can be accessed by individual writers or by a production company, in tandem with the writer. In 2013, the amount was fixed at 12,000 Euros for a single applicant or 16,000 Euros for a writing team and is repayable on the first day of principal photography on the developed film.

However, there may be no earnings at all in subsequent years unless a producer becomes attached and the project progresses towards production. That can be a slow process during which payment for the writer can effectively grind to a halt. Indeed, the Irish Playwrights and Screenwriters Guild (IPSG), now known as the Writers Guild of Ireland, the representative body for Irish stage and screen writers, puts the average income of *produced* writers (writing for film and television) at a mere 14,795 Euros per year (IPSG, 2013). Writers working on low-budget feature films may earn considerably less. The IPSG is concerned that 'screenwriters have very little share in the exploitation of the copyright they create [...] this impacts on their capacity to earn a significant income to maintain themselves as full-time artists' (IPSG, 2013).

Many of the screenwriters interviewed here are conscious that writing is not a hobby; it is their livelihood. Ailbhe Keogan is aware that she is 'responsible for bringing in part of the family income so I do try and get paid for my writing if at all possible'. Similarly, Margaret Corkery explains:

> I'm hard working and resourceful but I can't believe how little I've earned. In this recession, I must make it work. Think about writing in terms of a competitive-enterprise mentality. A way to make a living. I sometimes wonder – should I be putting all this energy into something that pays more?

Mackenzie recalls her early writing days when she had an idea and just wanted to get it down with little thought of the economics of the situation:

> I enjoyed the writing, in and of itself, and then my work attracted attention and that was a buzz too. Later, I wrote because I was paid for it. Now all those elements remain but the need to earn a living corrupts some of the pleasure of writing. [...] My writing life is my career, it needs to feed me and house me. Though I have to admit, the demands of the system, the deadlines, and the audience, can also impose a very productive, often very creative pressure on the writing.

Even when writers have periods of relative financial ease the film and television industry is a precarious business and tides can turn. McMahon, who has written for the Irish soap *Fair City* for a number of years reflects:

> Between commissioned screenplays and soap episodes I'd made enough money to buy a home and provide a certain quality of life for my family, but like so many, that house of cards came tumbling down. Now the bank wants to repossess and I'm as broke as a ten dollar hooker. But we're in preproduction on my next film, *Patrick's Day*, with a secured production budget of half a million dollars, so even if I can barely afford to put food on the family table, I have never felt more passionate about the twin privileges of writing and filmmaking.

Interestingly, these six screenwriters meet with the same obstacles and challenges that afflict most writers. The difference is that they have developed a resilience to weather the difficulties when they come, as they always do. As Ian Power observes, 'failure is not an option'. Rather than give up and walk away, which many of them consider doing on a daily basis, these writers persist until they find a way through. Over time, they develop the confidence to believe that they have the resources and the skills to find that path through the woods time and again, if they can just keep the faith and keep working.

From concept to page

None of the screenwriters interviewed express any fear about running out of ideas. Instead, they speak of teasing out a story idea from a maze of jumbled thoughts. Interestingly, they all exhibit a confidence in their own creative process and the eventual ordering of loose and disconnected ideas into shape and purpose. For example, Mackenzie lets an idea swim around in her head for some time before she sits down to write anything:

> Once I start, hopefully, the process accelerates the deeper I go in to story and ideas will accost me any time of day or night. But still I will write notes and structural outlines, lists of scenes, motifs and dialogue before I begin a treatment.

Keogan gets her story ideas 'from all over the place, from music, from novels, from podcasts, from the news, from the people in [her] life'. Mainly, she just listens out for voices that come to the surface from all of the inane chatter and data that constantly flows through her mind. She explains:

> I have developed a good filtering device which works for me. I don't quite understand it but I trust it. Basically, my mind will call attention to something that has risen to the surface. I'll examine it. I'll know if I should throw it back or keep it to explore further when I have more time. I have a shed full of these ideas, hanging up to dry. When I'm looking for a new project, I'll examine them again. Old ideas and reasonably fresh ones – I'll prod and poke them and eventually one idea will insist on itself. This then will be the root idea for a project that might take up two or three years of my life.

Foy also finds ideas in 'various places. Personal experience. A dream. Personal experience combined with a dream'. Just asking 'what if?' conjures up, for Foy, ideas, images, visual art and soundtracks:

> I don't know what I'll write a year from now so there's a fear you might be stuck. But you also need that fear to come up with something fresh. Complacency is the death of creativity. Anxiety is your friend.

Some writers are drawn to specific themes and thus explore ideas around it. For instance, McMahon is 'fascinated by what men are prepared to do to convince themselves they are men, and the illusory worlds they construct to protect their fallacies. The infinite vanity and stupidity of man means there is a never ending series of ideas out there for those themes.' Margaret Corkery, however, like Mackenzie, is painstakingly careful to review ideas before committing to one. As she observes,

> I can drum out loads of ideas. But I can take months to review them. Months. To see which one is a good one; one that combines the commercial and the artistic. Also, some stories I can do and some I can't. I *know* some stories and characters.

The way in which these writers speak about the different stages in their writing practice resonates with some of the stages of creativity identified by Shelley Carson. For instance, she labels the 'absorb brainset' as the 'knowledge-gathering and incubation stage' of the creative process whilst the 'evaluate brainset' is the stage in which we 'consciously judge the value of ideas' (Carson, 2010: 18). Both are vital stages in the creative process.

Once they have identified a story idea that is worth pursuing, how do these screenwriters proceed to tease that idea out? Foy likens the process to creating a piece of sculpture: 'I need to get it all down on the page, quickly, in very vague shape. I call this my "vomit" draft. From there I chip away at it until it starts to make sense.' This committing to paper without too much attention to detail is also referenced by Keogan, who comments:

> I consciously work in sequences and beats, otherwise I veer off course and lose the core of the story. I do not let my characters speak until I know what they have to say. Once I know who owns the story and

what journey they'll go on, I'll sit down and write a vomit draft of the screenplay in one or two sittings. This is generally a weak document but the heart/core of it is there.

Side by side this structured approach is a more 'playful approach', which includes gleaning a taste for the world of the project by listening to music, watching films and reading novels that resonate with the theme.

In contrast, McMahon and Power, initially at least, approach their writing via the creation of key scenes. McMahon explains:

It's impossible to advocate one methodology over another [...] but I'll often dive into a key scene so the characters can reveal to me how they might handle themselves under pressure, and I can fundamentally interrogate them from before and after that turning point.

Power's focus is also, primarily, on pivotal scenes:

I think about great scenes. I think about great conflicts. I think about how the story would be shaped based on rules I've made for myself over the years. Then I'll write up beats on white boards and start to build a structure.

From these insights into how ideas are executed on the page, there seems to be a shared consensus that it is imperative to actively tease out ideas rather than sit back and wait for 'inspiration'. The practice of almost 'playfully' courting ideas resonates with Keith Sawyer's research; creativity flows when 'you free your mind for imagination and fantasy, letting your unconscious lead you into unchartered territory' (2013: 5). The subsequent shaping of that idea into a treatment or a rough draft requires diligence and perseverance; in some ways it is a job of hard work, like anything else.

Writing practice

Once their core idea has been worked out, the question is, how do these screenwriters immerse themselves in the practice of writing? Some writers, for example, talk about structuring their writing day around specific tasks and optimum times of productivity. McMahon is the only writer who does not have a planned writing schedule. In contrast, Foy reveals that he works best when he has a deadline: 'To me a poison chalice is 'take as much time as you like.' Mackenzie shows up at her desk every day, whether she feels like writing or not. Power is equally consistent but is an early bird writer: 'I start early, around 5am or 6am, and run out of steam around 12 pm.'

As mothers of small children, Keogan and Corkery tailor their writing lives around their children's routines. Keogan maps her day:

> I am always behind on my work and with such limited writing time, I always tear into it. I don't have time to despair. I write four mornings a week when my children are in creche. Sixteen hours a week. When a deadline looms, I'm 100% focused. Scarily so.

Conversely, when there is elasticity in the deadline,

> I am sorting out my sock drawer or attacking the grill pan. Saying that, I am pretty much always thinking about some story or another. My ultimate dream would be to have a place to write that is not in my house. Ideally, a cabin in the corner of the garden.

Corkery also has a set writing schedule. It can vary slightly each day, but she takes it very seriously: 'I write from nine until one, four days a week. Lots of times I'll get in another three hours at night, after my daughter has gone to bed. I have to work very hard at it.'

The common denominator here is self-discipline and hard work. These screenwriters do not wait for some mythical muse to descend: they roll up their sleeves and work hard to tease out their ideas. They shape those ideas into treatments and then they apply themselves day by day, draft by draft, until they have a completed screenplay. But even that is not really enough, as Power observes: 'Anyone can write a first draft, but most "real" screenwriters can re-write; where true craft applies.'

The breakthrough

From these interviews, it is clear that all six screenwriters value their craft and are fully committed to the ongoing development and enhancement of their skills. They have shared how they generate ideas; how they shape those ideas into a working document, such as a treatment or a script; how they overcome the myriad challenges and obstacles facing the writer, often on a daily basis. But perhaps the most important question for emerging writers is, how did they get their break?

Was there a moment during the writing of their debut script when they knew that this project was a special one? For Ciarán Foy, the answer is no:

> I think I have that 'eureka' moment with every idea I start writing. Otherwise I wouldn't continue to write it. But you learn that so many factors come into play getting something off the ground. A good idea is just the beginning. You need agreeable financiers, a lot of luck, good timing, cast and crew to agree to be a part of it: so many things to fit into place. And I direct my own work too. In my estimation, for every five ideas I'm working on, one will be made. That's been my ratio so far.

The generation of many ideas in order to strike lucky with one is also familiar to Ailbhe Keogan. She says: 'The idea for *Run & Jump* was one of five I proposed to the Irish Film Board because I really wanted to get the First Draft Writer's Loan. I didn't think my first film would go into production. I just wanted to learn how to write screenplays.' Terry McMahon explains that both the idea and execution of *Charlie Casanova* were more like a 'desperation' than a eureka moment:

> Ashamed of my cowardice in the face of governmental attacks on the disenfranchised, I ended up standing in the high court watching my missus be sentenced to jail time for protesting, and I knew I'd have to return to a character I had been thinking about for a long time; the contemptible Charlie Casanova.

McMahon had no illusions about the challenge a script/film such as *Charlie* would be: 'far from thinking I might have something that would go to production, I knew it hadn't a hope in hell from inception; but I still had to write the bastard'.

Lauren Mackenzie had a strong sense that genre films were much easier to get optioned than dramas, and had been thinking about writing a horror script for some time before embarking on *The Daisy Chain*:

> I certainly remember that once I started writing *Daisy*, I was very engaged. I love psychological horror – the scariest monsters are always ourselves. I was also a relatively new mother and somewhat unhinged from the emotional and physical upheaval of babies.

The project took five years and a lot of to-ing and fro-ing:

> Once Aisling Walsh came on board, and subsequently attached Samantha Morton, things moved very quickly. But later, pushed by the financier, the edit and later marketing emphasised the genre to the film's detriment. For instance, the American DVD art bears no relation to the film and has disappointed many a buyer who was expecting something else.

Crucially, then, what were the factors that led to these first features being produced? What is of interest here is, why *that* script and not a previous effort? For Ciarán Foy, it was the fact that *Citadel* was based on a real life experience:

> I guess the personal aspect of it made for a character with a lot of depth. It's a psychological horror with one foot firmly placed in reality. The script was something I was very proud of, as the reaction from readers was the same every time – they were drawn in and genuinely terrified by it because it was real. It was harder, as I was drawing on a lot of memories and things that happened to me that I'd rather forget.

Keogan believes that it was the tone of *Run and Jump* that attracted interest:

> It was tackling real-life problems but in a humorous, un-grim way. People liked this. I studied films like *Little Miss Sunshine* with this in mind. People have since told me it was a fresh voice. Because it was my first effort, I was relatively unselfconscious, naive even and I think this came across on the page. It was freer, airier maybe? I do know that now I have people asking for scripts that are 'more Run-and-Jump', effectively turning those two verbs into a compound adjective, which makes me a little uneasy. I don't want to write the same script again.

When Ian Power saw the story that inspired *The Runway* on an old newsreel, he knew he was on to something. He recalls:

> I thought it had a universal appeal. It was the first script I wrote that I knew would get made when I finished writing it. That said, I was deliberately going for something very orthodox.

Previously, Power concedes, he may have been trying too hard to write something 'new'. With *The Runway*, however, he realised that he would have to make a simple film to begin with: 'Picasso could paint photographically real paintings before he moved into cubism (too grand a comparison perhaps but it is a truism that you have to learn the orthodox before you can do anything original).'

The screenwriters interviewed here illustrate, in their own work practices, a number of distinct stages identified by research psychologists as being integral to the creative process; a period of incubation; preparation; insight; evaluation; and finally, elaboration (Csikszentmihalyi, 1999: 79). The results for these screenwriters have been impressive; all six debut projects have won awards or been internationally recognised in some way. *The Daisy Chain* premiered in the Raindance Film Festival, London. It was nominated for Best Irish Film at the Jameson Dublin International Film Festival (JDIFF) and nominated for Best Achievement in Production and Best Actress (Samantha Morton) in the British Independent Film Awards. *Eamon* was selected for screening in the Discovery category at the Toronto International Film Festival, 2009. It won Best Independent Camera Award at Karlovy Vary Independent Film Festival in the same year.

Charlie Casanova was the first Irish film to be selected for competition in the South by Southwest (SXSW) Film Festival; it won Best Film, Best Actor (Emmett J. Scanlan) and Best Director at the Melbourne Underground Film Festival 2012 (MUFF); it was nominated for an Irish Film and Television Award (IFTA) in 2012 in the category of Best Film, Best Director and Best Script (Film). *Charlie Casanova* was picked up for UK and Irish cinema distribution by Studio Canal. *The Runway* was winner of Best First Irish Feature at the Galway Film Fleadh, 2010. It was IFTA Nominee for Best Film and for Best Director, both 2011, and winner of Best Film at the Lucas Film Festival, 2011; Best Film at the Buster Film Festival, 2011; Best Feature at the Celtic Film & TV Festival, 2011; Director's Choice Award at the Boston Irish Film Festival, 2011 and Best of Fest at the Palm Springs International Film Festival, 2011. *Citadel* won Best First Irish Feature at the Galway Film Fleadh, 2012; the MovieZone award for Best Feature at the Imagine Amsterdam Fantastic Film, 2013; the Midnighters Audience Award at the SXSW Film Festival, 2012; IFTA Nominee Director Photography (Tim Flemming) and IFTA Rising Star Nominee for Ciáran Foy, 2012. *Run and Jump* had its world premiere at the Tribeca Film Festival, 2013 and its Irish premier at the Galway Film Fleadh, 2013 where it won the Audience Award for Best Irish Film and Best First Irish Film.

Funding issues

Once a screenwriter has an idea that has been written up into a treatment or a first draft script, the next step is usually the acquisition of funding. The focus, in the first instance, is on script development; the working and re-working of the screenplay until it is polished enough to move through to the production phase. Five of the six writers followed the conventional route for screenwriters working in Ireland, in that they made an initial application for script development funding to the IFB. Only when the development phase is deemed successful by the IFB project managers and external readers is production funding awarded. Such funding is invariably partial, and additional funding must be obtained elsewhere, from European funding agencies such as, in the case of these writers, Creative Scotland, the Wales Creative IP Fund or Luxemburg Film Fund, to name just a few. However, as global recession continues and funding becomes more difficult to access, the screenwriter's response to the possibilities and challenges afforded by low-budget, or no-budget, filmmaking is of particular interest.

Of the six screenwriters interviewed, only Corkery and McMahon circumvented the conventional funding route; yet both succeeded in getting their films into production. Corkery sidestepped the IFB funding process altogether, applying and ultimately being selected for a 2007 low-budget feature film initiative, the *Catalyst* project. Aimed at first-time Irish filmmakers and emerging filmmaking talent, the project attracted 400 applicants. These were initially whittled down to 50, and later just 3 successful teams. The teams were mentored by industry experts, and each of the feature films was funded with a budget of 250,000 Euros. In contrast, McMahon's first-draft script of *Charlie Casanova* was rejected outright by the IFB and McMahon subsequently decided to go it alone and make the film anyway. The end result is a feature film that has garnered controversy, applause and accolades in equal measure. For the purposes of deepening our understanding of screenwriting and filmmaking practices such as this, McMahon's unique writing journey with *Charlie Casanova* will now be discussed in greater detail.

Case study: *Charlie Casanova*

'As expected the script (*Charlie Casanova*) was dismissed,' McMahon reflects; 'I naively decided to make it myself. With no money. As a constant reminder of what I wasn't doing, I got a tattoo on my body that said, *"The Art is in the Completion. Begin." '* As McMahon tells it, close to Christmas 2011, in the early hours of the morning, as his family slept, he sat in front of a recently opened Facebook account, sipping a whiskey. He typed the following into his status bar: 'Intend making no-budget feature, *Charlie Casanova*. Need cast, crew, equipment and a lot of balls. Any takers? Script at www.terrymcmahon.org. This is sincere, so bullshitters fuck off in advance. Thank you.' Within minutes, an interested party responded, followed by several more. Within 24 hours, 130 people had made contact. Nobody working on the film was paid; it relied solely on goodwill.

The first day of principal photography began three weeks after that night. McMahon recalls:

> Borrowed cameras and a crew comprised of many people I had never met before. The cameras had to be returned by midnight on the 11th day, so that's how long our shoot would take. During those eleven days of insanity we pushed with everything we had and the movie that would generate such extreme reactions was dragged into existence.

With no money from the IFB, McMahon was reliant on the generosity and financial support of friends and family. 'My father gave me three grand to cover bills, rent, etc. and the final production cost of shooting, feeding folks, etc. was 927 Euro.' The film was edited in the home of McMahon's friend, Tony Kearns. Another friend showed the film to Windmill Lane Studios and they were impressed: McMahon says 'they demonstrated astonishing generosity by taking care of all post (production), on the house'.

McMahon was under no illusion that *Charlie* would be universally liked:

> Because of the self-serving lying nature of the central character, I knew the form and function would be different from standard screenplays. Employing the novelistic notion of the unreliable narrator, I wanted the film itself to be a lie. Some people embraced that notion. Some despised it.

As it turned out, the IFB, supportive of McMahon in the past, was amongst those who 'despised' it, to quote McMahon. However, he is clear there was no 'conspiracy' on the part of the IFB: 'there was no real precedent for this kind of film in Ireland, either at script stage or during production'. However, once *Charlie* was selected for the South by Southwest Film Festival (SXSW), the IFB did support the project. Subsequently, they provided financial assistance for a 35 mm print when the film was selected for the Edinburgh Film Festival.

Charlie Casanova was McMahon's debut feature, and the unconventional nature of the screenplay, as well as the endeavour itself, took him on a rollercoaster journey. In his own words, the film went 'from anonymous obscurity on a budget of less than a grand to having its world premiere in competition at SXSW and a distribution deal with Studio Canal'. For McMahon, the film set an important precedent for those aspiring to a kind of indie cinema that might exist outside the IFB selection process, whilst still securing major distribution. These accolades aside, *Charlie* was also at the receiving end of much critical condemnation. For instance, writing in *The Irish Times*, film critic Donald Clarke (2012) declared that he would rather drink caustic soda than sit through another viewing of the film. Yet, McMahon contends that *Charlie* 'set out to be provocatively divisive'. He rejects what he perceives as 'a campaign by a coterie of critics that didn't just do untold damage to the life of the film on its opening week but exposed a poisonous conservatism within contemporary cinema criticism'. Ultimately, McMahon insists, writers have to be defiant and be prepared to sidestep funding bodies if necessary; an important message in these financially depressed times. He urges screenwriters:

Stop waiting for permission from funders or illiterate producers. Make movies yourself. Write, direct and produce your own movies. Act in them if you have to. Whatever it takes. With the proliferation of inexpensive equipment there are no excuses anymore. Make the motherfuckers on your mobile phone if you have to. Then, and only then, can you claim to have exhausted every avenue.

Advice for screenwriters

With hindsight and from the experience of having their first features produced, what advice would these screenwriters give to their younger selves and, by extension, other aspiring writers? 'Keep writing', says Power. 'After my first short I was signed to direct commercials, and didn't write anything for four years. The more you write, the better you get. I'd probably be on a third feature now if I hadn't taken that break.' Foy concurs:

Success is mostly about perseverance. Have several projects on the boil as production companies have more than your script to consider making. It'll be hard and there will be days when it will all seem hopeless, but it's 10% talent and 90% perseverance that'll get you there. At least I hope so! You can be lucky and hit the bullseye first time, or you can throw a dart 100 times and you'll probably hit the bullseye at some point. The trick is not to walk away on the 99th throw of the dart.

Keogan encourages screenwriters to spend more time honing the craft, 'and less time fuelling [their] ego with day dreams about being a success-ful writer'. Hard work is essential, and all the writers interviewed stress the need to be disciplined and professional. Keogan is keen to advocate that we make our own 'luck', a point also raised by a number of the other writers:

> I do work hard. I do meet deadlines. I do keep lines of communication open. That's not luck. That's being ready for when the luck playfully grabs you in a headlock. Luck is a tricky fella. You've got to tackle him to the ground, show him you mean business.

Mackenzie concedes that sometimes it can be a case of right time, right place, and she strongly urges writers to network:

> Writers need to be able to talk about the work clearly, intelligently, enthusiastically (it doesn't work to be too self-deprecating) and openly. A producer needs to have confidence that you can deliver and can collaborate. Fake it if you have to; something I've found women aren't as good at as men.

Nevertheless, whilst luck may play a part in a screenwriter's success, Mackenzie does make the point that ultimately, what is needed is 'Persistence. Draft after draft after draft'.

Likewise, there is no short cut to success for Corkery; she believes writing requires discipline, commitment and resolve:

> I will push myself and push myself. I kill myself. I have to work very hard at it. It can be the worst torture imaginable! But you have to do it if you want to make a living out of it. A very extreme level of application is required.

In failing to grasp that sooner, Corkery believes she wasted a lot time in her early 20s. In addition, once a writer's work is in the public domain, a very different set of challenges awaits. *Eamon* did well critically; and it did 'travel'. But Corkery suffered knockbacks, too:

> When you bring out a film, you have to deal with enormous levels of criticism. It was a tough experience. You have to be able take criticism, the worst kind. The most personal kind. But you put your work out there and you move on.

Conclusion

The interviews undertaken with these emerging screenwriters, who have all succeeded in having their first feature produced, have illustrated that, despite the difference in their backgrounds, budget, genre preferences and thematic preoccupations, they share a similar creative mindset. Importantly, they all exhibit strong levels of hard work, focus, consistency and persistence in their writing lives; they have, effectively, shaped their own success.

Csikszentmihalyi, Sawyer, Carson and others have cautioned against romanticising creativity: the tendency to attribute a mysterious, ethereal quality that defies definition or, importantly, intervention. The paradoxical reality, as evidenced by these interviews, is that much of a screenwriter's life is mundane, and that creativity is achieved through the daily grind. No matter what kind of creativity he studied, Sawyer found that 'creativity did not descend like a bolt of lightning that lit up the world in a single flash. It came in tiny steps, bits of insights and incremental changes' (2013: 2). Each of these screenwriters testifies to the power of conscious, persistent application; they consistently work hard, remain focused and, despite the knocks, keep their eye on the prize.

References

Carson, S. (2010) *Your Creative Brain: Seven Steps to Maximize Imagination, Productivity, and Innovation in Your Life*, San Francisco: Jossey-Bass.
Charlie Casanova (2011) Wr: Terry McMahon, Dir. Terry McMahon, Ireland: 94 mins.
Citadel (2011) Wr. Ciarán Foy, Dir. Ciarán Foy, Ireland/Scotland, 84 mins.
Clarke, D. (2012) 'Five Stars? I Don't f*****g Think so' in *The Irish Times*, 5 May 2012.
Corkery, M. (2013) Screenwriter's Interview (via telephone) 18 April and (via email) 5 September.

Csikszentmihalyi, M. (1999) 'Implications of a Systems Perspective on Creativity' in Sternberg, R.J. (ed.) *Handbook of Creativity*, Cambridge: Cambridge University Press, pp. 313–335.

Eamon (2010) Wr: Margaret Corkery, Dir: Margaret Corkery, Ireland, 86 mins.

Foy, C. (2013) Screenwriter's Interview (via email), 26 March and 15 September.

Irish Film Board/Bord Scannán na hÉireann (2013) *Irish Film 2013:A Year in Focus* [online], available: www.irishfilmboard.ie/.../Irish%20Film%2013%20A%20Year%20/n% [accessed 29 August 2013].

Irish Film Board/Bord Scannán na hÉireann. *IFB Funding Programmes* [online], available at www.irishfilmboard.ie/funding_programmes [accessed 5 September 2013].

Irish Playwrights and Screenwriters Guild (2013) 'Submissions Received by the Copyright Review Committee'[online], available at: www.djei.ie Innovation and Investment Intellectual property [accessed 2 September 2013].

Keogan, A. (2013) Screenwriter's Interview (via email), 2 April (via email) and 6 September.

McKenzie, L. (2013) Screenwriter's Interview (via email), 15 April and 5 September.

McMahon, T. (2013) Screenwriter's Interview (via email), 25 March and 6 September.

Power, I. (2013) Screenwriter's Interview (via email), 7 May and 5 September.

Run and Jump (2013) Wr. Ailbhe Keogan and Steph Green, Dir. Steph Green, Ireland/Germany, 102 mins.

Sawyer, R.K. (2012) *Explaining Creativity: The Science of Human Innovation*, New York: Oxford University Press.

Sawyer, R.K. (2013) *Zig Zag: The Surprising Path to Greater Creativity*, San Francisco: Jossey-Bass.

The Daisy Chain (2008) Wr: Lauren MacKenzie, Dir: Aisling Walsh, Ireland/UK, 89 mins.

The Runway (2011) Wr. Ian Power, Dir. Ian Power, Ireland/Luxemburg, 101 mins.

9
'Sorry Blondie, I Don't Do Backstory!' Script Editing: The Invisible Craft

Paul Wells

Introduction

In the Disney animated feature *Tangled* (2010), the knowing re-telling of the Grimms' fairy tale 'Rapunzel', the hero Flynn Rider resists Rapunzel's questions by responding, 'Sorry, Blondie, I don't do backstory.' Like the Proustian madeleine, the phrase resonated for me. It made me immediately consider what 'backstory' actually implies for animated characters, and further, in what ways the script development process for animation fundamentally differs from its live-action counterpart. I started to consider all of the aspects of animation's pre-production processes that remain invisible and un-recognised in the final outcome of a work, and why it remains important to somehow reclaim such aspects to recognise them as anything from key resources to lost skill sets, to points of academic interest and research. By the time my mind drifted back to *Tangled*, I had completely lost the plot.

Once I left the cinema, I considered these issues further. The burgeoning literature on screenwriting has, of course, given much attention to script development, the structure of a script, the processes of adapting scripts for the screen, and the value of the script itself as an object of study. Inevitably, most of this has been directed at traditional live-action film and television, with either lip service paid to animation or an assumption that it operates in the same way as orthodox forms. In the canonical works of the so-called 'screenwriting gurus', this leaves Robert McKee writing nine lines about animation, stressing 'the law of universal metamorphism' and its tendency towards action, farce and high adventure in maturation plots (1999: 85). Whilst Christopher Vogler, in his desire to impose the Hero's Journey schemata on Disney's *The Lion King* (1994), becomes dissatisfied with the shift of tone in Act Two, the speed of Simba's transition to adulthood, the role of Rafiki, and the under-developed female characters, he mostly fails to recognise that this is an *animated* film (2007: 258–267). Vogler's involvement in script development for Disney does nevertheless acknowledge that his voice was but one of many contributing to the evolution of the screenplay, and serves to illustrate one of the key challenges in understanding how animated films are 'scripted': that for virtually every animation made, from studio feature films to independent short films to television series, there is a distinctive process at the heart of its development, execution and completion.

This is not to say that there do not exist common principles, and that it is not possible to engage with these processes; indeed, a literature is emerging that addresses the specificity of the form, either by determining the possible written methodologies pertinent to features, episodes and shorts (e.g. Webber, 2000; Scott, 2003; Wellins, 2005; Wells, 2007; Besen, 2008), or by revealing production processes as possible models for imitation or inspiration (e.g. Cook and Thomas, 2006; Furniss, 2008; Wells and Hardstaff, 2008; Selby, 2009, 2013). Most of these texts, like many of the publications about screenwriting craft, show the linear development of a process of construction, and although some acknowledge that creative processes are subject to drafts and changes, responding to a variety of conditions and sets of feedback, few dwell on one of the key aspects of creating animated films: the impact of editorial interventions and the role of the script editor. It is this neglected aspect of the production pipeline that informs the discussion in this chapter.

Defining the script editor

Writing in the late 1970s, Brenner describes the script editor as a 'person on production staff who analyzes scripts, writes or re-writes when necessary, and confers with writer at all stages of teleplay development. Usually works with producer' (sic) (1980: 308–309). Some 20 years later, Parker discusses the same role:

> One of the traditional means to the first commission within UK television is in fact to work as a script editor on a series, a role which in America is normally held by a writer. However, this job is usually seen to be the first step to a producer's job and obtaining one as a writer will need some effort. The route which has become favoured in recent

years is to start off as a reader and then progress to script-editing or
to development work.

(1998: 205)

Whilst taking these definitions into account – though for me, they still
carry with them the idea that the script editor is somehow a 'lesser' role –
I wish to look at the editorial process in a wider sense, and how it more
specifically informs the production of animated works. It is important
to see the editorial process in two ways: firstly, as part of the creative
choices the animator, artist or director impose upon themselves; and
secondly, often fundamental to the collaborative screen production process, when an external agent intervenes, either in the service of directing
the writer or creator to change or re-draft material, or directly re-writing
the material themselves. In essence, these two processes can connect
and run in parallel, though that is dependent on the nature of the
production.

Arguably, then, and partially suggested by Parker, the notion of script
editing might begin at the point of submission of a script, when in film,
for example, the work is placed in the hands of a script reader who
will make recommendations based on criteria already set by the Head
of Development, story editors, producers, etc. (Grove, 2001: 123–129).
Equally, in productions where changes to the script occur frequently in a
collaborative devising and development process – certainly common in
animation – the lead writer's work may also be monitored and modified,
here by a script supervisor (Wells, 2007: 107). A script editor may also
work with the director or producer to manage the planned feedback to
the writer, before and throughout a production, and act to record or
add changes to a script. In whatever eventuality, script editing is often
a more fluid role than has been previously acknowledged, is certainly
an undervalued role, and yet is seemingly intrinsic to the continuity of
many projects.

This, of course, then begs the question of what the script editor does,
and how this functions within the context of animation production.
To answer this question is to also speak to a variety of definitions
of 'script', and the particular emphases on visualisation in the pre-
production of animation. As an aside, it is true to say that animation
does not attract traditional 'writers', except for those who write for television in all formats, but rather image makers, often adept with ideas
and concepts, but less able in relation to traditional written storytelling
structures. Many find writing 'treatments', 'step outlines', 'scripts', etc.
difficult, and prefer to work out their narratives in character designs,

sketches, storyboards and shooting scripts. Most animation productions embrace both models of working, where there is an oscillation
between the textual and the visual in the development of the work.
Depending on the production, the 'script editor' can take on multiple
functions here. In the following examples, I wish to look at three essential processes that the script editor engages in – notation, excision and
iteration – which speak both to orthodox script-editing skills and those
required for animation.

First principles

To begin with, it is worthwhile addressing the script editor in the context
of television, in that, firstly, this was my own first experience of engaging with the role, and secondly, this is the place where many budding
screenwriters undertake the role, often having to respond to a different
set of demands than they may later encounter in film production. It is
helpful to note, then, what a script editor typically does on conventional
television series. It is often assumed that 'editing' is only about taking
things away from an already complete script, when actually it is mainly
concerned with re-writing, replacement and review, and is constantly
pre-occupied with problem solving and resolution in advance of production itself. My own script-editing work on British soap operas, useful
to draw from here, was largely characterised by the following tasks:

- ensuring that the episode objectives had been achieved, and that the
  overall agreed series narrative arc was advancing across a series of
  episodes
- making sure that the approximate length of the episode was
  achieved, excising 'over long' episodes with recommendations for
  immediate possible cuts
- writing additional or replacement 'holding' or 'bridging' scenes
  that either ensured postponement of particular 'reveals', or that
  introduced 'fresh' repetition of important expository information
- editing and/or re-writing extended monologue/dialogue
- re-writing scenes for fast turnaround pertinent to production needs,
  such as inserting apology and confession scenes; enhancing dramatic
  irony; increasing or decreasing exposition; and creating dialogue to
  support prop and environment use.

These tasks effectively placed the role of the script editor between that
of the lead writer and the producer/director, and directly affected the

final outcome of the episode; yet the role was nevertheless in the service of a script written by an experienced writer, and responding to agreed storylines and character profiles established by the programme development teams. The process was also exclusively 'textual', albeit informed by considerable verbal discussion. Admittedly this is a process particular to episodic series and serials, but it is also an essential part of animation for television in the guise of what is known as the series 'bible'. As with a live-action series, the bible contains an overview of the story world, the characters and storylines; but crucially it includes pertinent visual material, such as character designs, environments, and examples of props and costumes. At a conceptual level, the bible also represents a confluence of production conditions that impact upon the script/storyboard/shooting script, namely:

- the need to create a specific world defined and limited by its own **terms and conditions**
- the consideration of the relationship between narrative and aesthetic requirements, and the **economy** of the chosen technique
- the relationship between **character and story events**, and the specific elements that will be **animated**
- the imperative of the **soundtrack** in the determination of the imagery, and the timing of the animated elements
- the realisation of the **performance** of character action implied in the script, and mediated through voice artists and animators.

Fundamentally, then, the work of the script editor in animation is not merely the act of working with text, but taking into account the core aspects of what is required to specifically produce animation. Whilst there will always be practical factors attached to evaluating and editing the live-action script, its main function is to foreground the story with its facilitation thereafter a matter for the producer and director. The focus on pre-production in animation essentially 'front ends' these considerations, and makes these issues instrumental aspects of writing and developing a script in the first instance.

Most animated works seek to create a particular world with their own terms and conditions. This is partly about using the form effectively to create a distinctive environment with its own (sometimes surreal, but nevertheless consistent) internal logic. These then operate as 'rules' within what could be a wholly anarchic context, creating the specific consistency that is the mark of an artistic or critical intention with a particular outcome. The feature film specifically is heavily reliant on its pre-production process to ensure such coherence; the cartoons of the golden era in Hollywood had strict length and time constraints on production, even when in the hands of 'auteur' directors. Television series require a bible in order that different writers and directors can refer to the codes and conventions established for the series, whilst also bringing their own individual creativity. The independent production relies on the particular vision of its principal creator to know, create and sustain a world. In all of these cases, the story world also defines the approach of the script editor, who is as marshalled as much by the intrinsic codes and conventions of the animation and its contextual infrastructure as they are the narrative content.

An Vrombaut and John Grace created a highly specific world for the popular children's series *64 Zoo Lane* (1999–2003, 2010–present), which had clear instructions about its characters, plot, structure, language and humour, as well as the following Do's and Don'ts:

- Animals can move freely within one continent, but cannot travel to other continents.
- Stick to native animals (no dromedaries in Australia or penguins in the North Pole).
- If a character appears in a story set in one continent, it cannot appear in a story set in a different continent.
- There can be no humans, human footprints, litter left behind by humans or any other signs of human civilisation.
- Props should always be made of materials the animals can find in their natural environment. Keep props simple (no machines).
- Don't set a story within a story.
- Avoid flashbacks.

This gives a consistency to the work that children can engage with and soon grasp the parameters of, but they are also conditions that script editors had to take account of in the submitted scripts, which sometimes overlooked the rules. Grace often recounted that no matter how many times he referred writers to the rules and the characters, advising them to research some of the 'real world' characteristics of animals, animals would still appear in the wrong continent, acquire 'magic' props, and meet humans. All of this the script editor would need to re-draft, edit and correct.[1]

The same kinds of issues arise in the Hot Animation children's series, *Bob the Builder* (1999–), but point up the importance of what I wish to call here, notation. The intervention of the producer or nominated script advisor at the outset of a production is an important editorial contribution and is usually configured as 'notes' back to the writer. Notes from the script editor and/or producer become fundamental to the development process and are prescriptive aspects in the ultimate finalisation of the script. Here I wish to address an example of a *Bob the Builder* episode that underwent nine drafts, and which works to exemplify the key functions of script-editing processes in animation.[2]

Notation

The *Bob the Builder* script bible is very clear about the nature of the relationships in the series, and of its tone. Fundamental to this is Bob's relationship to his machines: Scoop the JCB, Muck the dumper, Dizzy the cement mixer, Lofty the crane and Roley the steamroller. The machines provide an important 'spectacle' in an apparently local and everyday situation, and play two vital roles. Firstly, they speak to the awe and empathy that children often have when seeing big vehicles and playing with mechanised toys. Secondly, the machines represent a set of cheeky and playful children themselves, and so offer a further point of relationship with the children watching. Though Pilchard the cat is also a key character, *Bob the Builder* relies less on children's seemingly innate empathy with animals, and more on children seeing themselves reflected in the antics of the machines. Bob is essentially their paternal figure, but more an encouraging friend. Wendy, his business partner, is maternal and slightly more organisational and authoritative. Whilst Bob's builder's yard might suggest something urban and modern – which it does allude to through its use of technology – it is nevertheless set in the traditional English rural idyll of children's 3D animated programming, thus including Farmer Pickles, Travis the tractor and the naughty scarecrow, Spud, a minor villain.

Each episode has an 'A' and a 'B' plot, concerned with a type of building task, and must at some point include the catch-phrase (or a variation of it), 'Can we fix it?' 'Yes we can!', normally led by Scoop. Humour is important to each episode, and is largely based on sight gags and slapstick. This normally implies the kind of mutability and elasticity of the 2D cartoon, and is not usually associated with 3D stop motion puppets, but in the case of *Bob the Builder* the machines were constructed to be treated as 'squash 'n' stretch' characters. This directly affects what can be written and how it can be written, and is intrinsically related to the capacity of animation to achieve a particular and distinctive outcome.

The bible reminds writers that they should try and find original jobs for Bob to undertake, though nothing that would take him too far out of his remit as a builder: 'We do not want to see him as an astronaut, acrobat or aerobics teacher.' Each plot should also include a logical role for some or all of the machines. No other vehicles are permitted and places with crowds avoided, most stories taking place in the locations for which sets have already been built.

Importantly, then, both for writers and editors, the established conventions and material limits of the programme determine the parameters of not only the story, but specific elements of it. This is often expressed in some detail, especially in relation to puppet capability. For example:

> Remember these are not real people – the human characters and Spud will always need a metal magnetic base to walk on. Please avoid climbing up ladders.

> Bob and Wendy can't actually fit through the doors on the office and house so we can't show them going in or going out. They have to be already out with the door just closing. Bob cannot talk directly to Wendy when he is in the yard and she is in the office. However, if Bob is in the workshop with the door up, then he can speak directly to the characters in the yard.

> Bob and Wendy don't wear watches so please make use of clocks on walls in office and front room and also town hall clock.

The writing decisions, then, are often determined by technical conditions. Any writer considering a farce plot, for example, where entries and exits determine much of the humour, would already be constrained by Bob and Wendy's issues with doors. Even the number of machines able to attend any one job is limited by the size of the set. It is important to remember that such issues are critical when making a series with real materials: computer-generated animation in this respect has more flexibility, albeit still informed by the retention of established assets and virtual sets, but clearly these can be manipulated and changed more easily. The script editor's role under these circumstances, then, is not merely 'creative', but as someone checking that these technical issues have been respected. Should too many of the machines be on set, for example, each with lines and responsibilities, scenes would necessarily have to be re-written to scale down the machines, as well as revisions to dialogue and action. This is a crucial reminder that script editing is often more about pragmatism and problem solving, even when affording the opportunity for an inventive contribution.

A further and fundamental aspect of guidance for writers of *Bob the Builder* is in relation to dialogue. The bible suggests, 'avoid complex grammar, figures of speech and specific words which a young audience will not be familiar with'. Addressing a children's audience can be problematic for adults not familiar with children, and requires some research in relation to specific vocabulary and register. Equally, this must also accord with the fact that building activities are part of an adult world, so in essence Bob and Wendy explain ideas and issues of a more mature nature in simple language, whilst the machines for the most part pose questions or remain reactive to a situation, each using their individualised catchphrase. Again, the script editor needs to check for the inclusion of these catchphrases to reinforce the identity of each character, and to secure a child's investment and empathy by repetition and ritualistic familiarity. From Scoop's 'No prob, Bob' to Muck's 'Muck to the Rescue' to Lofty's 'Err, yeah, I think so', these catchphrases play an important role in the infrastructure of a script, where writers are instructed, 'don't come up with "clever" variations on these'. Clarity and directness become key watchwords, with an expectation that monologues are avoided in favour of concise scenes with clear exchanges. These are important factors in creating the story world, becoming the core conditions to which the writer must conform, and for which the script editor must ensure adherence.

In an episode that I wish to address here, the producer and script editor's notation becomes very important. Firstly, the proposed title, *Rhythmic Roley*, was rejected immediately on the basis that it might not be meaningful to children, and more importantly, because it was not indicative enough of the ensuing story content. Titles pre-figure and pre-suggest the story, hopefully attracting viewers, but not giving the whole narrative away. Whilst script editors often make no comment on titles, it is sometimes their responsibility to make sure that they adequately reflect the episode content; and if not, to suggest alternatives.

One of the first script notes is to cut 'flowers being loaded into Muck's dumper'. Whilst it is often the writer's first imperative to find decorative imagery to help visualise a scene, in this instance, the flowers add nothing to the story, and in animation terms are expensive to produce. The writer and the script editor need to be as aware as the animator of the places where animation itself can be reduced, or where unnecessary set dressing can be reasonably omitted. Later, Bob is discovered wearing a dressing gown and slippers, a costume that would probably not be used again, and so once more, on pragmatic grounds, this is cut.

The core premise of the script is the idea of Bob's machines becoming a band, but this is never fully rationalised. The script editor suggests that their music is essentially percussive, using the already established functions and possibilities of the machines and the environment. The script is described as 'complicated and overlong' and that its concluding scene, in which the machines stand in for a local park band, feels 'tagged on'.

Notations on a later draft suggest that the script does not really work because the creation of the bandstand seems outside Bob's normal building remit; nevertheless, this is the only one remaining aspect of the episode by the final draft. As the drafts develop, the concept of the band changes, but the notes are predominantly the same, always concerned with maintaining the story world, making sure the animated sequences are efficient, and sustaining a pragmatic approach to actually making the episode. The notes thus function as significant editorial interventions in advance of a final definitive script, which is thereafter used in the production.

Excision

The Simpsons is one of the most popular and long-established animated situation comedies of all time. It is essentially written by a team: a show runner, a lead writer and a collaborative group of contributing writers, with input from the cast following table readings of draft scripts.[3] As a devising process, this can have enormous benefits in making sure that there is a high degree of creative intervention and in the maintenance of quality comic invention. For the lead writer and the script editor, however, this can be a challenging process because it means that the script is subject to considerable change, the balance between story structure and the imperative to sustain 'gag' beats being hard to maintain when the devising and writing remain fluid.

There is also the additional demand that the script editor can both reconcile the structure of a scene in regard to its comic outcomes and timings, and be able to write or modify gags if necessary. Editing gags has its own problems. Sometimes, if a sequence does not appear funny enough, the temptation is to add further jokes, when in actual fact the most important thing is to re-visit the premise in order to generate alternatives. This kind of intervention can often privilege more surreal or non-sequitur jokes, which can be accommodated, particularly in animated comedy; but as Smith points out, it is important not to introduce the 'one-eyed monkey' as a solution to script issues, as it inevitably sets in train a further series of problems to justify the logic of its inclusion (1999: 22). Upsetting the balance between the already established set-up and cueing of the agreed jokes, and their pay off, is often also a consequence of the arrival of the 'one-eyed monkey', even if it sometimes seems amusing and fresh. Older material can thus seem stale and unfunny simply because it has survived drafts and interventions, and so the script editor must make sure that newer material actually solves a problem or improves the quality of the script.

In the episode 'Bart vs. Thanksgiving', significant editorial interventions occurred as the script developed. These were generated by the whole writing team, but were executed by the script editor before the episode was signed off by the showrunner to go to animation. The episode has a clear three act structure and, as is typical in a lot of script development, the premise is established quite successfully only for problems to arise in the second act, largely in this case due to over-invention, in turn problematising the nature of the ending and its intended emotional tenor. In Act One, Marge prepares thanksgiving dinner for the extended Simpsons family. Typically, Bart misbehaves, resulting in Lisa's hand-crafted table centrepiece being destroyed in the fireplace. Bart refuses to apologise, which becomes the preoccupation of the rest of the episode. The first 18 pages of the 54-page draft have very minor re-writes and gag edits, the main cuts being lines given to Marge's sisters.

In Act Two, Bart leaves home as a consequence of his refusal to apologise. The screenwriters thus give themselves *carte blanche* about what Bart then encounters before the inevitability of his return home. It is at this stage that, in some ways, the invention runs ahead of the purpose of the story. Bart leaves home, tries to steal from Mr Burns to support himself, lands 'on the wrong side of the tracks', and eventually realises that he wants to go home. In some senses, whilst the writers know that they do not want Bart to undergo a clichéd narrative about learning the error of his ways, or compromise his comic mischief, they must not sacrifice the core expectation that Bart and Lisa will resolve their issue; the audience knows that beneath their sibling conflict is shared affection.

There are numerous cuts between pages 19 and 38, such as a Bart 'preparation to leave' scene which only signals prevarication, and arrests the momentum of the story. The sequence with Mr Burns, which initially features an extensive chase and a long dialogue scene with

Smithers, is considerably reduced, ostensibly because the animation required for the chase would need much work and much expense, adding little to the narrative. This is also the case for a dream sequence featuring a Pilgrim's Thanksgiving, initially included as part of Bart's moral turnaround. A scene set in a Plasma Centre is cut, reduced to a reference in voiceover, whilst a character on 'the wrong side of the tracks' who 'sticks needles in his arm' is also excised. Once again, some of this is pragmatic: additional characters who are not necessary or have no potential as long-standing characters are removed; sound is sometimes used to avoid animating complete scenes; and scenes which might offend or alienate viewers are reviewed for relevance. Crucially, even though this is about Bart straying into a challenging terrain, and a vehicle for gags, the cuts revolve around the idea of Bart remaining allied to thoughts of his family, not extraneous situations.

Ultimately, even though at first Bart is pre-occupied with the fact that he will be called to account for his absence and the stress that he has caused, the writers realise that the ultimate focus should be on the narrative route to his apology to Lisa. Bart negotiates his anxiety in a reverie, which echoes the Disney cartoon *Pluto's Judgment Day* (1935) in showing him in a trial situation. The use of the reverie here also forces the cut of an earlier dream sequence, making this sequence more effective as the method by which Bart rehearses his return in a comic idiom, and so that his actual re-connection with his family can work on more emotional terms. As indicated earlier, this balance between the general scepticism of the humour and the emotional parameters of the relationships is a hard one to maintain, but is necessary to the overall tone and outlook of the series.

Pages 39–54 conclude the episode, and again extraneous scenes that do not service the denouement of the story are cut. Lisa sits at her desk writing a log: 'Dear Log, my brother is still missing and maybe it's my fault because I failed to take his abuse with good humour. I miss him so much already.' At this point, Bart calls to her through a vent pipe on the roof. Lisa then joins him, and key lines are cut where Bart apologises to Lisa and even offers her money to accept his apology. Another scene in which Marge and Homer overhear this exchange is also cut, as it disturbs what will be the emotional arc between Bart and Lisa. What was a rather glib resolution and sustained conflict to Bart and Lisa's cut dialogue is replaced by the following:

```
                         Lisa
          Just answer one question. Why did you do
          it? Because you hate me, or because you're
          bad?
```

```
                    Bart
     I don't know! I don't know why I did it!
     I don't know why I enjoyed it! And I don't
     know why I'll do it again!
```

This exchange is much more in tune with the core character traits of both characters: Lisa is not especially concerned with Bart apologising, but about whether it is a fundamental rupture in their bond; Bart is just as clear that his actions are not often that motivated, but about arbitrary pleasures. The following lines are then also cut:

```
                    Lisa
     Okay. I'll tell you what. Since you
     have yet to develop the first glimmer
     of a conscience at the age of ten, I
     think you should have an advisor...

                    Bart
     Like, whattaya mean?

                    Lisa
     Someone who could tell you when you're
     going too far...like Jiminy Cricket
     did for Pinocchio.

                    Bart
     Well, I don't happen to have a little
     cartoon character telling me right
     from wrong.
```

This cut is made on the basis of resisting the opportunity to engage in ironic, self-reflexive humour about Bart and Lisa's status as cartoon characters – a common trait in animated cartoons per se – in order to maintain an emotional tension in which Lisa ultimately asks Bart to find the spot inside him that recognises he has hurt her feelings, and then apologise accordingly.

Excision, then, is a key aspect of the script editor's work, not just in a spirit of pragmatism or in managing the multiple possibilities of animated comic invention, but to ensure there is consistency in the dialogue and action to secure the intended emotive tone and empathetic outcome.

Iteration

Animation as the 'art of the impossible' offers the seductive quality of being able to depict anything that might be imagined. As I have sought to indicate, though, these apparent freedoms are always con-strained by the terms, conditions and costs of the technique, the genre of writing, and the mode of exhibition. The example from *Bob the Builder* sought to stress the value of the show bible and notation; and the use of *The Simpsons* to demonstrate the problems of comic devising and the importance of excision in sculpting the final script. These exam-ples deal exclusively with script as text in animation, and so this final example seeks to examine the script-editing process when the 'script' of a film exists only as visual material. Essentially, it is quite straightfor-ward to see how the script editor functions when dealing with language, and conventional notions of the screenplay; but when productions only work with sketches, storyboards and shooting scripts, the role is conceiv-ably different. It is equally easy to see that when developing a text, it is subject to obvious re-drafting; however, in animation, interventions in visual story planning are not an illustration of an idea, but an iteration of script on the same terms and conditions as text. Editorial conditions thus change and are made on specifically visual terms.

Animated World Faiths, a series telling the stories of religious icons and their belief systems, was essentially developed by visual means.[4] The most immediate benefit of working in this way is its flexibility and ulti-mate pertinence as the starting place for the animation itself. The first attempt of this method is normally small thumbnail sketches and nota-tion that establish the characters, story and core action. The sketches can be moved around and placed in a different order if necessary, or easily discarded in favour of other visual ideas. For animators happier working through drawing and re-drawing, this is a much more useful approach to 'writing', and the editorial work comes from looking at the largely representational panels and finding the right order for the narrative, identifying important absences, and helping with the layer-ing of further plot lines. This method also allows for the maximum visual experimentation at the most cost-effective time in the production pipeline.

The next stage is to begin to find scenes and sequences that define the narrative, but which are then further refined by consideration of the composition and position of the camera in each image. The stress in much animation comes from trying to tell the story in purely visual terms, so attention needs to be given to how each panel narrates its plot point. The script editor at this stage normally checks the relationship between each panel, noting what comes before and what comes after, and whether this has a transparent visual logic. Usually, after finalising a thumbnail run-through, this process then moves on to creating more formalised storyboards which take into account what will actually be animated, and how sound might be deployed. These images are then used to create an animatic (a moving image version of the thumbnail sequences, within an improvised provisional soundtrack), and become the basis for the development of a shooting script. Script editing using this method, then, is effectively a process of reflection and recognition of how each iteration of drawing communicates both information and meaning.

One episode of *Animated World Faiths*, 'The Story of Guru Nanak', was visually edited in pre-production through the following considerations:

- checking the depiction of characters in relation to their physical gestures and actions to ensure that what they are feeling and doing is clear
- checking the depictions of environments to ensure that they either communicate where the characters are, or support their actions appropriately
- checking that non-figurative, more abstract, or symbolic imagery can be read clearly and quickly
- checking the overall appropriateness of the image in communicating a story point
- checking the composition and framing of the image for its capacity to support specific camera moves
- checking the elements within the image that are intended to move, and that the suggested choreography of the move communicates clearly and effectively (i.e. eye-line moves, head-turns, hand-gestures, walk-cycles, use of props, etc.)
- checking the relationship between the panels to ensure implied narrative relationship and continuity is clear
- checking if the intended sound supports/counterpoints might replace the intended image (Figures 9.1 and 9.2).

Script editing on these terms and conditions requires a high degree of visual literacy, and whilst this is not notation free, or without recognition of possible dialogue, the non-reliance on text insists that there is a clear understanding of what animation as a specific language of expression is capable of. Whether through the visual transitions achievable through metamorphosis, the condensation possible by securing the maximum degree of suggestion through the minimum of imagery, or the using of associative potential of signs, symbols and iconographic

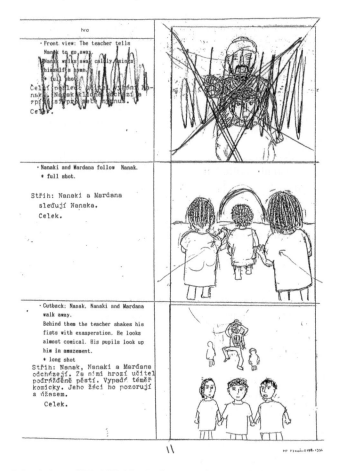

Figure 9.1   Animated World Faiths: Dialogue and potential shots are often excised in visual script editorial practices

images (Wells, 1998: 68–126), animation extends the range of variables in defining and limiting the narrative.

Conclusion

This chapter has sought to draw attention to the pre-production editorial processes that are instrumental in the script development of animated works. The use of notation, excision and iteration are fundamentals in securing the most efficient terms and conditions for work

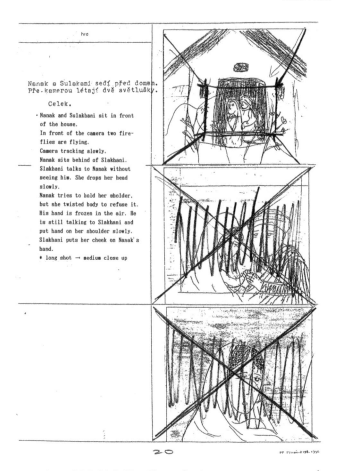

Figure 9.2 Animated World Faiths: Shot selection, camera moves, and specific choices of what is animated are fundamental to the specificity of animated narratives

made specifically in animation and its particular conditions. Constant attention needs to be paid to the limitations and freedoms of each technique; the place of animation in relation to genre and audience; and its own distinctive credentials in the construction and manipulation of images. Though animation production pipelines are many and various, with numerous collaborative roles and functions, script editing, whether in the hands of a specific person or across a number of roles, is an invisible craft that nevertheless secures the most visible and often iconoclastic of outcomes. Though it has often been the case that the scriptwriter has been undervalued in many cases, the role of the script editor, and the editorial process in general has also been often made invisible. This is accentuated in the animation production process because there are usually so many roles and contributors in making animated films, that the fundamental pre-production interventions of the script editor – visual or textual – are often forgotten, yet are completely crucial in ensuring that the production process is predicated on pragmatically grounded, narratively assured, and animation-sensitive scripts and storyboards. To note its fundamental place and purpose is to properly recognise the pre-production process as where an animation is really made.

Notes

1. John Grace, who sadly died in 2006, was a colleague of mine at Loughborough University, and these recollections are drawn from our informal conversations about the series.
2. The scripts referred to here are drawn from the Hot Animation Collection housed at the Animation Academy Archive at Loughborough University. Specific names of scriptwriters, editors and producers are not referred to.
3. The material here was produced in association with *The Simpsons* producer and showrunner, Al Jean, in November 2010.
4. The scripts referred to here are drawn from the Right Angle Productions Collection housed at the Animation Academy Archive at Loughborough University. Specific names of scriptwriters, editors and producers are not referred to.

References

Besen, E. (2008) *Animation Unleashed*, Studio City, CA: Michael Wiese Productions.

Brenner, A. (1980) *The TV Scriptwriter's Handbook*, Cincinnati, OH: Writer's Digest Books.

Cook, B. and Thomas, G. (2006) *The Animate! Book: Rethinking Animation*, LUX with Arts Council England, London.

Furniss, M. (2008) *The Animation Bible*, London: Laurence King Publishing.

Grove, E. (2001) *Write and Sell a Hot Screenplay*, London & New York: Elsevier/Focal Press.

McKee, R. (1999) *Story: Substance, Structure, Style and the Principles of Screenwriting*, London: Methuen.

Parker, P. (1998) *The Art and Science of Screenwriting*, Exeter: Intellect Books.

Scott, J. (2003) *How to Write for Animation*, Woodstock & New York: The Overlook Press.

Selby, A. (2009) *Animation in Process*, London: Laurence King Publishing.

Selby, A. (2013) *Animation (Portfolio)*, London: Laurence King Publishing.

Smith, E.S. (1999) *Writing Television Sit-Coms*, New York: Peregee.

Vogler, C. (2007) *The Writer's Journey: Mythic Structure for Writers*, Studio City, CA: Michael Wiese Productions.

Webber, M. (2000) *Gardner's Guide to Animation Scriptwriting*, Annandale, VA: GGC Inc.

Wellins, M. (2005) *Storytelling through Animation*, Hingham, Massachusetts: Charles River Media Inc.

Wells, P. (1998) *Understanding Animation*, London & New York: Routledge.

Wells, P. (2007) *Scriptwriting*, Lausanne: AVA Academia.

Wells, P. and Hardstaff, J. (2008) *Re-Imagining Animation: The Changing Face of the Moving Image*, Lausanne: AVA Academia.

10
Scripting the Real: Mike Leigh's Practice as Antecedent to Contemporary Reality Television Texts *The Only Way Is Essex* and *Made in Chelsea*

Peri Bradley

Introduction

This chapter aims to investigate what can now be regarded as Mike Leigh's institutional conventions intended to closely recreate reality, as the tradition from which *The Only Way Is Essex (TOWIE)* (2010–) and other television 'dramality' programmes such as *Made in Chelsea* (2011–) have emerged. The terms 'dramality' and 'reali-drama' have emerged into common usage from the media, whose mainly critical attitude is based in the fact that these programmes purport to be 'reality' but actually include fictional elements designed to promote drama. The narrative construction and industrial practices involved in the production of these recent dramatised, reality television texts can be traced back to and aligned with Leigh's improvisational workshops that resulted in films like *Bleak Moments* (1971) and one of his most iconic works, the television drama *Abigail's Party* (1977). Leigh's commitment to reproducing reality on film and television in as authentic and convincing a manner as possible for the purposes of social realism involves a unique approach to screenwriting methods that, whilst not popular with financiers, attracts critical acclaim.

As an example of a contemporary television text that employs methods like those of Mike Leigh, *TOWIE* uses a 'hands off' tactic in order to reaffirm the real, but in this case in the name of entertainment rather than social commentary. The screenwriting process and its narrative effect are purposely obscured to maintain its genre reputation as observational and detached, rather than manipulated and scripted. More widely, the rise and popularity of reality television has resulted in interesting changes in some screenwriting practices, where encouraging guidance is favoured over specific scripting of action and dialogue in order to maintain a realist aesthetic that allows 'drama' to emerge from situations.

This chapter thus investigates the work of Mike Leigh in its historical and industrial context as a precursor to reality television texts such as *TOWIE*. The relationship between the authorial works of Leigh and the hybrid television 'dramality' will be analysed in order to comprehend how screenwriting practice has been forced to develop in order to incorporate the aesthetics of reality television, a genre that saturates the contemporary industrial landscape.

Mike Leigh

According to Goodridge,

> Mike Leigh occupies a unique position on the world stage. His extraordinary rigorous process of filmmaking by rehearsal, instinct and improvisation involves extensive commitments from actors and crew members that has resulted in some of the most truthful and insightful character studies of the last two decades.
>
> (2002: 45)

Mike Leigh has been lauded as one of the great British filmmakers of his time; yet, he suffers from criticism for his methods and also from comparison to Ken Loach, another admired and acclaimed UK filmmaker of a similar ilk. As critic Tim Robey of the *Daily Telegraph* states,

> Like Marmite and Moulin Rouge, Mike Leigh has a tendency to divide people [...] He's a compassionate miserablist who finds comedy in the most painful of situations; in the eyes of his detractors, these same films are impossibly grim and full of condescension and caricature.
>
> (2007: 2)

The television show *TOWIE* is received in much the same way: its reliance on Essex 'caricatures', and their relationships and interactions to entertain and also cause controversy, tend to stimulate the same extreme and opposite reactions. Audiences either adore or loathe the show, and some of this extreme reaction, mostly from middle- to upper-middle-class factions of British society, might be said to result from the fact that it explores the same issues of class that Leigh examines in his work.

As Tony Whitehead (2007) points out, Leigh is invariably placed in the category of socially conscious filmmaking with Loach, but because of his so-called contradictory use of improvisational methods to enhance realism, employed next to his excessive characters that tend to belie realism (although Leigh states that this is actually a form of 'heightened realism'), he is considered somewhat inferior to Loach. As a result of realism still being regarded as a defining factor in British cinema, Leigh's use of comedy and satire, as expressed by an exaggeration of the characteristics of the British working class in particular, is often cited as the reason for his work being criticised. Not only is it said to veer away from the conventions of reality, seeming to somehow court the baser human instincts of laughing at others' misfortune or ignorance, it also heightens our sense of the film as an artefact rather than 'reality'.

Leigh's texts, whether film or television, are treated by him as a collaborative process whereby he devises and directs, rather than 'writes' the work. As with any collaborative process and any authorial director or 'auteur', the creative process begins and ends with the choices and control imposed by the artist. Leigh has always been very careful about the team of actors and filmmakers he works with on his rigorous method of production. The script is very carefully teased out of the actors through a process that involves intense one-to-one consultation with Leigh about all aspects of their character. It is only once this is completed and Leigh is satisfied that the actors are brought together to perform an improvisation of a 'bare-bones' outline (as opposed to a full screenplay). As Leigh himself states,

> For me the process of filmmaking is one of discovering what a film is by making it [...] the actual depths of the film, the writing and conception, are entangled with the whole, so I always embark without a script [...] at the point of casting, there is absolutely no story.
>
> (cited in Goodridge, 2002: 45–49)

This method of working does not run completely counter to normal screenwriting processes for film and television, as explained by Rosenthal,

Your outline is a plan, you hope a very good plan, for something that has yet to be born or created. It is the sketch, the plan, the guide that shows you the possibilities and the problems [...] but it is not the work itself. This means that your script is going to have an independent life, which your treatment can only hint at.

(1995: 161)

Although Leigh's work can be seen to proceed from a similar basis, his methods of practice tend to divert from the norm with his next step, in which he allows the actors themselves to supply the dialogue that emerges from the situations, confrontations and locations that he has placed them in. This inclusion of actors in the creative process means they are being asked to reach into the depths of their own experience, and to know their characters' actions and reactions so well that they become second nature. As a result, what emerges on screen is an undeniable authenticity on the part of the actors. However, what is also evident is Leigh's concept of a 'heightened reality', one that borders on a type of 'surreality' that in fact almost *denies* authenticity. For example, when developing a pivotal scene, he might inform the actor of their character's actions, but not tell this to any of the other actors taking part in the scene in order to derive spontaneity. This can be seen in *Abigail's Party*, when the uptight Laurence, a man with middle-class aspirations, dies of a heart attack. At the time of the first rehearsal, Tim Stern, the actor playing Laurence, was the only one who knew his character's fate, and so what emerges from the scene is a sense of actual shock and panic. As Leigh states of his own work,

A lot of people never really find out what they are taking part in until they see the film [...] because through genuine, organic improvisations, you can engender truthful, spontaneous material – that's what you see on screen.

(cited in Goodridge, 2002: 50)

We can therefore see that Leigh's methods are employed with specific purpose and planning to enable an authenticity, or 'verite', that is central to the ethos of his filmmaking practice. To facilitate the verisimilitude essential to his work, this lack of a script is designed to allow the creative abilities of his cast to stimulate his own artistic process. This would seem to be at odds not only with the screenwriter, who creates 'natural' dialogue that is both entertaining and poetic, but also with industrial practice, which normally demands that a script be written before any financial backing can be provided. As such, Leigh's claim that,

> I work up the scene to the point where it's absolutely structured. They learn it by rehearsal, not by it being written down. Good actors can do that. And what I do in my writer capacity is not just dialogue but by subtext; I'll set something up in relation to what I can see. I can only script a scene when I actually see it [...] It's writing through directing. And it can only be done by absolutely understanding not only the actor but the character and the rhythms of the character.
>
> (cited Goodridge, 2002: 53)

could be, and is, questioned and criticised, with assertions that he exploits his actors by asking them to produce the dialogue and then simply writing it down. Leigh disputes this, denying that he is simply performing a type of journalistic function. Rather, he states that he structures the actors' journey so that they have a sense of where their character begins and where they are going; and that it is from his meticulous planning and intense involvement with every step of that journey that makes the dialogue as much a collaboration as any other part of his directorial control. This view is certainly supported by Richard Porton who states:

> All of Leigh's scripts are the product of an intimate process of collaboration with unusually talented casts, although it is important to emphasise the fact that his work is no more improvised than Fellini's: after a fairly lengthy rehearsal period, Leigh incorporates the actor's contributions into a final script and remains as much in control as any traditional director.
>
> (2002: 177)

This is also supported by Michael Coveney, who sees Leigh's method of work as 'far from exploiting the contribution of the actors by using them to make up his scripts for him' and that 'in fact liberates them into a condition of creative artistry rarely available to them elsewhere in their profession' (1996: 9). Placing Leigh's methods into the context of received wisdom concerning the art of screenwriting, particularly for television, means that comparisons can be drawn that set up a recognisable relationship between the two case studies chosen for this chapter: *Abigail's Party* and *TOWIE*. This relationship also addresses the issues surrounding the impact of the rise of reality television on screenwriting, and the differentiation between 'high art' texts such as

Leigh's, identified as docu-dramas, and 'low art' populist shows herein named 'reali-dramas'.

Abigail's Party

Abigail's Party is a play originally produced for the stage that appeared on the BBC's *Play for Today* slot in November 1977. *Play for Today* is considered to be part of the 'golden age' of television, showcasing new creative talents such as Trevor Griffiths, Dennis Potter and, of course, Mike Leigh (BFI, 2013). It was known for its emphasis on gritty social realism, but was also a platform for other groundbreaking genres such as science fiction and comedy. *Abigail's Party* can be seen as a hybrid genre combining social realism and comedy, a genre that Leigh has become known for. It is a stylised and extremely mannered suburban situation comedy, and a biting satirical commentary on the aspirations and tastes of the new middle class that emerged in Britain in the 1970s. The play originally ran at the Hampstead Theatre in 1977. There were 104 performances in all, and such is its resonance with the British psyche that it has been and is continuously reproduced in amateur and professional productions across the country – and the world.

For Leigh, the location of his drama is vital and impacts closely on the action and the dialogue. He chose to situate *Abigail's Party* in Essex, or according to him, 'theoretical Romford' (cited in Coveney, 1996: 116). The significance of this particular area is its middle-class status and, notably, the influx of the aspirational working classes who were earning more money and therefore able to overcome more traditional class barriers. In the play, Beverly Moss invites her new neighbours of two weeks, Angela and Tony, to a 'sophisticated' drinks party, a display of conspicuous consumption and newfound wealth. She also invites her divorced neighbour Susan (or, as she refers to her, Sue), who in her restrained manner and careful speech is coded as of a higher class than the others. Susan's 15-year-old daughter Abigail, of the play's title, is holding a party at her mother's house, and as the strains of punk music filter through and provide a jarring juxtaposition to Beverly's choice of Demos Roussos, Leigh makes his audience aware of the radical shift in 1970s culture and the tensions between youth, class and the establishment.

Against this backdrop, Beverly's husband Laurence arrives home late from work, just before the party begins. The get-together starts in an awkwardly British and typically middle-class way, until Beverly and Laurence begin an embarrassing marital squabble. As Beverley forces more drinks on her guests and the alcohol begins to take effect, Beverly flirts more and more openly with Tony, creating an increasingly uncomfortable environment for their visitors and an ineffective and powerless Laurence. After a tirade about art and music, which reveals his more middle-class aspirations, Laurence suffers a fatal heart attack. Within this bare bones structure, all of the obsessions, prejudices, fears and petty competitiveness of the protagonists are ruthlessly exposed whilst also engaging with the anxieties and shifting undercurrent of 1970s culture and society.

Leigh's work, *Abigail's Party* in particular, has been and is still discussed in an intellectual manner and, even if it is criticised, it is always placed in the 'high art' bracket. As Porton comments,

> Like Charles Dickens, the most blatantly theatrical of nineteenth-century novelists, Leigh uses comic hyperbole to indict the established order. Usually facilely pigeonholed as examples of British realism, Leigh's films are as indebted to British comic traditions and the theatre of the absurd.
>
> (2002: 165)

However, Porton's comment that,

> Leigh's fascination with the often 'vulgar' particularities of working-class, lower middle-class, and nouveau riche life, moreover, coincides with the recent theatrical attraction to 'spatial politics', which bears the imprint of Henri Lefebvre's influence [...] *Abigail's Party* [...] examines social geography in a more intimate fashion, revealing the implications of kitsch in all its horrific, and – on occasion – strangely appealing, glory.
>
> (2002: 170)

also positions the play alongside the second case study text, *TOWIE*. If we consider this contemporary series in light of the previous quotation, we can also see a similar examination of social geography: *TOWIE*, too, is seen as 'revealing the implications of kitsch in all its horrific, and – on occasion – strangely appealing, glory'. In theoretical terms, it is necessary here to place both case studies within the framework of social realism as a construct that is capable of engaging the audience in a social and even political discourse that questions established cultural mores.

Lacey defines social realism as capable of revealing 'the situation of the working-class at the level of its culture and everyday practices' (2007: 5), which indicates that not only is *Abigail's Party* a work of social realism, but that *TOWIE*, in its portrayal of the nouveau riche with working-class roots, is still engaging with the same issues, albeit in an updated, contemporary industrial and cultural environment. As described by Rolinson in his chapter, *Small Screens and Big Voices: Televisual Social Realism and the Popular*, social realism translated from film, theatre and literature onto television as 'a key social realist arena, given its ability to address mass audiences in the domestic sphere' (2011: 172). The immediacy of the televisual aesthetic lends itself particularly well to the genre of social realism and, as can be seen from *Abigail's Party*'s enduring impact and popularity in both television and cultural terms, one that effectively addresses and connects with the audience.

Although we are now happy to accept *Abigail's Party* as a work of social realism, at the time it was criticised for its stylised 'realism' and awkward, uncomfortable dialogue and situation, and was accused of holding up the lower classes for ridicule and derision. With similar critical reception, the British television show *TOWIE* can be seen to operate in the same manner, yet predominantly for the purposes of entertainment, not social commentary. Its improvisational tactics, which seek to provide realism and authenticity, are often what it is most criticised for; yet, they are also a large part of the show's public appeal. In line with Leigh's work, *TOWIE* attempts to conceal its constructedness whilst also employing it to explore contemporary society. Although I am not trying to claim that *TOWIE* was designed for anything but entertainment, its involvement in cross-media platforms and the everyday yet universal issues it deals with, means that it still functions as an observational if dramatised mode similar to that of the soap opera. It is here, and in relation to Leigh's work, that the show finds interesting connections with screenwriting practice.

The Only Way Is Essex

TOWIE is based in Essex, England. It shows, as Grace Dent's article in *The Guardian* puts it, 'real people in modified situations, saying unscripted lines but in a structured way' (*The Guardian*, 23 October 2010). It is part of the new wave of hybrid reality television shows called 'dramality' or 'reali-drama'. If we are to believe the portrayals given of Essex, then the population of this area is stereotypically uneducated, 'tanorexic', appearance obsessed and, in the context of the apparently dying British class system, part of the vulgar and common masses. One can dip into any episode of *TOWIE* and experience the compelling and, for some, simultaneously repellent experiences and antics of the cast of supposedly 'real' and 'ordinary' people. In one episode particularly relevant to this study, 'Botox Party' (Series 2: Episode 8), we see Chloe and Maria, two of the show's main female characters, walking on treadmills at a gym that appears more like a stage set, chatting to Chloe's cousin Joey Essex about the advantages of Botox in maintaining a line-free face. The following conversation reveals a fairly stereotypical representation of intellectually limited Essex 20-somethings, where, arguably, the audience is encouraged to laugh at them rather than with them:

> Joey Essex
> What are you doing tonight?
>
> Chloe
> We're going to a botox party.
>
> Joey Essex
> (puzzled look on
> his face)
> What is it?
>
> Maria
> (indicating between
> her eyebrows)
> Injections and it paralyses your
> muscle in your nerve, or whatever!
>
> Joey Essex
> (even more puzzled
> look on his face)
> Why do you want that?
>
> Maria
> So basically you can't frown
>
> Chloe
> So you can't get lines - so when you
> go like that...
>
> She attempts - and fails - to raise
> her eyebrows.
>
> Joey Essex
> But say you become paralysed!
>
> Chloe
> No - put your eyebrows up like
> you're really surprised about
> something.

```
Joey obligingly raises his eyebrows.

                   Maria
Yeah, do that. See, you've got
two lines - we'll never get that!

                   Chloe
This gets rid of them...
(waves her hand across
her face)
...because...
(pauses, looks to heaven
for inspiration)
...by now I should have about four
lines.

               Joey Essex
Why? Oh, because you got that done,
you aint got it?

                   Chloe
No, because I can't move me 'ead.

She attempts to raise her eyebrows,
to demonstrate.

                   Maria
Would you 'ave it?

               Joey Essex
No! I 'd never 'ave that!
```

On the surface this is a fairly mundane dialogue, yet it has been constructed and then edited in a way that is presented as comedy. In the same episode, Amy Childs (who left the show to pursue a solo career after appearing on *Big Brother* in 2011) chats in her beauty salon to her assistant, Paloma, about preparing for the Botox party. She states that she does not want too much Botox to prevent herself from looking like the 'back of a spoon', and talks about the fact that men, such as Sylvester Stallone, now also have the treatment. Amy and Paloma then proceed to try and pronounce Stallone's name, which results in a comedy double act where they have to break it down into syllables and ultimately pronounce it 'Silverlester'. This further confirms for the audience that the characters are uneducated, and their pronunciation emphasises their working-class roots. The cast of *TOWIE* are thus represented in the same manner as Bahktin's vulgar masses or grotesques, whose moment of carnival sees them dominate the screen for a short while where chaos reigns, but with order and reason returning at the end of the show. Nevertheless, the cultural reach of the series can be seen in its huge popularity with audiences to such an extent that the words 'vajazzle', 'reem' and 'jel', terms first used in *TOWIE*, have entered contemporary UK vernacular. The word 'vajazzle' now appears in the *Oxford English Dictionary*.

Critical analysis of *TOWIE* can be recognised as emanating from the same established school of thought that critiques Leigh's work: that of the middle-class establishment, who seem to perceive the exposure of such working-class vulgarity to the public as a threat not only to middle-class taste and discernment but also to the established order. This is apparent in the quotation below from *The Guardian* television reviewer Stuart Heritage (2011), containing similar elements to those levelled at Leigh by critics such as Dennis Potter in response to *Abigail's Party*. For Potter,

> This play was based on nothing more edifying than rancid disdain [...] it was a prolonged jeer, twitching with genuine hatred, about the dreadful suburban tastes of the dreadful lower middle classes.
>
> (cited in Medhurst, 2007: 170)

In his accusation of classism against Leigh, Potter fails to recognise that Leigh offers up an extreme but mostly accurate portrait of the complexities of the British class system in all its gory detail, not in order to jeer but in an attempt to inform and understand. In a similar way, I argue that Heritage fails to identify *TOWIE*'s engagement with not only the cultural issues and concerns of contemporary society but also how they are expressed in an alternative way through the radical shift in the form and content of a multi-platform and convergent media. He complains:

> Narratively speaking it had a structure that was somewhere between scattershot and nonexistent. A couple got lost in the woods, an old lady went swimming, a Playboy model got a spray tan, a boy legitimately decided that he wanted to be known as Joey Essex, a woman asked where South London was, and a pig urinated on the floor and then started drinking it. In fact I've made it sound much more exciting than it actually was. Nothing was captivating enough to make you want to tune in for a second 45 minutes, unless you harbour an inexplicable fascination with incontinent pigs.
>
> (*The Guardian*, 21 March 2011)

Heritage may be expressing a view that a percentage of the audience shares, but he ignores the fact that *TOWIE* is an interactive text that many audience members both access and interact with via, for example, Twitter and Facebook, discovering a very different narrative coherence. Heritage expresses concern about the narrative 'hyperreality' of *TOWIE* where the 'story' resembles the random events that often occur in everyday life, his main criticism being that it makes no narrative sense and therefore has little entertainment or any other value. He also claims an inability to keep track of the dialogue and pronunciation, thereby effectively placing the cast as 'other' in terms of class and taste to those who affiliate themselves with *The Guardian* and its middle-class readership.

Unlike Leigh's work, *TOWIE* may not be designed as social realism and commentary, but it still operates to reveal the social order and its tensions, and the fascination of the middle classes with working-class culture. The disdain and open contempt for the show is therefore embedded in British class structures, the lower level status of television in the hierarchy of the media, and also in its reality television form. However, to understand further how this show can be analysed in a similar manner to Leigh's work, we also have to consider how both function in the context of screenwriting practice.

Screenwriting and dramality

The cultural struggle between the elite and the popular has been a long and on-going one, and an investigation of how this still operates in terms of screenwriting practice reveals that, although opinion appears to be split, there is a case for defending dramality as a creative endeavour that still complies with traditional principles of story arcs and narrative structure. According to television writer and author William Smethurst (2005: 37–38), there exists a basic narrative structure that can be followed but one that nevertheless allows the screenwriter creative agency. This includes:

- *Situation*: visual setting – main characters – the beginning of an engaging story that involves conflict to maintain audience interest.
- *Complication*: initial situation needs to be complicated – false trails laid – aims and ambitions of character frustrated – clear indication of where the story is heading – audience interest maintained.
- *Reversal*: situation for protagonist should now reverse – if it began well it should worsen – if it began badly it should improve.

- *Climax*: the central issue should reach a climax – for television this should include action, movement and pace.
- *Resolution*: something must have changed – or it can be a twist resolution – where everything returns to normal.

Smethurst's paradigm provides points in the structure that create audience curiosity and interest, including narrative 'hooks' and conflict to keep the audience engaged with the text. His model therefore offers the screenwriter a broad and non-prescriptive guide of how to compose a narrative, one that actually promotes the author's creative flow rather than stifling it. In this way, Smethurst seemingly supports Leigh's concept of allowing enough creative space in the narrative construction process that the result is both imaginative and innovative.

Furthermore, as Nicola Lees points out in her book, *Greenlit: Developing Factual/Reality TV Ideas from Concept to Pitch*, format is vital to the development of a reality television show, functioning as its blueprint for all stages of development and execution (2010: 101). This includes a set of 'format points' that drive the narrative of each show and series, which in effect work in the same way as the basic structure identified by Smethurst. Because these format points happen at the same time and in the same way in every show, every week, the production team does not have to find a completely new approach each week, essentially allowing a range of stories to be told in the same way.

The genre and format of *TOWIE* fall into more than one category. It appears to be part 'observational documentary' and part 'docu-soap', giving us unique access into the day-to-day lives of organisations and individuals, where

> A narrator might set the scene, or the subjects themselves relate what's happening. Observational documentaries follow the same characters from week to week and are likely to return for more than one series. Each episode tends to have a self-contained story that is resolved by the end of the show. Careful casting ensures the characters are compelling enough to sustain a whole series.
>
> (Lees, 2010: 100)

The difference with *TOWIE*, however, is the 'staging' that takes place, thus creating the need for a new category or genre: dramality or reali-drama. What this adds to the observational documentary and the docu-soap is that dramatic effect has been staged purely for the purposes of entertainment. Dramality also involves the promotion of what Silverblatt calls 'cultural myths', which are identified as 'stories that tell a culture about itself' (2007: 224). Silverblatt states that 'whether a cultural myth is true, it often assumes a *mythic reality* over time, as it is told and retold over time' (2007: 225). This is certainly true of *TOWIE*, in which the mythical status of Essex and its inhabitants are confirmed and reaffirmed on a weekly basis, where people are displayed as tanorexic, uneducated, fashion-conscious and appearance-obsessed party animals. Although this does not make Essex a 'mystical place that represents an idyllic lifestyle' (Silverblatt, 2007: 228), such as Laguna Beach in *Laguna Beach: The Real Orange County* (2004–2006), it does represent it as a mystical place that hovers somewhere between an actual geographical location and an ephemeral television set that is both dislocated and hyperreal. This notion specifically aligns *TOWIE* with *Abigail's Party*, and with Leigh's working practices more generally, in that through improvisation and semi-scripting it seeks to obtain a 'heightened realism' with an emphasis on the vulgarity associated with lower middle and working classes.

In terms of writing for this sort of television, as Duncan observes, such shows are often considered by the industry as 'writer proof' (2006: 343), meaning that they use researchers instead of screenwriters. However, as Duncan goes on to say of reality television drama series such as *TOWIE*,

> these types of reality TV series do use the *series episodic technique of multiple storylines*. And in unfolding these storylines, they also use the *two-or four-act structure*. This is achieved not by a writer writing a script but by producers in an editing room using the principles behind writing an episode. To aid in this process, producers cast the 'real' people using character types that will engender conflict [...] These types of reality series use producers who understand story and structure and represent a clear opportunity for writers to use their skills in the editing process.
>
> (2006: 343)

As such, *TOWIE* is part of a new television genre that, as Duncan identifies above, through improvisation and subsequent editing provides a new form that combines reality, drama and comedy. It might be seen as a direct response to the phenomenal rise of reality television, whereby the writer provides the story and a scene outline, and the actors improvise the scenes during the actual production. This is comparable to such texts as Larry David's HBO series *Curb Your Enthusiasm* (2000–), where Larry David and other guests and celebrities play exaggerated and comedic versions of themselves. The story each week is constructed but the dialogue and actual action is improvised by the characters. There is a type of retroscript, which is a plot outline with a vague description of the dialogue, allowing space for improvisation, thereby adding realism and characterisation to the performances, in a very similar way to how both Mike Leigh and *TOWIE's* producers operate.

It is interesting to note here that one of *TOWIE's* former producers, Daran Little, is a BAFTA-nominated screenwriter who worked for many years as a storyliner and writer on the television soap *Coronation Street* (1960–). This direct fiction/non-fiction connection reinforces the idea that *TOWIE* resembles nothing more than a soap opera in aspects such as narrative structure, form and content. In a 2011 article from the *Telegraph* newspaper, Little's involvement in the show is commented on:

> Darren Little was story producer on the debut series of the 'structured reality' show, known to fans as *TOWIE*, and tasked with bringing out the 'drama and comedy' in the real lives of the characters. He told Radio Times: 'I met them and felt contaminated by their incestuous lives, but three weeks later we started to film and from there, a phenomenon was born'.

TOWIE has been such a popular success that it won a BAFTA in the viewers' choice category at the 2012 Television Awards. Little, who described the programme as a natural evolution of *Big Brother* (1999–), a show that would 'film fame-hungry but seemingly talentless young people in their natural environment', now works on another dramality show, Channel 4's *Made in Chelsea* (2011–). Although employing the same improvisational techniques as *TOWIE*, *Made in Chelsea* explores the super-rich and upper-class echelons of British society. The series presents grotesquely exaggerated representations of this particular class group, but it has not proved as popular with audiences as *TOWIE*, and does not attract such extreme and virulent panning from critics. This might be attributed to the obviously more highly educated cast, and the more closely aligned moral and ethical values that they share with the mostly middle-class media producers. What can most certainly be observed about *Made in Chelsea* is that unlike *TOWIE*, it does not engage with the same class issues and tensions as Leigh's work, albeit employing similar improvisational techniques.

Conclusion

It is perhaps reassuring that in this age of the rise of reality television, there is still a place for the skill and talent of the screenwriter. It should also be acknowledged that despite the unconventional approach of both Leigh and the producers of *TOWIE*, the screenplays for the majority of Leigh's films can still be purchased, and *TOWIE* is widely recognised as 'constructed', even at times 'scripted'. In fact, *TOWIE* carries a disclaimer at the start of the show stating that some of the scenes have been created for the purpose of entertainment. In light of this, it seems that even reality needs some help from the creative imagination of the screenwriter who, whether writing an actual screenplay or not, is contributing to contemporary and innovative drama that is in line with the continually evolving industrial and cultural environment.

Regarding screenwriting practice, far from diminishing the role of the writer, the creation of dramality can be seen as a natural development within the context of the rise and overwhelming popularity of reality television. Screenwriting skills such as creating plots, structures, narrative arcs and characterisation are still instrumental to the formation of an entertaining and compelling reality text. When considering Mike Leigh's improvisational techniques as a fundamental aspect of his critically regarded realist texts, the screenwriter's role in the production of dramality and other hybridised forms of reality television can still be deemed crucial and creative. Within the industrial landscape, Leigh's works of social realism may seem far removed from the much scorned and disparaged *TOWIE*; however, it is clear that his rigorous and thorough improvisational practices and his engagement with the tensions of the UK class system can still be seen at work, albeit in a much more constrained and demanding timescale, in this particular example of the hybridised genre of dramality.

References

BFI Screenonline, *Abigail's Party*, available at http://www.screenonline.org.uk/tv/id/461315/synopsis.html (accessed 4 October 2013).

BFI Mediatheques, *Play for Today*, available at http://www.bfi.org.uk/archive-collections/introduction-bfi-collections/bfi-mediatheques/play-today (accessed 4 October 2013).

Coveney, M. (1996) *The World According to Mike Leigh*, London: Harper Collins.

Dent, Grace, 'Grace Dent's TV OD – Essex Girls Amy and Sam are 20, but Look Like 39-Year-Olds Vainly Trying to Pass for 24' in *The Guardian*, available at http://www.theguardian.com/tv-and-radio/2010/oct/23/tv-od-the-only-way-is-essex (accessed 6 May 2012).

Duncan, S.V. (2006) *A Guide to Screenwriting Success: Writing for Film and Television*, Oxford: Rowman and Littlefield Publishers.

Goodridge, M. (2002) *Screencraft: Directing*, Hove: Rotovision.

Heritage, S. (21 March 2011) 'The Only Way Is Essex: Beyond Trash TV' in *The Guardian* Blog, available at http://www.theguardian.com/tv-and-radio/tvandradioblog/2011/mar/21/the-only-way-is-essex (accessed 4 October 2013).

Lacey, S (2007) *Tony Garnett*, Manchester: Manchester University Press.

Laguna Beach: The Real Orange County (2004–2006), Cr. Liz Gateley, Dir. Various, USA.

Lees, N. (2010) *Greenlit: Developing Factual/Reality TV Ideas From Concept to Pitch*, London: Methuen.

Made in Chelsea (2011–) Wr. Daran Little (2011–2012), Dir. Various, UK.

Medhurst, A. (2007) *A National Joke: Popular Comedy and English Cultural Identities*, London: Routledge.

Porton, R. (2002) 'Mike Leigh's Modernist Realism' in Ivone Margulies (ed.) *Rites of Realism*, Durham: Duke University Press, pp. 164–184.

Rolinson, D. (2011) 'Small Screens and Big Voices: Televisual Social Realism and the Popular' in David Tucker (ed.) *British Social Realism in the Arts since 1940*, Basingstoke: Palgrave Macmillan, pp. 172–212.

Rosenthal, A. (1995) *Writing Docudrama: Dramatizing Reality for Film and TV*, Newton, Focal Press.

Silverblatt, A. (2007) *Genre Studies in Mass Media: A Handbook*, New York: M. E. Sharpe.

Smethurst, W. (2005) *Writing for Television: How to Write and Sell Successful TV Scripts*, Oxford: How-To Books.

The Only Way is Essex (2010–) Crs. Tony Wood and Ruth Wrigley, Dir. Various, UK.

The *Telegraph*, 31 May 2011, available at http://www.telegraph.co.uk/culture/tvandradio/8546072/TOWIE-producer-says-he-felt-contaminated-by-characters.html (accessed 6 May 2012).

Whitehead, T. (2007) *British Film Makers: Mike Leigh*, Manchester: Manchester University Press.

Part III

Screenwriting and Authorship

11
Based on a True Story: Negotiating Collaboration, Compromise and Authorship in the Script Development Process

Alec McAulay

Introduction

Ian Scott's *In Capra's Shadow: The Life and Career of Screenwriter Robert Riskin* identifies the 'brilliant, individual and intuitive contribution' (2006: 10) Riskin brought to a number of Capra's films, notably in terms of creating socio-political content and relevance. Rika Pelo, arguing that Tonino Guerra is the per-eminent author of the cinema of alienation (2010: 118), points to consistencies of voice and theme in the oeuvre of the screenwriter. In the process, Pelo re-configures so-called 'auteurs' Tarkovsky and Antonioni as 'creative collaborators' with Guerra. Such identifications of a unique, authorial screenwriter voice across a range of films are a rarity in the discursive arena of film. They self-consciously posit film authorship as a site of contention, overtly or implicitly challenging the hegemony of auteur theory's privileging of the director as author. Both Scott and Pelo show that, inevitably, identifying the thematic commonalities and unique, consistent voice of a screenwriter-as-author involves 'retracing the handwriting of the screenwriter in the shadow of the director's more visible approach' (Pelo, 2010: 113).

Scheeres and Solomon, commenting on collaborative undertakings in academic research, describe the 'struggle from a position of compliance to one of productive disruption' (2000: 114). I suggest that a similar productive disruption is required in our understanding of screenwriting practice in order to make the screenwriter's authorial contribution as visible as that of the director.

* * *

189

Whilst attending film school in New York in 1998, I was struck by a thought during a class discussion on *Chinatown*. All film and media schools incorporate the critiquing of great films in their curriculum, but none that I know of screen failure films. This is an interesting conceit, not least because, as Nash notes, 'Failures test us and teach us' (2013: 151). In filmmaking as in life, we can learn from our mistakes. That thought seemed all the more pressing when I studied for my MA Screenwriting a decade later, and again took part in screenings and critiques of cinema classics. Of course, no one sets out to make a bad film, and yet bad films are plentiful. The question is, how does that happen?

Received wisdom on the script-to-screen process infers that it is one of continual improvement and enhancement. Directors, producers and editors bring notes to the drafts; actors bring an 'improv' tradition; 'happy accidents' generate wonderful scenes; editors 'save' the movie; and composers 'bring it to life': this forward momentum is overwhelmingly represented as progress towards a Platonic ideal of the film. And yet it stands to reason that the script-to-screen process does not always work effectively; that, theoretically at least, the ideal film is not always the one projected on screen, and that the best film achievable may in fact have been Draft 5 of a script that progressed in diminishing quality from that point on for another six drafts due to some misfire in the collaborative process. Whilst the regret for a film's failure may be shared by all its collaborators, the thought that a flawed version of the script undeservedly usurped a better version is arguably exclusive to the screenwriter, a notion that Price states exists because 'critical discourses, concepts and metaphors [...] have persistently pushed the screenplay text into a peculiar ontological state of non-being' (2010: 42). The hunch that one authored a better version of the film than that seen on screen is a Pyrrhic victory reserved for screenwriters, and one little explored.

This chapter therefore attempts to expand the dialogue on the screenwriter's experience of the collaboration and negotiations inherent in the script-to-screen process. The approach is informed by Giddens' conceptualisation of the self as 'a reflexive project [...in which] we are not what we are, but we are what we make ourselves' (1991: 75), and as such offers a reflective practice account of the script development process on one production. Whether this will serve as commentary on a great film, a failure film, or something in between, I cannot say, as at the time of writing the film is still in post-production. However, it will hopefully illuminate some common issues that screenwriters have to deal with as they negotiate their way through script development, contributing to research that lacks concrete examples from the writer's perspective.

Background to the project

On 31 May 2012, I received an email from Stephen Bilston,[1] an American film director based in Nagoya, Japan. It read:

> I was curious if you're still interested in doing a low-budget production of your script, *Don't*. I just read it again and would love to do a low-budget shoot of it here in Nagoya later this summer. Any thoughts?

Don't is about a young man encountering a supernatural presence when he moves to a new building. It is based on a true story. I had sent it to Stephen in February 2012 after it came up in a conversation about a different project. After I read his email, I quickly replied that I would be very interested in hearing his ideas for the project. He came back the next day:

> I think it's near ready for production with a few minor tweaks.

That was 1 June 2012. Five months and seven drafts later, the film went into production. During that period of script development, characters were added and deleted, their genders, nationalities and motivations changed, the structure oscillated between linear and non-linear, and even the title changed. The supernatural element was enhanced, reduced, and then enhanced again – just not as much. Stephen fell in and out of love with the project, at one point suggesting that we pull the plug on the whole endeavour. Needless to say, the process was energising, life affirming, maddening and deeply stressful: fairly typical of development.

Against this background, this chapter will explore issues of collaboration, compromise and authorship by offering a case study of the script-to-screen process of *Don't*. Screenwriting research encompasses theoretical considerations of how to navigate development (e.g. Peter Bloore's *The Screenplay Business*, 2013), and generalised after-the-fact reflections on particular – usually successful – films (e.g. Kevin Conroy Scott's *Screenwriters' Masterclass*). However, screenwriting practice requires that emerging screenwriters be provided with more resources offering detailed recordings of historical, contextualised cases of screenwriters re-writing their screenplays, usually in response to notes from collaborators such as directors and producers. There is currently a paucity of such materials, possibly because creative practitioners prefer that their free expression not be called to account at a later date; or, perhaps, because screenwriters are reluctant to reveal how their efforts have been enhanced by notes, or alternatively diminished, in order to reach a slightly unpalatable compromise.

Whilst considerations of the screenplay as an art form begin to emerge (e.g. Corley and Megel, this volume), practising screenwriters are aware – sometimes painfully – that the industrial context in which it sits continues to regard the screenplay as malleable, violable and open to incursion. Critical screenwriting theory, by way of explanation, posits the blueprint model of the screenplay as a staging post on the way to somewhere else (e.g. Batty and Waldeback, 2008; Nash, 2013); however, this model remains under-realised in critical and pedagogical terms. It is hoped, then, that the following outline of the development of *Don't* can in some small way fill this existing gap, enhancing our understanding of the micro considerations writers are faced with when they negotiate the development stage of screenwriting practice.

Genesis of the idea

Nagoya lies 250 kilometres to the west of Yokohama, where I am based, and so the five months of notes and re-writes took place over a series of email exchanges and Skype conversations. Those emails and my notes on those conversations provide the basis for this narrative. In order to understand the negotiations that took place, it is necessary to have some background on the screenplay narrative. What follows is a true story; or at least my sincere recall of the event.

* * *

In the summer of 1993 I was a young, single man looking for a new place to live in the provincial Japanese city of Okayama. I found an apartment building that I liked – old, dark, but well located – with a few empty units. Particularly appealing was apartment 701. However, 701 was for sale, not for rent, and instead I was shown apartment 501. No one had lived there in years. The balcony was covered in pigeon droppings, but the place was spacious, near the river and had good views of the castle. I figured that if I gave it a good clean, it would be a decent home.

The day after I viewed the apartment, the estate agent called me into her office. The building's concierge had relayed information that they now wanted to pass on to me. The apartments were big and occupied by families. No single men lived in the building. However, some years previously a single man had lived in apartment 501. One night, his girl-friend visited. They argued violently, and she stabbed him. The man died in the room. His girlfriend then went out onto the balcony and jumped to her death. Apparently, the estate agent was legally bound to tell me this. She smiled and said, 'Do you still want the apartment?'

My Japanese girlfriend at the time warned me off, telling me that the Japanese believe the ghost of a suicide stays where it dies. I felt inclined to pass, but the estate agent had taken pity on me and contacted the owner of apartment 701, convincing her to rent to me whilst keep-ing the property on sale. It was higher, brighter, with better views and had a spacious balcony. They offered to reduce the rent by 5000 yen if I promised to keep the tale of 501 a secret. I agreed.

On moving day, my football team-mates helped me and we went out afterwards. I came home at just after midnight to my first night in my new apartment. Tired and a tad squiffy, I pressed '7' on the lift. The lift ascended, and stopped – at floor 5. There was no one around. Apartment 501, the murder-suicide apartment, was right in front of me. I assumed I had pressed the wrong button, and went to press 7 – but button 7 was already illuminated. I had not pressed the wrong button.

I pressed 7 but nothing happened. I pressed 'close doors' and still nothing happened. No matter what I did, the doors stayed open. My heart racing and my palms sweating, I stared at the door of 501. I do not know how much time passed, or what made me decide to act, but in the end I bowed deeply and uttered the phrase, *Yoroshiku onegai shimasu*, a standard greeting of new arrivals to neighbours which basically means, 'Be kind to me'. I remained deep in my bow, and after a few moments the doors closed and the lift ascended to floor 7.

Idea to script to commission

I always thought that this story would make a good short film. How-ever, a true story that makes an entertaining dinner party anecdote needs much more to become a screenplay. The short film format lends itself to narrative experimentation (Batty and Waldeback, 2008: 122), but I felt that this tale was best served by conventional screenplay craft, what Alexander Mackendrick labels 'the imperative need for positive action to produce tension towards crisis' (2004: 12). The encounter of my protagonist with a ghost would only be dramatic if the external conflict resonated in some way with his own internal conflict, forcing him to make a potentially life-changing choice that the audience could empathise with. This is at the heart of the transformational arc as proposed by Dara Marks, which 'tracks the protagonist's internal struggle to rise to meet the external challenge by overcoming internal barriers' (2009: 29).

For the protagonist's encounter with the ghost to render an emotional impact, then, I felt that it needed to be the climax of rising conflict, with significant but easily understood external consequences. I developed 'a clear premise and unity of opposites' (Egri, 2007: 171) by deciding to write *Don't* as a cautionary tale, depicting how one young man on the verge of making a disastrous decision is forced, in extraordinary circumstances, to consider the potential consequences of his actions. The structure would be non-linear; an elliptical structure that would work back to its middle point. However, the tale itself would be simple: the protagonist, Archie, after moving house flirts with a woman in the bar before returning home. He is considering cheating on his girlfriend when the lift stops, the inference being that the supernatural presence, the tale of the murder-suicide lovers resonating thematically throughout, brings him to the realisation of the right thing to do. It would be an old-fashioned morality tale, but with a strong central character who goes on a journey and is faced with a choice, ultimately leading to a redemptive arc.

In transforming the tale from my story to Archie's, I was taking the initial actions that turn 'a true story' into being 'based on a true story'. As a screenwriter, my duty was not to the facts of what happened that night in 1993, but to the essence of Archie's story. What exactly constitutes the 'essence' of a story is a tricky issue, perhaps especially so when 'a true story' is purportedly depicted. Coincidentally, during the development of the script, BBC Radio 4's *The Film Programme* broadcast a four-part special that summer on the biopic, with Mark Gatiss interrogating the genre largely in terms of how it negotiates its 'based on a true story' aspect. Gatiss recalls the story of the first producer to express an interest in the Joe Orton biopic, *Prick Up Your Ears* (1987): 'I want to make it' says the producer, 'but I have two questions: Does he have to be a playwright? And does he have to be gay?'

The Orton biopic anecdote is told for laughs, but whilst writing *Don't* I was sensitive to the kernel of truth that it contains regarding compromise, embellishment and omission. That truth is brought forth in Gatiss' comparison of two biopics on Cole Porter, *Night and Day*

(1946) and *De-lovely* (2004). Gatiss notes that the former excises any mention of Porter's homosexuality, portraying him as resolutely hetero-sexual and devoted to his wife. *De-lovely* makes Porter's homosexuality a central concern. However, Gatiss is dismissive of *De-lovely* and declares *Night and Day* to be 'a biopic that absolutely mangles the truth but somehow does present something quite authentic about its subject.' 'Authentic' is a term often portentously deployed in discussion of film, but Gatiss invokes it to mean the key to a character, what makes them tick, what drives them to make the decisions they make and undertake any action, or generates the contradictions that make us all so human and flawed. A biopic is necessarily reductive, and the conventional struc-turing is to valorise this key element as defining of the subject. For Cole Porter, Gatiss imagines the 'key' was something other than his sexuality, therefore the misrepresentation of that aspect of his life is forgivable if the film succeeds in an 'authentic' representation on some deeper, more meaningful level.

This notion of honing in on the 'authentic' is central in screenwriting practice. McKee sees authenticity as residing in detail that comes from research, and like Gatiss sees emotional authenticity as allied to 'believ-able character behavior' (1999: 188). It is this authenticity that the screenwriter must author on page and protect through development. When Lionel Trilling in *Sincerity and Authenticity* declares that 'the prescriptions of society pervert human existence and destroy its authen-ticity' (1974: 161), he may well be commenting on the experience of screenwriters in the script-to-screen process. The tensions that arise when creative endeavour meets business practice may chip away at the authentic heart of the screenwriter's story. Alternatively, of course, a shared creative vision can mean an enhancement of the screenplay is achieved, but I would argue that enhancement can only take place if the screenwriter identifies the authentic essence at the heart of their story that they will choose to champion, all the while being aware of the contiguous nature of that authenticity. This is Ferrara's reflec-tive authenticity, 'the *cognitive* moment of that relation, oriented to knowing something about oneself, and the *practical* moment of that relation, oriented towards committing oneself to something' (2009: 27). This complements Fromm's rejection of relativism, when he states, 'The problem [...] is not that there is *an* interest at stake, but *which kind* of interest is at stake' (1942: 215). Be it the insight into character that Gatiss makes salient, or the imperative to do the right thing in life that I identified as the essence of *Don't*, the screenwriter finds their authentic essence and does not allow it to be compromised.

In *Don't*, I felt that I had a story of a likeable young man who is on the verge of making a disastrous life choice, only to be brought back from the brink by mysterious forces that make him realise the error of his ways. Watching friends, family or colleagues lose their way because they made a wrong choice is a universal experience. Regret is a terrible thing, and we all have moments we wish we could go back to and rectify with the benefit of hindsight. This was the collective memory of the audience that I wanted to tap into. This, I decided, was the 'authenticity' I had to protect through development. This was the story I wanted to author. Compromises and sacrifices would be made, some more bitter than others, but any deviation from this element would, I felt, mean a de-legitimisation of my own sense of ownership and authorship of the story. This would be my guiding light through development.

Script development

In early June, the initial conversations were about a change of title. From a shortlist of five, Stephen chose *Dark River*. Kurokawa, a common Japanese surname, literally translates as 'dark river', and so we invented this name for the female suicide. The choice of *Dark River* meant the nearby river, mentioned only in passing in the first draft, was now foregrounded as more of a brooding presence.

On 5 June 2012, I delivered the second draft with some minor tweaks. In the middle of the month, we had more Skype meetings. Notes were being generated by script meetings Stephen was having with his team in Nagoya, which included our director of photography, production manager, art director, locations manager and first assistant director, all individuals whom I had yet to meet. Not being able to participate in those meetings was both a blessing and a curse. My initial reaction was to want to be there, to fight the corner for favoured elements of the screenplay. On the other hand, the team consisted of a group of film-makers committed to the project who were reading the script cold, in the sense of not being privy to the notes Stephen and I generated in our Skype meetings. That is a wonderful readership to have. If the new drafts did not inspire them, it may well be because the writing was not having the desired effect.

The Nagoya group requested that Archie's girlfriend, Nobue, be more prominent. In the first draft she had only one line and she appeared in just two scenes. It was felt that increasing her on-screen presence would make it easier for Stephen to pitch the role to an actress. Whilst I agreed with the note and saw that more screen time for Nobue kept the consequences of losing her current for the audience, the challenge in the second draft was to give her more of a presence without losing the overall pace and economy of the story. The result was that Nobue was given a more active role in the scene where Archie moves into the flat, and is brought back in the post-move celebration scene at the bar, where her early exit frees Archie to flirt with Sayuri (the name given to the temptress). With these changes, the script went from seven pages in Draft 1 to eight pages in Draft 2.

More notes on finer details led to Draft 3 and then, on 24 June, I delivered Draft 4. In between, Stephen's team had suggested that in the climactic scene, Archie actually be dialing Sayuri's number in the lift rather than looking at her card, another excellent note as it takes the character to the brink.

Over the summer, Stephen and I both travelled and communication slowed somewhat. Stephen sent an email on 12 July saying he thought Draft 4 was 'nice'. The word 'nice' has the same emasculating effect on screenwriters as it has on potential suitors. That word, and the fact that Stephen was keen to meet in person (we never did) to talk over Draft 4 put me slightly ill at ease. Stephen was casting, securing locations and working on other projects. The bar setting had become a bowling alley. Sayuri worked there and past flirtation with Archie was implied. A new character had appeared, a mad Old Woman living in the building, who possibly became unhinged when she witnessed Kurokawa's suicide. A key line delivered to Archie by the concierge, 'I heard the THUD! when she hit the ground,' was given to the Old Woman, preceded by 'Her name was Kurokawa.' The Old Woman was a stock horror character designed to allow an unsettling gaze onto Archie, and make the audience jump out of their seats with her sudden appearances. The current draft ran to 13 pages.

No more was said about Draft 4 until 14 August, when the following arrived from Stephen:

Sorry for not being able to touch base as regularly as planned. *Dark River* has been moving along nicely with almost every location secured and most of the roles cast. I had a few thoughts regarding the script that I wanted to run by you. Some major changes but I feel like it could work better and help simplify things.

1. Cut out the bowling alley telling the story to his friends and just make it linear. So for example, the film starts with Archie heading to the apartment, he meets the realtor, goes out for drinks, gets a call from the realtor, is told about the suicide, etc.

2. Bring in Nobue earlier. IF we go with the above approach then Nobue could meet him at the apartment and help translate to the realtor. This would allow us to get to know Nobue earlier.
3. Return to the idea of the office lady flirting with Archie and being the aggressor.

Hopefully these ideas make sense. Let me know your thoughts.

The non-linear structure we had until Draft 4 consisted of starting in the bowling alley with Archie telling the story to his friends. We see the story in flashback, up to the point where the estate agent calls him in to explain the murder-suicide event. He then receives another call from the estate agent whilst telling the story, with the offer of 701, and at this point the story proceeds linearly until the end. Whilst I felt the partial non-linear structure served the story best, I was willing to explore the possibility that I might be wrong on this. The other notes, however, were more problematic. I replied the next day as follows:

1. Linear is fine. I'm not sure how it will affect running time 'til I give it a go – we'll see how that one goes.
2. I take your point on wanting to foreground Nobue more. I don't think she should translate – double the screen time. But there is a bigger problem than that. If she is in the apartment viewing scene, the audience will need to know that she is Archie's girlfriend, but that they are not going to live together. That will plant the question 'Why?' in their heads, and as we are not going to answer that question, we shouldn't pose it in the first place. We do not want Nobue to have a through-line of her own – short films really can't handle more than one major character. So let's have her on screen so that the audience is aware of what is at stake for Archie. My first idea is perhaps we go back to Archie telling the story, but instead of bowling, he is watching Nobue do something (yoga?). Anyway, these are early thoughts, let me mull it over ...
3. Fine on going back to the OL. I did like your idea of having Archie make the call from the lift; I take it you are happy to stick with that?

Stephen replied straight away:

I agree with you on point 2. We definitely don't want her storyline to conflict with Archie. However, it would be nice to see how a more linear approach would serve the story. Let's give that a go and see what happens.

Draft 5 was the linear version. I also introduced a doll for Old Woman to carry. Whilst re-writing I felt there was a problem in the climactic scene in that Archie is reacting to a closed door. This seemed thin and static, and we somehow had to raise the tension by giving Archie something more visually disturbing to react to (a closed door is only scary if someone eventually has to open it). By having Old Woman carry a doll that is then abandoned on floor 5, Archie would have a 'face' to react to. I sent off Draft 5 to Stephen on 16 August. Stephen replied the same day:

I like it.

The next day, on 17 August, I got another email from Stephen:

You're going to HATE me. I just re-read draft 1 again...and I liked it. Humh...thoughts?

Clearly, this was unexpected, and somewhat of a blow. Processing this message, I recalled a workshop I attended where the presenter had said that whilst some notes from directors are about the script, others are a cry for help. This was undoubtedly the latter. It seemed to me that Stephen had become too immersed in the project and had developed tunnel vision. The fact that he had returned to Draft 1 suggested we all needed to step back from the project and take stock of what we had, and remind ourselves of what we set out to achieve. At this point, the ownership I felt of each draft was undiminished, and there was no note that had been incorporated that fettered the project or in any way diluted my 'voice'. On the contrary, in terms of making the film more clearly a ghost story, each re-write had taken the narrative forward. The linear/non-linear aspect was a non-issue, as I had written each version to allow for either to be realised in the edit. The script had taken on a handful of horror tropes – a dark river, a mad old woman and her foreboding pronouncements, a scary doll – which enhanced the genre appeal. At the same time, I could easily live without these elements if Stephen wanted to go back to a simpler, more stripped-down telling of the tale. As a result, I rejected the option of trying to write another draft that balanced all these elements in favour of a conversation with Stephen about his vision and passion for the project. As essential as a director's passion is, it can get lost in the logistics of pre-production and the competing voices of script development. Instead of looking how to go forward, then, I felt it best to re-trace our steps to this point, to see where Stephen had lost that initial passion. This also seemed the best way to ensure that the project would actually make it into production. I emailed back:

> Well, the short answer is; as director, you need to find your 'vision' of the film, and it sounds like you are not there yet. Or, more likely, I imagine you have competing visions and are not sure which way to go.
>
> I won't go into a long answer 'til we talk, partly because I am not sure what draft you are referring to. Is it the very first one you read, with no old woman, no dark river, etc...?
>
> I think all the elements are there across all the five drafts, it is just up to you what you want to include and/or leave out. Personally, in terms of structure, I prefer the elliptical structure with Archie's narration (Draft 4). It is more dynamic. Draft 5 is, as you said, simpler, but what you lose is some of Archie's devilishness and charm.
>
> I'll try and get the Skype on so we can go through it. As I said, I think it is a case of deciding what to keep, and what to lose.

Stephen replied on 18 August:

> I just like them all. I'm going to do some combining this weekend. I'll send the 'director's cut' on Monday.

I sent an encouraging response, but this was not the reply I had expected. One part of me was uncomfortable with the fact that Stephen assumed he could go to a director's draft at this stage. On another short film I scripted, the director's draft led to a whole new second act, with the director then trying to take sole writer credit. That is why I had negotiated a sole writer credit at the outset with Stephen on *Dark River*, and hoped that he would remember that. If the writing credit was to be shared on this project, it would have to be negotiated from a default setting of sole credit to me.

On 20 August, Draft 6 arrived: Stephen's draft. He wrote in his email:

> I did some editing. Changed some things and still tried to bring Nobue in sooner. Also, introduced an idea with Nobue and Archie moving in together. Let me know your thoughts.

Before I even read the draft, I knew we were in crisis. A line had been crossed. The essence of this story was a charismatic young man who is on the verge of losing his loving girlfriend through a moment of weakness. What was presented here was a protagonist who is considering cheating on his girlfriend on the day they move in together. My fears were confirmed when I read the draft. The fact that Stephen had written a draft that did not work was not the point. Writing and re-writing is our time to experiment and play; we are allowed to fail. The point is to recognise the failure, learn from it, and use that learning to hone a better draft. I did not 'blame' Stephen for this violation of the essence as I had identified it: the fault lay with me as I clearly had not communicated my point effectively enough. Screenwriting requires talent, time to write, and the ability to collaborate and compromise. It also requires perseverance, which more than anything else, became the salient quality I had to fall back on at this point.

Whilst the emotional essence of Archie's story had been severely compromised – obliterated, in my view – there were logistical problems with the story. Apart from Nobue and Archie now moving in together, the Old Woman had been cut, and along with her, our dark river motif and the 'thud' line. The screenplay had been slashed from 13 pages to 7, with narrative consistency and rhythm sacrificed to achieve this economy. I wrote back the same day:

> I can see that you are after economy here. Getting it down to 7 pages is quite a challenge. We should try and talk about that at some point, because I do have some major issues with this draft and email always makes things sound harsher than intended. But I hope we know each other well enough now that we can be honest and know that any comments and criticism are for the benefit of the project.

> With regard to this draft, it certainly is more sparse, but I think we have lost more than we have gained. One thing about this draft is there are inconsistent elements so I don't really 'get' bits of it (see my notes) making it difficult to comment in broad terms. I have attached scene-by-scene notes to highlight some of these problems. Right now, there are two main points I would make.

> 1. Having Nobue move in does not work. Archie should be a charismatic rascal. Having him try to connect with another woman on his first night living with his girlfriend makes him a bastard. The fact that he does it walking into his new home makes him a stupid bastard. The audience will dislike him.

2. I think Old Woman has to come back. We have lost the sense of foreboding she brought. The line 'I heard the thud' is one such moment. Also, with no Kurokawa line, we have no Dark River, so the title no longer makes sense. I thought water would be one motif you'd thread through the film, but that seems to be gone.
3. From the way you've put this draft together I assume you want a leaner, tighter, less populated story. If so, let's chat and figure out how to achieve that.
4. I attached two pages with 11 notes.

I felt this could go one of three ways. The first possibility was that Stephen would see that Draft 6 was not working, decide that all the drafts did not work and call a halt to production. The second scenario was that he would accept my misgivings on Draft 6, and we would talk through his need for economy and find a way to achieve it in Draft 7, to be written by me. There was a third, worst-case scenario, where Stephen would insist that Draft 6 was what he wanted, call it a locked script and forge ahead into production. Having gotten to know Stephen better over the preceding months, I felt the last scenario to be unlikely, though not impossible. I made a mental note that if this scenario played out, I would withdraw from the project, and take no credit on the final film. The tale that I felt ownership of was 'loveable rascal' Archie's tale. The 'stupid bastard' Archie in Draft 6 was a stranger; Archie had become some callous dolt who I did not want to take responsibility for.

Whether or not I would have followed through on this mental note to myself is now a moot point, as Stephen replied the same day:

Thanks for the quick reply. I'm definitely trying to make it shorter. I can see your points. Sadly, we're running out of time. We really need to land on a solid draft this week or I'm going to need to postpone another month.

Do you have any ideas what to do?

Once again, rather than re-write in a way that I might have *thought* Stephen wanted, and to retain my desired sense of authorship, I felt my role was to re-kindle Stephen's passion for the project, which had clearly demised. I wrote back straight away:

Well, not sure what to suggest because I don't really know what the problem is. That's why we should talk so I can figure out what you really want.

We started out with a simple, true tale that you loved. What is it that has cooled your reaction to that first draft? Is it simple over-familiarity? (I fall in and out of love with my projects...) Is there something 'missing' – more tension needed? A clearer threat to Archie? If you can tell me what is not there, I can try to put it in...

This was the definite low point on the project for me as a screenwriter. There was a moment when I realised that I had delivered five drafts with the end result that the director's enthusiasm seemed to have drained rather than grown. He had gone from excitement to exhausted bewilderment, and we were now at a stage where Stephen was talking of postponing (which I was sure would mean cancelling completely) production.

We set up a Skype meeting where I fought for the project, but in terms of keeping it a story about my Archie, the brash, cool, vulnerable and immature young man. Stephen and I talked it through, and we realised that a simple tale well told was what we had been seeking from day one, what we should hold on to, and what would best serve our need for economy. I pressed my notion of the essence of the story, and Stephen seemed to regain some of his early passion for the project. He agreed that Nobue should not move in, but insisted that she should be more 'sassy'.

On 22 August, I finished Draft 7. We open on Nobue jogging by the river. She gets to say 'Four men with big balls!' to the bowlers. There is a non-linear structure, with Archie telling the tale whilst bowling. The exchange with Sayuri is a cutaway seen from Japanese friend Tadashi's point-of-view. Old Woman is gone but the concierge delivers the 'thud' line. It came out at seven pages, and I emailed it to Stephen with the following message:

I think we've really nailed it here; we have the economy without sacrificing Archie's attraction, and Nobue is actually more vibrant and vivacious.

On 23 August, Stephen wrote back:

This works! I'll move this draft into production and start working on a shooting script. I still want to play with the moving in scene and trying to add more conflict sooner. There is still something that seems to drag. I keep asking myself around page 4–5, 'Is anything happening...why do I care?'

Although Stephen's reply was more guarded than I had hoped, we were going into production, with Archie as I had originally envisaged him, his emotional journey intact. I wrote back the next day, cautioning on the rush to conflict. Short films are usually either big on plot, with a penchant for twisty endings, or character thumbnail sketches; but rarely combine both. I felt we could have both, and sent Stephen a link to Lynne Ramsay's *Gasman* (1998) as an example of a slow build to conflict after having established characters, the conflict coming out of character rather than for its own sake. Stephen's only comment on *Gasman* was that he loved it.

Shooting began of Draft 7 in November 2012. I was on location for part of the shoot and some changes evolved at that time. However, I realised during shooting that a fundamental shift had taken place in my own sense of authorial claim on the story. Matthew Lott, the actor who plays Archie, completely inhabited Archie. He was gracious enough to approach me whilst shooting to discuss the character. I told him that Archie was now his, and that he should take ownership. The writing had been developed thoroughly. I had been given my space to work and experiment, and now it was the actor's turn to do the same. Stephen had assembled a cast of fine actors who would now bring their craft to the story and would enact, as well as enhance, what Stephen and I had achieved on the page. We had established a shared vision of the emotional journey we wanted the audience to go on: the actors seemed to understand that vision, and possess the skills to realise it; and the crew was in place to work with Stephen, committed to making it happen. I felt sure *my* story would be the one shot, but I also believe that films come to life in the edit. As that process is ongoing at the time of writing this chapter, I cannot comment on the outcome; except that an exchange is still taking place between myself and the Nagoya team. We are still making the film. We are still writing the film.

Conclusion

As Giddens suggests, 'Rituals of trust and tact in day-to-day life [...] touch on the most basic aspects of ontological security' (1991: 47). The script-to-screen process is one such ritual of trust and tact. Giddens notes the 'threats and opportunities' (ibid.: 57) that modernity presents to our sense of self as we experience such rituals. The script-to-screen process is perhaps impossible to fully grasp, let alone teach in the classroom, unless it has been experienced. But what research like this can do is raise awareness of the tensions that evolve around authorship and ownership of a screenplay, situating them not as occasional, but inherent in the development process. As Gubrium and Holstein note,

> It is not that narrators lose all control of their own stories, nor that stories are no longer about those whose experiences are communicated. Rather, ownership is increasingly mediated by widely available communicative frameworks and, thus, is more diffusely proprietary than ever.
>
> (1998: 180)

Jennifer Moon talks of 'emotional insight', a type of 'learning that results in a behaviour change that seems to be more profound than simply knowing something' (2004: 51). What screenwriting research can do, and must do, is provide further case studies and analyses of writers re-writing, reflecting on *in situ* practice, expressing both the craft they impose on the story and the creative imperative that allows them to say, both during and after collaborative development, that *this* story is *my* story. Only then can we truly understand notions of collaboration, compromise and authorship in screenwriting, and for those of us who teach, impart them onto our students in effective and practice-based ways.

My experiences on *Dark River*, at times fraught and maddening, came to a satisfying conclusion because as a writer I feel that I had a clear notion of what I wanted to say. The emotional insight brought to the process, mediated by it, and stored for deployment on future projects, is an essential skill. It is one all screenwriters should embrace in the site of contention that is the script-to-screen process.

Note

1. This is a pseudonym and is being used for the purpose of protecting the identity of the real director.

References

Batty, C. and Waldeback, Z. (2008) *Writing for the Screen: Creative and Critical Approaches*, Basingstoke: Palgrave Macmillan.
Bloore, P. (2013) *The Screenplay Business: Managing Creativity and Script Development in the Film Industry*, Abingdon: Routledge.
Chinatown (1974) Wr. Robert Towne, Dir. Roman Polanski, USA, 130 mins.
Corley, E.L. and Megel, J. (2014) 'White Space: An Approach to the Practice of Screenwriting as Poetry' in Craig Batty (ed.) *Screenwriters and Screenwriting: Putting Practice into Context*, Basingstoke: Palgrave Macmillan, pp. 11–29.

De-lovely (2004) Wr. Jay Cocks, Dir. Irwin Winkler, USA, 125 mins.

Egri, L. (2007) *The Art of Dramatic Writing*, Milton Keynes: Wildside Press.

Ferrara, A. (2009) 'Authenticity Without a True Self' in Phillip Vannini and J. Patrick Williams (eds.) *Authenticity in Culture, Self, and Society*, Farnham: Ashgate.

Fromm, E. (1942) *The Fear of Freedom*, London: Routledge.

Gasman (1998) Wrs. Lynne Ramsay and Harold Manning, Dir. Lynne Ramsay, UK, 15 mins.

Giddens, A. (1991) *Modernity and Self-identity: Self and Society in the Late Modern Age*, Oxford: Polity Press.

Gubrium, J.F. and Holstein, J.A. (1998) 'Narrative Practice and the Coherence of Personal Stories' in *The Sociological Quarterly*, 39(1), 163–187.

Mackendrick, A. (author) and Cronin, P. (ed.) (2004) *On Film-Making: An Introduction to the Craft of the Director*, New York: Faber and Faber.

Marks, D. (2009) *Inside Story: The Power of the Transformational Arc*, London: A&C Black.

McKee, R. (1999) *Story: Substance, Structure Style and the Principles of Screenwriting*, London: Methuen.

Moon, J. (2004) *A Handbook of Reflective and Experiential Learning*, London: Routledge-Falmer.

Nash, M. (2013) 'Unknown Spaces and Uncertainty in Film Development' in *Journal of Screenwriting*, 4(2), 149–162.

Night and Day (1946) Wrs. Charles Hoffman, Leo Townsend and William Bowers, Dir. Michael Cutiz, USA, 128 mins.

Pelo, R. (2010) 'Tonino Guerra: The Screenwriter as a Narrative Technician or as a Poet of Images? Authorship and Method in the Writer–Director Relationship' in *Journal of Screenwriting*, 1(1), 113–129.

Price, S. (2010) *The Screenplay: Authorship, Theory and Criticism*, Basingstoke: Palgrave Macmillan.

Prick Up Your Ears (1987) Wr. Alan Bennett, Dir. Stephen Frears, UK, 111 mins.

Scheeres, H. and Solomon, N. (2000) 'Whose Text? Methodological Dilemmas in Collaborative Research Practice' in Alison Lee and Cate Poynton (eds.) *Culture & Text: Discourse and Methodology in Social Research and Cultural Studies*, St. Leonards, NSW: Allen & Unwin, pp. 114–131.

Scott, I. (2006) *In Capra's Shadow: The Life and Career of Screenwriter Robert Riskin*, Lexington: University Press of Kentucky.

Scott, K.C. (2006) *Screenwriters' Masterclass: Screenwriters Talk about Their Greatest Movies*, New York: Newmarket Press.

Trilling, L. (1974) *Sincerity and Authenticity*, Boston: Harvard University Press.

12
Sarah Phelps on Writing Television: Adaptation, Collaboration and the Screenwriter's Voice

Kate Iles

Introduction

In a *Southbank Show* interview with Melvyn Bragg to coincide with the launch of *Pennies from Heaven*, Dennis Potter stated emphatically, 'I don't write *for* television, I *write* television'(14 February 1978). Potter's implication was that television fiction is driven by those who create the texts upon which it is based; that it is derived from those who create the blueprint: the screenwriters. Quite simply, his words emphasised that without the screenwriter, television fiction would not exist. This is an idea advocated today by television writer Sarah Phelps, whose work over the last ten years has encompassed nearly a hundred episodes of the BBC soap opera *EastEnders*, episodes of television drama series *No Angels* (Channel 4) and *Being Human* (BBC3), and two high profile BBC adaptations of work by Charles Dickens: *Oliver Twist* in 2007 and *Great Expectations* in 2011. Phelps acknowledges the power of the screenwriter's ideas and craft as central to her practice, and it is this sense of both authorship and ownership that earns her not only great recognition for her work, but greater recognition than her counterparts in the world of film, where the role of the director continues to dominate.

With particular reference to Phelps' Dickens adaptations, which have significantly raised her profile in the last five years, this chapter will thus explore how 'writing television' works for Phelps, both practically and philosophically, and how her approach impacts on those working in collaboration with her. Through extensive interviews with the writer and her production colleagues, and an examination of her written texts, together with the resulting broadcast productions, it will investigate the defining role of the screenplay in establishing the key visual, narrative and psychological markers in television drama.

Finding a voice

For Phelps, along with a love of words and ponies, television was her chief childhood preoccupation: 'I am a child of the small screen. I grew up watching it and I remember being transported by TV shows when I was a kid. It was the theatre in the corner of the room' (author's interview, 2013). She never envisaged that writing was a career option and came to it relatively late, having worked as a costume assistant at the Royal Shakespeare Company (RSC) before being invited to take part in a writing for radio workshop and, in 1997, landing a job on the BBC World Service twice weekly radio soap opera, *Westway*. Although she has a degree in English, Phelps has never studied screenwriting and remains sceptical of the armoury of technical writing manuals with which screenwriting students are expected to engage. As she says, 'This [screenwriting self-help] is a multimillion pound industry and it is largely useless. It has a tendency to smother creativity.'

When asked how she approaches her own writing, Phelps is adamant that she will never write treatments, scene breakdowns, outlines, character backstories or any of the other preparatory elements that are typically expected from students. 'I simply sit down with a blank computer screen and write. I need to feel my characters moving and hear them speaking before I can decide what to do with them.' She refuses to acknowledge a system or formula behind her writing, but an analysis of her work reveals key characteristics that make it clearly identifiable and attractive to drama commissioners, directors and audiences alike.

The chance to work on *EastEnders* in 2002 was Phelps' professional breakthrough. By 2004 she was a lead writer on the long-running soap and by the time she departed in 2007, she had written 97 episodes and was recognised by both fans and the popular press as one of the show's best writers. She was noted for her ability to handle storylines and characters unflinchingly, but with a distinctive degree of warmth and humour. The series was already a personal favourite: 'I was a bit obsessed with it. *EastEnders* told stories about the people we were, or the people our grandparents were.' Remarking that '*EastEnders* draws a huge number of viewers to the rest of BBC1's content. You mess with them at your peril', she is fiercely defensive of its place at the heart of the schedule. Her challenge, after the relative obscurity and creative freedom of *Westway*, was to find a way of working with a set of iconic characters and relationships that would inspire both her and the audience. The relentlessly industrial, conveyor belt process of soap opera production is a daunting one for many writers, and as Phelps attests herself, 'It's a behemoth, a factory, so you need to find those characters who make your blood beat, who give you a blast of oxygen which forces you to write about them.' This visceral approach, Phelps taking a scalpel to her characters to find where their heart is, is what made her work so recognisable to an army of *EastEnders* viewers.

Asked about her favourite storylines, Phelps points to two: the return of Dirty Den to Albert Square after his apparent death at the bottom of a canal ten years previously, together with Jean Slater's attempted suicide and daughter Stacey's unexpectedly compassionate, measured response to her mother's depressive illness. Both of these major storylines required the kind of subtle character building and psychological excavation that runs counter to soap opera's reputation for car crash melodrama and hyperbole. Of Den's reuniting with his daughter, Sharon, Phelps says:

> I liked writing the sharpness of wit but I also loved what those characters meant to each other, the complexities of what they felt for each other. It was murky and dangerous territory and the situation humanised Den. He was never a superhero; he was a wideboy. He fancied himself and a myth had grown up around him. There was something of a Greek Tragedy about him. That terrible deception: Den had let his daughter think that he was dead; how grubby, how cruel, how sordid. But it was so human. You tell a lie and then that lie takes on a life of its own. When is the right time to step out of it, to tell the truth? Never, really. And Den told so many lies in his life, to everyone. An arch deceiver, always scrabbling to stay on top.
>
> (Walford Web (Sarah Phelps interview), 2009)

Commenting on the difficulties of addressing issues such as depression and suicide in a mainstream soap, Phelps is surprisingly upbeat. She sees a loyal audience who know their characters inside out as an opportunity for exploring challenging subjects, not a barrier to it:

> The fan base means that you can sometimes travel to dark places and the audience will come with you. I think it's about the bond of trust between the show and the audience. No one wants to be lectured to, or horrified or gratuitously scared, or feel like they've been hit over the head with a pious brickbat of an issue. The skill is in presenting

a character like Stacey Slater who looks like she's a right selfish little madam, all about herself, and then slowly, stealthily peeling back that mask so we can see and understand how she is like she is; see her heart and soul.

(Walford Web, 2009)

This energetic and psychological approach to her characters is a defining quality of Phelps' writing, and that she speaks about them with precise understanding demonstrates just how much she invests in analysing and investigating them and their backstories, to find out 'what their truth is and what makes their heart beat'. It is also the means by which Phelps draws a degree of creative energy from what many television screenwriters would consider inflexible characters who offer little for the imagination to work with.

None of this intensive background work takes the form of lengthy character outlines, mind maps or written biographies: the materials screenwriting students are routinely asked to produce. Nevertheless, for Phelps, the key information influencing what her characters do and say is part of a complex, nuanced relationship with them. Her characters lead her into situations and exchanges with complete credibility and integrity, and the fluidity with which she talks about their motives and relationships demonstrates the strength of the bond she has with them.

A conversation with Dickens

Phelps wrote for *EastEnders* until she 'could feel [her] oxygen running out', and having honed her craft under its relentless spotlight, she turned to working with another set of iconic characters with a passionate fan base when the BBC asked her to start work on an adaptation of *Oliver Twist*. She claims that the call came, 'not because I'm an aficionado of Charles Dickens, but because they suddenly found themselves without a writer about six weeks before production was due to start, and they needed someone who could turn it around really quickly'. There was, in fact, already a connection at the BBC between Dickens adaptations and its flagship soap opera. In 2005, the corporation had taken a radical new approach to Dickens' classic novels by adapting *Bleak House* into easily digestible 30-minute episodes, scheduled twice weekly directly after *EastEnders*. As Christine Geraghty (2012: 14) has argued, this adaptation scripted by Andrew Davies, who had forged his reputation with high quality Sunday night classic serials, was deliberately targeted at *EastEnders*' large, youthful audience. It was produced and marketed with the observation that 'the Dickens novel was very much the soap opera of its day' (BBC Press Release (Danny Cohen), 2003) as a central premise.

It was a strategy that paid off. Audience figures for *Bleak House* were high, the press response largely positive, and the series won Best Drama Serial at both the BAFTA and Royal Television Society awards in 2006. It might have been expected then that BBC1 should wish to repeat this success with an *Oliver Twist* adaptation screened nightly during the week before Christmas 2007, this time pushing the 'Dickens for a soap opera audience' idea further by asking one of *EastEnders'* most celebrated writers to adapt it. Andrew Davies, it should be noted, has never written an episode of a soap opera.

Tackling *Oliver Twist*, says Phelps with characteristic gusto, was 'like a rush of oxygen straight into the face', but she is predictably enigmatic when asked to deconstruct the adaptation process. There are over 50 film, television and stage versions of the story, but Phelps did not watch any of them, apart from Lionel Bart's musical film, *Oliver!*, which she had seen as a child. Nor did she engage with the vast library of scholarly analysis pertaining to Dickens' life and work. There was no attempt to doggedly transpose Dickensian dialogue, prose or even plotting into a condensed television format. 'I read the novel twice and then put it to one side and started writing', she explains. The only steer from the BBC was that she could not include expensive rooftop chase scenes. But this apparently dismissive attitude to the practical business of adaptation, and the lack of any clearly defined method in her approach, is misleading. In fact, Phelps developed a powerfully intelligent connection with Dickens, his view of life, his characters and his potential television audience, which becomes obvious through a closer examination of the production and those who worked on it with her.

A major challenge in adapting *Oliver Twist*, asserts Phelps, was that 'it's a novel which everyone thinks they know but actually they don't', and so managing the audience's expectations was very difficult. She was surprised, for example, by how Oliver himself disappears from much of the book, by its rampant anti-Semitism, the sentimentality and the sanctimoniousness of some of the prose, and the messiness of some of the plotting. But, as she points out, 'the thing that's most annoying about Charles Dickens is that just when you are getting ready to throw the book across the room, he absolutely slams you with an image, a detail, or a character'. As she observed with the *EastEnders* audience, with a solid and devoted fan base, Dickens was able to take his readers to dark, difficult places they would not necessarily feel comfortable with.

The degrading cruelties of the Victorian workhouse and the brutality of the 19th-century criminal justice system are two such places deliberately exposed in *Oliver Twist*. 'He used his stories to make people care', Phelps remarks, and it is a principle that clearly lies behind her own versions of his work.

On reading the novel, Phelps says that she had to find out what Dickens had to say to her, what William Goldman defines as the screenwriter's individual emotional connection with the source material. Goldman is adamant that 'in any adaptation you have to make changes. You simply must', yet he adds, 'While you are altering, you must remain faithful to two things: the author's intention and the emotional core of the original as it affected you' (1984: 324). In conversation with Phelps, it is clear that although she sees writing as a seamlessly organic process, there were issues, individual storylines and relationships that she responded to in particular, and which drove her adaptation.

One of the things Phelps admires about Dickens is what she describes as 'his furious engagement with the world as he saw it and the use of his writing to address some of its inequalities'. In *Oliver Twist*, she identified one of his chief preoccupations as the prejudice of Victorian society towards its children, who were at once commoditised and pampered, and also the source of terrible exploitation and deprivation. Contemporary parallels were not hard to find in the way that 21st-century children are both targeted for their influence on the spending patterns of their parents, and vilified for their bad behaviour and educational underperformance. Phelps comments that at the time of writing the screenplay, the tabloid press was awash with references to children as 'urban rats' and 'hoodlums'; precisely how Fagin's children would have been perceived by many of Dickens' readers. Cultural attitudes to children are thus what form a key thematic foundation to her adaptation: Dodger and his associates are portrayed as the urban rats of their day; Bill Sikes as the hardened, battle-scarred, repeat offending, scrounging member of the underclass they might grow up to be. The need to create a version of the story that would resonate with her own concerns, as well as the preoccupations of the modern television audience, was key to her approach: 'Hopefully the story responds to the nature of the era in which we are. What I really wanted to write and what I really hope I achieved is an *Oliver Twist* for our times.'

Phelps identifies other important elements which formed her first impression of Dickens' novel, and which would be central to her script: the implicit scandal and tragedy surrounding the fate of Oliver's mother and its terrible impact on the Brownlow family; an obsession with the haves and the have-nots, and their desperation to avoid or escape poverty; the doomed love affair between Nancy and Bill Sikes; the anti-Semitism running through Dickens' portrayal of Fagin. Having processed these initial observations, Phelps notes that she needed to be able to describe the story in one sentence, what Goldman suggests encapsulates what it is 'really about' (1984: 313). For Phelps, it was simply this: 'The orphan child comes home.' Distilled to what she calls its crystalline base, this was, for her, the focus of Dickens' multi-layered story: 'For me, as a writer, this sentence is the light that guides me.'

Viewed as a whole, this search for home against the enormous odds of the horrific and usually fatal conditions of the workhouse, enslavement at an undertaker's, homelessness, the perversion of the 19th-century judicial system, and the plotting of those out to stop Oliver or profit from his death, is precisely what Phelps' *Oliver Twist* becomes. Putting the character of Oliver resolutely at its centre, over five episodes we follow him from the loss of his mother through the confrontation of a set of apparently insurmountable obstacles to his final restoration with his family in the form of Mr Brownlow.

Creating a character for Oliver that would convincingly make him a strong, likeable protagonist required considerable deviation from the novel, in which Dickens repeatedly describes him as 'poor Oliver', continually 'stammering' and 'weeping'. Phelps says:

He's always weak and whimsical, almost a portrait of what a Victorian readership would feel a deserving pauper child was. He reacts to life rather than does things. I was very clear I didn't want a whiney, horrible Oliver. He's a gutsy kid who's searching for something. He's already gone through so much in the workhouse system that when he gets home you want him to be safe and you think he deserves it.

When Phelps' Oliver asks for more, he does it because he wants to, not because he has drawn the short straw amongst the other workhouse kids. Dickens' Oliver pleads with Sikes: 'For the love of all the bright angels that rest in heaven, have mercy on me' (Dickens, 2007: 140). In Phelps' version, he looks him in the eye and says, 'I'm not scared of you.'

The other character radically altered for a contemporary audience is Fagin, who is portrayed by Dickens with unapologetic anti-Semitic spite, rarely mentioned without the preface 'vile' or 'withered', and usually referred to contemptuously as simply 'the Jew'. Fagin is, says Phelps, the one character on whom Dickens fails to shine a revealing spotlight to even try and find out what is going on beneath the surface. 'It made me angry,' she says, 'which is good for a writer.' As such,

> Rather than sweeping it under the carpet, I wanted to look at it in its nasty, squinty, horrible little eye. Victorian readers still believed in the idea of the child murdering Jew and I felt I needed to rehabilitate Fagin, to establish him as Oliver's rescuer and source of safety. I kept thinking, 'who is Fagin, really? Does he really want to be here surrounded by kids demanding sausages when he's trying to keep a kosher household?' I imagined him as this incredible erudite dandy, a victim of the European pogroms whose dream would be to attend sophisticated soirees discussing Spinoza. I wanted all that frustration, that sense of being an outsider and a pariah.
>
> (*Oliver Twist: Behind the Scenes*, 2008)

Fagin is thus given a voice in Phelps' adaptation through the invention of Ezekial, the pet raven who functions as a familiar to whom he talks and is able to express his inner self. In her screenplay, the court scene in which Fagin is condemned to death is rewritten to give full voice to the institutionalised anti-Semitism of the age. The sadistic judge who passes sentence tries to force Fagin to show his repentance by praying, publically, to a Christian God. But with only his faith left to him, Fagin refuses and is sentenced to hanging. For Phelps, he is condemned to death primarily because of his Jewishness.

No such creative liberties were necessary with Nancy and Bill Sikes, apart from the fact that Phelps wrote Nancy with a mixed race actor in mind (Sophie Okonedo was eventually cast in the role). This was 'because it's absolutely plausible and because I'm sick of watching period drama where every single person is white'. Phelps comments that in contrast to Fagin, it is clear from the novel that Dickens had shone a spotlight on Sikes' character and backstory, and so he is more three-dimensional than the brutal thug of popular imagination. She cites scenes from the book where Sikes acts with unexpected tenderness towards Nancy, and she made a point of dramatising the disturbing visions of Nancy that he experiences after her death. 'Dickens writes Sikes as a man with a conscience, turned bad through experience and necessity. You can feel him getting excited when he writes about him and Nancy.' In her version, Bill has a tragic moment of reflection after Nancy's murder and deliberately hangs himself in an act of contrition, rather than falling to his death accidentally. Phelps writes the murder scene with penetrating simplicity: 'Sikes looks down at Nancy's body and understands with sudden clarity that there is no more Nancy, just the space where she was and that he's done it. Him. And he is gripped with the most appalling fear' (2007). In a telling final scene Phelps has a wretched Artful Dodger witnessing his friend Fagin's hanging in front of a baying mob, before heading off into the streets with a self-conscious swagger, and with Bullseye by his side, her indication that he is destined for an adulthood even more brutal and damaged than that of Sikes.

This process of excavation and subtle highlighting of characters, themes and events to suit a mainstream television audience is also clear in Phelps' manipulation of the novel's plot, which she says struck her as 'messy and barely plausible', particularly towards the end. This lack of structural coherence is a possible consequence of the novel's initial monthly serialisation in 24 parts during 1837 and 1838, which could have meant that Dickens wrote each episode without a clear vision of where the story was eventually headed. For the sake of compression and dramatic impact, Phelps reinvents the character of Monks, Dickens' chief architect in the attempt to disinherit Oliver, to become the grandson of Oliver's benefactor, Mr Brownlow. Thus, Phelps' interest in the family tragedy that results from Oliver's mother's disastrous relationship with his father is given extra prominence. The Brownlow home is elevated to one of the three main settings, along with the workhouse and Fagin's den. Oliver and Monks are half brothers, as they are in the book, but their father is Brownlow's son. 'In order to infuse the Brownlow household with a sense of danger, with a viper at the heart of the nest, I made him into Brownlow's treasured grandson' (2008). As such, his treachery is even more pronounced.

Phelps' bold, creative approach to Dickens, rather than strict fidelity to the original text, was one of the BBC's main selling points when it came to publicising the series as a highlight of the 2007 Christmas schedule. 'This gripping take on Charles Dickens' classic remains faithful to the spirit of the novel while delivering a modern, thrilling, tragic and occasionally comic edge', enthused the BBC press release (2007). 'Oliver Twist. Haven't we been here before?' the *Daily Telegraph* (2007) asked rhetorically in its preview of the series. 'Not like this you bloody haven't' came the emphatic reply. It is a strategy that played well with the audience, if not necessarily with Dickens fans (one Amazon reviewer damningly described the script as 'horribly bowdlerised' (2011)). Viewing figures were high, averaging 6.5 million over five episodes, and press reviews generally positive, *The Guardian* describing it as 'Dark, funny and real. It manages to feel modern but also faithful. Somewhere between melodrama and gritty realism' (2007). For Phelps, the success of *Oliver Twist* marked a dramatic shift in her professional profile. The specific recognition afforded to her by the press and within the industry is testament to her emergence as a bankable screenwriter with a distinctive individual voice. Despite her love of *EastEnders,* she has never returned to write for the 'behemoth' where she established her reputation.

Speaking to the director, and to the audience

On the strength of *Oliver Twist's* success, Phelps was able to pitch her next project directly to the BBC. This was her take on her favourite Dickens novel, *Great Expectations,* and once again she distilled its essence into a single sentence that would guide her screenplay: 'A boy who sells his soul and buys it back by becoming a man'. As such, it is Pip's moral and existential journey that makes up the backbone of Phelps' adaptation. His love for and pursuit of Estella, which, for example, dominates David Lean's 1946 film, is given less prominence here. *Great Expectations* is regarded as a more complex novel than *Oliver Twist*. It has a larger cast and is written through Pip's first-person narrative voice, which poses particular problems for a screenwriter since the reader only sees what Pip sees and only experiences his internal responses to events. Nevertheless, Phelps was aided structurally by the fact that the novel is divided into three distinct stages that translate directly to the three hour-long episodes she was asked to deliver. As ever, she wanted to be rigorous about only keeping what was important to the story, to cut out some of the narrative bagginess, and to make explicit some of the subtleties and implications of Dickens' writing. She was clear from the outset that she was not adapting *Great Expectations* for an audience of Dickens scholars and existing devotees, but rather wanted to find a way of giving a mainstream television audience access to what she considers his greatest novel.

Phelps describes *Great Expectations* as a 'fierce, savage, heart-breaking book' with edge-of-the-seat storytelling and very high dramatic stakes. 'It's definitely not a comedy and I was criticised for taking the comedy out. But one of the things I don't like about Dickens is his comedy; I find it whimsical and fluffy, based on hilarious names and so on.' Phelps saw the comedy represented by secondary characters such as Chumblechook, Mr Wopsle and Wemmick's Aged Parent as a distraction from the book's main narrative and thematic thrust. With a disciplined approach to the economies of storytelling learned from *EastEnders,* it was an area she was quick to excise.

As with *Oliver Twist*, there were key elements that dominated her reading of *Great Expectations*, and which informed the areas of emphasis in her adaptation. She notes:

> It's a cruel story of deceit and damage, grief and betrayal. Miss Havisham is one of my favourite literary characters; a damaged woman consumed with the theatricality of her grief. Her relationship with Estella is manipulative and sadistic. She deliberately subjects her to a hyper-sexualised and corrupted education to make her an instrument of her own revenge. The two death masks that hang in Jagger's office are a reminder of the noose that hangs over Magwitch as soon as he comes back to repay Pip. Pip is a lost kid suffering from survivor's guilt, something that's clear from the first page where we find him contemplating the graves of his parents and his five tiny siblings. I didn't see the joke in any of this so I couldn't write it.

Phelps was impressed by Dickens' use of location, and this provided rich pickings in her adaptation. London is a key character in the book and is given similar prominence in her screen version, along with Satis House and the wide expanses of marshland where Pip grew up. 'The language of description is haunting and vigorous and I loved the shifting, transitional nature of the landscape of the marshes. It relates directly to Pip's experiences of life and the landscape of his heart. Satis House is absolutely the physical heart of the story.'

The screenplays for both *Oliver Twist* and *Great Expectations* are very clear demonstrations of Phelps' ambition to create for these adaptations a distinct identity driven by the demands of the medium and its audience. These are more than skeletal scaffolds to be interpreted freely by the rest of the creative team; they are vivid and highly specific in their description of locations, lighting, sound, costume, movement and the emotional tone of each scene, alongside dialogue and setting. Even particular camera angles and movement are deliberately implied here.

In the opening scene of *Great Expectations*, we are 'very close and very tight' on Pip in the graveyard. Magwitch's first appearance is 'limping, blundering, fast and clumsy', accompanied by 'the sound of harsh rattling breathing, a thumping heart, an atmosphere of intense and absolute purpose' (*Great Expectations*, episode 1). Before Pip sees Magwitch, we sense through the camera 'that close feeling on the back of his neck, the sense of being watched'. Phelps is clear to give the director absolutely everything she can so that her intentions are never in doubt. Our first glimpse of East End street life in *Oliver Twist* is one of 'Absolute noise and colour! A chaos of activity. Costermongers, hawkers, traders, shouts and cries, carriages passing... and Oliver in the middle of it. Filthy, confused and hollow-eyed with hunger, his feet bleeding, bruised and raw' (*Oliver Twist*, episode 2).

Her screenplays are full of additional asides that make it obvious where the focus of attention should lie. In *Great Expectations*, our first vision of Joe Gargery and the treacherous Orlick is typically detailed and dynamic. Joe is 'gilded from the fire (of the forge's furnace) like a Nordic God'. Orlick 'emulates everything about Joe, the way he stands, the way he folds his arms, right down to the way he always keeps a hammer riding on his belt'. Neither of these descriptions is taken directly from the book, but they point very adroitly to the role both these characters will assume in the adaptation, and particularly the jealous love Orlick feels for Joe.

The character of Magwitch and the role he plays in Pip's story and eventual redemption is clearly signposted in Phelp's screenplay. He is given 12 of the 97 pages of the first episode, disproportionally generous in comparison with his presence in the first stage of the novel. Phelps is drawn to Magwitch as one of the characters on whom Dickens shines a light to the discomfort of his audience. In the novel, he is unflinching in his depiction of the dehumanising brutality of the hulks and the deportation system, and the injustice of Magwitch's fate when he returns from Australia having honestly earned his fortune to repay Pip. Phelps' screenplay draws us into his terrible situation on an emotional level in a way in which the book, through Pip's narration, is unable to. In her description of the action, she writes of 'filthy hands with broken nails as the man (Magwitch) falls and claws his way back up – a glimpse of his legs, the heavy irons rubbing raw on his shins, we wince to look at them'. When Pip offers him the stolen pie, sealing the lifelong connection between the two, Phelps ensures through the screenplay that there can be no ambivalence about the significance of the action:

> and there's a long moment. This one gesture, the battered slice of pie on the boy's shaking hand held out to him will change the course of everything. Magwitch stares from the pie to Pip's face. Like all his strength and toughness, all that hard-bitten urgency has entirely departed from him. Like his heart has suddenly hollowed out with some terrible, inconsolable loss.

In the book, Dickens leaves Magwitch at this point until he is brought to the forge by the soldiers after being rearrested. But Phelps decides to stay with him after Pip leaves, to see him use Joe Gargery's file to free himself from his chains and confront his adversary, Compeyson, before his violent, savage apprehension at the hands of soldiers and their dogs. Phelps, rather than compressing the book, is actively expanding it here to enhance her audience's interest in this character and the themes he represents.

It is this kind of creative, actively dramatic and visual approach that enables Phelps' screenplays to connect powerfully with an audience who might be unfamiliar with the source material. Alongside Magwitch, Miss Havisham is one of the key figures whose precise role in Pip's story is one that Phelps needed to distil accurately. Gillian Anderson (2013), who was cast in the role having previously won praise for her portrayal of Lady Dedlock in *Bleak House*, attributed her involvement to the strength of the screenplay and the 'beautiful, mysterious and heart breaking' (BBC website) depiction of her character. Once again, Phelps expands her presence with additional scenes and lines of dialogue that leave the audience in no doubt as to Miss Havisham's cynically destructive role in Pip and Estella's futures. Quizzing Pip about the deaths of his parents and siblings, she asks, 'Do you never wonder why you survived, Pip? Why you were chosen to live?' and tempts him with the answer, 'Perhaps you were meant for something special. Perhaps it is intended that you, like Estella, will be different and extraordinary.' Moving outside Pip's perspective for the sake of the television audience, Phelps also has Miss Havisham confronting Estella, having witnessed a moment of affection between her and Pip. Here we are left in no doubt about her agenda for her adopted daughter, as she reprimands her for not being in control of 'her passions': 'We will begin again. And this time you will learn.' At the end of the exchange, Miss Havisham asks Estella, 'What is love?' 'Death', comes the reply, and Phelps adds forcefully in her description of the action here, 'We glimpse the sheer unadulterated hell of her life.'

This kind of embellishment, reinforcing of the novel's key emotional and narrative markers, sometimes at the expense of more peripheral material, can also be seen in Phelps' approach to dialogue in both *Oliver Twist* and *Great Expectations*. Her screenplays only rarely mirror Dickens word for word. Iconic sound bites do remain; for example, Oliver still says 'Please sir, I want some more', and Magwitch still terrifies Pip by threatening, 'I'll cut your throat'; but virtually all of the rest of the dialogue is Phelps' own, heavily peppered with the flavour of Dickens. Again, Phelps is challenged by the need to stay close to the spirit and period of the original whilst giving her characters a voice that will resonate with her audience.

Julian Rhind Tutt, who played Monks in *Oliver Twist*, commented: 'Sarah's got this great talent to engage you by using dialogue which you know is not contemporary, not strictly 1835, but which somehow rings absolutely true' (*Oliver Twist: Behind the Scenes*, 2008). This approach was not universally admired, however. One disgruntled Amazon reviewer of *Great Expectations* complained, 'I only counted 10 lines in the whole series by the great man himself'; yet other reviewers on the website recognised that Phelps' aim of making the story accessible to new audiences had paid off: 'I was pleased to see the series keeping close to his [Dickens'] book but in a fresh way suited for the understanding of 21st century television audiences.'

Phelps' signature screenwriting style, her ability to write television full of detail, movement, emotion and colour, is no barrier to her collaboration with directors. Unlike many writers she is often on set, and Coky Giedroyc who directed *Oliver Twist* is an enthusiastic admirer:

> She writes with an incredible flair and energy which is extraordinarily visceral and visual. She dispenses with any sentimentality, she uses a rough vernacular from the street and she writes with muscular pace and brittle tensions. She creates complicated characters who live and breathe and who sit in the real world. There is never a dull moment in Sarah's writing, never a boring lull.
>
> (Author's interview, 2013)

Giedroyc points to a scene from the series' final episode, where Sikes tries to abscond with Oliver after Nancy's murder, as a key example of the kinetic, dynamic writing which is so appealing to directors and which expresses the essence of what 'writing television' is all about: '...and then we see that Sikes, wild eyed, breath harsh, is carrying Oliver in his arms. Oliver's head hangs down, blood on his shirt by his shoulder...blood on Sikes from carrying Oliver, running, running.' 'It is the powerful forward momentum of the writing', comments Giedroyc, 'which makes directing her work so exciting. Scenes never hang around too long. Rhythms are bold and at times disjointed. In one sentence she can encapsulate a scene, a whole emotional and physical world that I can bring to life for the screen.'

Conclusion

Coming from one of the UK's leading television drama directors, this endorsement from Giedroyc is a testament to Sarah Phelps' success in developing a screenwriting voice that is not only a vivid expression of her own personality, but which dictates very specifically how her work is to be translated onto the screen. As a passionate viewer of television and a writer with, to date, almost 100 broadcast hours to her credit, she has developed an acute understanding of the demands of her audience. Her most recent screenplays demonstrate very clearly how, over the course of her career, she has systematically crafted a style of writing that is vigorous and specific enough to withstand the production process. In doing so, she has ensured that she can directly and successfully engage with her audience through dialogue, image and action.

Phelps' current project, *The Crimson Field*, will form a key part of BBC1's 2014 commemoration of the outbreak of World War I. It is six-part series set in a field hospital on the Western Front, and will be her first original broadcast drama, giving her the opportunity to write television which is entirely the product of her own imagination. Actively endorsing the screenwriter's defining role in television fiction and Phelps' own distinctive reputation, Channel Controller Danny Cohen specifically referred to *The Crimson Field* at a press launch for 2013–2014 drama output as a 'brand new, original series from Sarah Phelps'. Even before the first draft screenplays have been completed, expectations for narratives, characters and settings researched and created by Phelps herself are, with good reason, exceptionally high.

References

An Interview with Sarah Phelps (2010) *WalfordWeb: EastEnders on the Internet*, available at http://www.walfordweb.co.uk/ww/spotlight/1265/interview-sarah-phelps [accessed 17 June 2013].
Danny Cohen Announces Host of New Commissions for BBC1 (2012) *BBC Media Centre*, available at http://www.bbc.co.uk/mediacentre/latestnews/2012/danny-cohen-mgeitf.html [accessed 28 February 2013].
Dennis Potter: Man of Television (The Southbank Show) (1978) Wr. Melvyn Bragg, Dir. n/a, UK, 60 mins.
Dickens, C. (2007) *Oliver Twist*, London: Penguin.
Geraghty, C. (2012) *Bleak House: BFI TV Classics*, Basingstoke: Palgrave Macmillan.
Giedroyc, C. (2013) Author's Interview, Wednesday 1 May, London.

Gillian Anderson Talks about the Script and the Sets (2013) *BBC Great Expectations*, available at http://www.bbc.co.uk/programmes/b018wmhr/clips [accessed 4 March 2013].

Goldman, W. (1984) *Adventures in the Screen Trade: A Personal View of Hollywood and Screenwriting*, London: McDonald & Co.

Oliver Twist (2008) Wr. Sarah Phelps, Dir. Coky Giedroyc, UK, 180 mins.

Phelps, S. (2007) *Oliver Twist*, original screenplay.

Phelps, S. (2011) *Great Expectations*, original screenplay.

Phelps, S. (2013) Author's Interview, Friday 8 March, Suffolk.

13
Working the Writers' Room: The Context, the Creative Space and the Collaborations of Danish Television Series *Borgen*

Eva Novrup Redvall

Introduction

Writers are where it all starts. That is how Head of DR Fiction at the Danish Broadcasting Corporation DR (formerly Danmarks Radio), Nadia Kløvedal Reich, explains the DR approach to producing quality television drama (cited in Pham, 2012). Since the late 1990s, the strategy of DR's in-house drama production unit, DR Fiction, has been to focus on original ideas of writers based on the concept of 'one vision'. The notion is that one person needs to feel ownership and have an overall vision for a project in order to create successful series like *Forbrydelsen/The Killing* (2007–2012) or *Borgen* (2010–2013). In the DR production framework, this person is singled out as the head writer, but he or she normally works closely with other writers as well as the in-house producers of DR Fiction. It is a highly collaborative process, and several series in the DR framework are based on the use of writers' rooms for producing quality drama series.[1]

Historically, there has been little tradition of working with writers' rooms on quality drama series in the European television industry, where writers are sometimes described as going from shell to shell (Redvall, 2012a and 2012b: 17). Contrary to the long US tradition for writers' rooms, mainly used for comedy but also for drama series, many European production cultures have only gradually begun working with writers' rooms outside of the telenovela and soap opera format. DR Fiction began experimenting with a 'head writer–episode writer' structure when the department deliberately tried to imitate working methods from the USA in the late 1990s (Redvall, 2011).

Since then, the use of the writers' room has become an established part of several one-hour drama series structured across ten episodes, but the rooms can be small with usually only one head writer working with two episode writers during the storylining of new episodes. However, despite their limited size, the rooms are understood as writers' rooms similar to those known in the US television industry and regarded as crucial to the production of quality drama series. This is not only because they are able to produce material at the intended speed required for production, but also because they promote communication and collaboration as early as the development stage of production.

Based on observational studies of the writers' room used for the television series *Borgen* (2010–2013), and interviews with key producers and writers at DR, this chapter will analyse what can be regarded as the creative benefits of working with writers' rooms.[2] As discussed at many industry events, such as The European TV Drama Series Lab in 2012 (Redvall, 2012a), there can be many challenges to establishing writers' rooms. For example, a fundamental issue is the expense of hiring several writers over just one, and, as several showrunners and writers describe, the absolute need for 'egoless' writers who can function in a process of developing material together (Redvall, 2012a: 17, 21).[3] In the DR Fiction framework, one of the lessons learned during the early trials of collaborative writing was that not all head writers are good leaders, and that many writers do not take well to having their work rewritten. As will be discussed, scholarly literature on US writers' rooms points to several problems, from their hierarchical structure and the precarity of the work situation, to issues of gender, race and age when casting the rooms, to questions of copyright and credit. Nevertheless, there are many creative benefits in working with writers' rooms, and this chapter attempts to outline some of them.

With the success of series such as the crime thriller *The Killing* and the political drama *Borgen*, we have seen over the past few years a sudden interest in the working processes of what some journalists have called 'the Danish TV hit factory' (Gilbert, 2012). At the European TV Drama Series Lab, the rise and success of series from DR was thoroughly debated, and several explanations pointed back to the working structures of the writers (Redvall, 2012a: 13–14, 2013a: 15, 62). How these writers actually work, then, is an important aspect of studying these series, which is why this chapter focuses specifically on the use of the writers' room. Using observations and interviews from one such writers' room in the DR framework, the chapter will analyse how a context for the writing process is created, one that facilitates communication around production at an early stage of the development of new work: a creative space for externalising and 'entering' an idea in a collaborative manner.

Team writing and writers' rooms

As described by scholars and industry analysts, a strong tradition for team writing in European film and television culture does not exist (e.g. Finney, 1996; Born, 2005). This has begun to change in the Danish television industry, in part due to DR's establishment, in the late 1990s, of a collaborative structure whereby a head writer works with several episode writers. Series such as *Borgen*, *The Killing* and *Arvingerne/The Legacy* (2014) are all based on the work of several writers. However, each series has one creator with overall creative control and authorial designation, and the series is presented as 'by' that one creator in both the opening credits and the public realm. In studying the work of specific writers' rooms at DR, a clear sense has emerged that the head writer is indeed in charge, but that the process is highly collaborative and is based on extensive input and feedback from writers and other contributors. Before analysing the creative advantages of this way of working, however, it is worth introducing some of the recent research on US writers' rooms as a source of comparison and contrast.

In the US television industry, the tradition of team writing and writers' rooms goes back to the early years of broadcasting, particularly for sitcoms (Caldwell, 2008: 211; Henderson, 2011: 1). Production scholar John Thornton Caldwell refers to this collaborative process as 'writing by committee' (2008: 211), and he has also discussed how this practice is often regarded more as an industrial pursuit rather than an artistic endeavour (2008: 201). Caldwell's research does not paint a pretty picture of the state of US writers' rooms. He describes the early writing teams for sitcoms such as *The Dick van Dyke Show* (1961–1966) as populated by 'collegial, good-humored turn-takers', in contrast to the function of the writers' rooms of today, which he describes as 'intense, strategic pressure points in the development of a television program' (2008: 211). Writers are expected to work 80-hour weeks and late nights if needed (2008: 215), and depictions of the rooms sometimes sound like 'nonunion digital sweatshops of below-the-line workers' (2008: 214). Notes on the work coming out of the rooms are interpreted as ' "orders" from ostensible superiors to clients in the production chain' based on some 'implicit theory of the audience' (2008: 221), and whilst there is some discussion of the potential creative benefits of brainstorming and developing ideas together, the overall impression is a rather grim portrayal of a space marked by stress, anxiety and 'professional one-upmanship' (2008: 216). Other studies focusing particularly on the work of writers and writers' rooms in Hollywood point to potential dangers relating to the casting and politics of the rooms in terms of gender, race and age (e.g. Bielby and Bielby, 2002; Henderson, 2011; Phalen and Osellame, 2012).

As often highlighted by writers themselves, the writers' room is a place where one cannot go unless invited. For example, the creator of *Dexter* (2006–), James Manos Jr, has stressed that writers' rooms are 'sacrosanct' and off limits to actors and executives (cited in Redvall, 2012a: 14). This exclusivity helps to create an aura of mystery around them, and few academic researchers have been granted access to observe what goes on in the room. Felicia Henderson describes her study of the work 'behind the closed doors' in writers' rooms as auto-ethnography, inhabiting the role of a 'boundary-crosser' by using her experience as an industry professional to develop her research (2011: 1). Several media production or screenwriting scholars have a background of working in the industry, and thus draw on their own experiences in their research.[4] Practice-based research like this can offer many interesting perspectives on the industry, and having industry networks is useful for helping researchers gain access to these often well-guarded sites of production. There are, however, still surprisingly few studies based on experiences or observations of the working practices of a writers' room.

One recent exception is Patricia Phalen and Julia Osellame's study of what they call 'rooms with a point of view', which draws on a six-week observational study of a US prime-time drama series and interviews with 45 television writers (2012). Choosing an exploratory approach to the work in the room, their study addresses several critical points raised by the writers that relate to, for example, the hierarchical structure of the room and examples of sexual harassment. Positively, the study also sees writers characterise their working space as 'the good room', a place that has the right chemistry and a feeling of safety so that people do not hold back their ideas out of fear (2012: 10–11).

Other publications like Tom Stempel's *Storytellers to the Nation* (1992) have offered an 'insider's history' on the work of American television writers through numerous interviews. More recently, Lawrence Meyers (2010) has gathered established writers for round-table conversations about various aspects of working in writers' rooms, with the promise of providing practical advice for succeeding in television. Much can be learned from writers talking about their work, but the writers involved in such talks are usually successful 'above-the-line' stars rather than 'below-the-line' writers who might have more sweatshop-like experiences as described in the work of Caldwell. Accordingly, when US showrunners discussed working in writers' rooms at the European TV Drama Series Lab, they mostly focused on the many positive sides of their successful rooms, insisting on 'the fun' of collaborative writing (Redvall, 2013a: 13).

In her study of US writers' rooms, Felicia Henderson has stressed how her work in the industry has been marked by no one experience being like another, since 'every show's culture is unique' (2011: 1). Similarly, US showrunners often remark that all rooms are different and that all showrunners work in different ways (e.g. Frank Spotnitz in Redvall, 2012a: 17). It seems worthwhile to explore how to understand the unique culture of a particular series and the nature of writers' rooms that are perceived as examples of best practice. The following analysis is such an attempt: to synthesise the nature of the context, the creative space and the collaborations of one particular series (*Borgen*), focusing on the possible creative benefits of working in writers' rooms, which, as discussed, are sometimes criticised for being a structure chosen on the basis of production demands; of being able to produce a certain amount of material in a limited amount of time, not for artistic reasons. As highlighted from the previous research, there can be many conflicts and challenges related to working in writers' rooms, but there are also strong creative arguments in favour of organising the writing of a new series around a collaborative room based at the heart of production. This is what will now be discussed.

Context of the writers' room

Having a writers' room at the site of production situates the writing process in the same space as the other people working on the same project. As an example, the writers' room for *Borgen* was located in a production hallway in DR's headquarter DR-Byen, together with the offices of the producer, the researcher, the production designer and other crew working on the series. The studio containing the main sets for the series was downstairs. This gathering of people working on the same production in the same space has been a controlling idea for how best to organise the work processes at DR Fiction since their establishment of so-called 'production hotels' in the late 1990s. Instead of having different personnel scattered across different departments and locations, the intention of the then Head of Drama, Rumle Hammerich, was to gather people working on the same project specifically to facilitate collaboration. Based on a belief that good film and television production is all about communication, Hammerich wanted to strengthen the opportunity for dialogue and for constant encounters rather than having conversations about projects confined to formalised meetings (2012).

Scholars analysing the emergence and organisation of the US studio system have pointed to the division of labour as a central element to the mode of production (e.g. Bordwell et al., 1985). According to Janet Staiger, this division led 'to the separation of the planning phase and the execution phase' (1979: 18), and in screenwriting studies questions around this division are often discussed as being a traditional divide between conception and execution (e.g. Maras, 2009). As is the case with most major production units, the DR Fiction framework for production is based on a clear division of labour and different degrees of specialisation. However, having so-called production hotels creates a space where those who might traditionally be separated by divisions between conception and execution have the opportunity to interact during all stages of the process.

Amongst the practitioners at DR, having a writers' room close to the rest of production is regarded as a valuable asset. Producer Camilla Hammerich finds it to be crucial, since having writers present provides the opportunity for making writing and production come together at an early stage, thus allowing for certain logistics to guide the writing process during the storylining stages (2012). *Borgen* researcher Rikke Tørholm Kofoed emphasises the value of having communication on a production 'happen by itself', since no one has the time for constant, formalised meetings (2012).

From observing the work of the *Borgen* writers' room, it was clear that the writers often interacted with other people working on the production and drew on their expertise. There was a solid sense of respect surrounding the work of the writers from other personnel, who would not unnecessarily disturb them and whom the writers would consult on matters of research, backstory or more practical matters such as building plans for sets and information about locations. The writers would also have coffee and sometimes lunch with others from the production, and based on these informal meetings others would know what was being written about in the room, occasionally contributing their own ideas or anecdotes. As well as facilitating communication between different personnel, the presence of writers also allowed others to have a sense of the material being written in the room at an early stage, which seemed to create a shared sense of excitement as to where some storylines might end or how the writers would deal with challenging scenes.

Having the writers' room at the centre of the production creates a clear sense amongst the writers that there is a machine waiting to be fed. Creator of *The Killing*, Søren Sveistrup, describes how he needs to feel production breathing down his neck before being able to make the final choices for his screenplays (2012). The many demands of production also seem to be more naturally integrated at an early stage of production, when a writer can easily verify things with the researcher or producer by just opening the door and asking a question. Rather than a finished screenplay having to be adapted to production demands, the presence of writers during the outlining of stories gives the possibility of discussing aspects in a constructive manner at an early and potentially cost-saving stage of the development. This is a clear advantage for writers and others working on the production. *Borgen* writer Jeppe Gjervig Gram reveals that he finds inspiration in writing close to production. As an example, he mentions being able to visit the set if he needs 'to visualise the physicality of a scene' (2012). He also argues there is great value in having writers present who can answer production questions related to their material.

In relation to what has been discussed as the New Danish cinema, Mette Hjort has argued that the collective nature of many projects by Lars von Trier and the structure of his production company Zentropa's so-called Filmbyen ('The Film Town') seems to have facilitated collaboration on many different levels, what she has called 'a site of synergy' (2005: 20). Having the writers' room as an integrated part of a production space can be regarded as an attempt to create a site of synergy, where practitioners can have long and informal discussions during development, writing and production, rather than being scattered in different departments and only brought together for formalised meetings. The importance of inhabiting the same space has been raised continuously in interviews, and whereas most Danish television production takes place in somewhat isolated companies spread across Copenhagen, DR Fiction is one of the few players in the industry with both the physical capacity to accommodate people in the same space and the financial capacity to keep them there for substantial amounts of time.

The creative space

Whereas the physical existence of a writers' room close to other personnel makes the context of production ever-present and facilitates interaction, the very fact of having a writers' room creates a particular type of space for the process of writing itself. It is a space one can enter, and where the story can materialise visually, for instance, on white boards and through mood boards. Sociologist Sara Malou Strandvad has discussed the screenplay as 'the externalised idea' and the written materialisation as important to concretise discussions of what the idea will be (Strandvad, 2008: 164). The writers' room in this sense can be regarded as a room in which the idea is able to materialise gradually, and where those present can discuss directions and developments based on different ways of making the story come alive.

As an example, during the development of new series *The Legacy*, the room became full of images, books and art linked to the work of the legendary female artist at the core of the story, as well as mood boards depicting the personalities of other characters in the cast. Suggested outlines for all episodes in the first season were on one wall, whilst the story beats for individual episodes were developed on white boards. The glass windows in the room were also used for writing. The room, and the kind of room that it developed into, became a shared space where an atmosphere for the series could be created; and where, on a very basic level, story beats and storylines could be moved around easily, weaving material together to form a treatment and other documents. The visualisation of story segments and ideas also made the process one of movement and physicality rather than writers spending entire days sitting in front of computer screens. In the *Borgen* writers' room, head writer Adam Price would rarely sit down during a working day, pacing back and forth between white boards and writing down results of the constant discussions with his co-writers. The structure of working for *Borgen* was to spend two weeks storylining an episode, which would then be presented as an oral pitch to the researcher and producer on the final day. Keeping the development stages of the story on the boards seemed useful for discussing how the stories emerged, as well as enabling possible changes to the material since everyone could see, for example, the number of scenes containing a character or how many scenes it took for a storyline to evolve.

As well as the writers' room becoming a place where the story can materialise, it can also be helpful in establishing a particular type of mood for the writing process itself. Many writers testify to being inspired by specific rooms or locations. In the DR context, Søren Sveistrup argued that he felt the rather shabby location of the old TV Byen ('The TV Town') was more suited to the writing of *The Killing* than the shiny glass offices and modern furniture of the new DR Byen (2012). Furthermore, although the location of a writers' room might be given, those inhabiting it can create a special atmosphere that will help to facilitate the material being written. The very existence of a writers' room thus provides a unique scene for the writing process, one where a writer can enter and share.

This sense of physicality can also make a difference when communicating ideas to others at an early stage of development. The writers' room bestows an idea of concreteness, even if little is yet on paper: whereas the everyday work is regarded as off-limits to producers or executives, there are advantages of using the room as a setting for pitching a project to others. Observing the development of *The Legacy*, it was interesting to see how an important pitch meeting was held in the writers' room with the head writer at the desk, pitching from the white boards, with the executives as guests of the vision in the room. Having commissioners enter the space as opposed to having writers go and pitch in the offices of executives seemed to be of great advantage, the appearance of the room and the work manifesting itself on the walls helping to communicate ideas clearly.

Writers' rooms can also be creative spaces where particular rules apply. These can differ from series to series, but as analysed in the work of Phalen and Osellame, writers often talk about the need for a room where they feel safe and free to fail (2012: 11). In Danish feature film writing, some screenwriters talk of the importance of creating 'a dumb room' for an idea, where one is allowed to say anything; one needs to create a space for the spontaneous, 'dumb' ideas rather than people holding back from fear of not sounding clever enough (Redvall, 2010: 141). Whereas the screenwriter discussing the dumb room for feature film collaborations refers to an abstract, mental space, the television writers' room can be a place where rules or ideas of creative restraints apply. In the case of *Borgen*, the writers made 'a musketeer oath' when moving into the writing of the first series that all writers had to agree on a particular suggestion before settling on an idea (Gram, 2012). The writers tried to keep specific production demands out of their creative process during the initial stages of development; and the producer was asked not to comment too much on production issues and logistics when hearing the content of an episode for the first time. This did prove to be difficult, however, with many of the discussions around the first episode outline focusing on practical concerns such as the number of exterior vs. interior scenes, or the number of scenes featuring particular actors. Nevertheless, having other people enter a room that 'belongs' to the writers does create a sense of writers being in charge, and where storytelling issues should be at the core of all discussions.

Collaborations in the room

As highlighted above, writers' rooms create a context and a space for collaborative writing processes that can take on many forms. In the DR Fiction framework, the writing collaborations of different series seemed to have found their own unique structures and paces, even though the fundamental structures around production were the same. The most established structure was that of *Borgen*, which being in its third season was perceived as having well-functioning routines. The *Borgen* writers' room centred around head writer Adam Price working with two steady co-writers, Tobias Lindholm and Jeppe Gjervig Gram, during the first two seasons. For the third season, however, Lindholm stepped out of the room and three new writers were attached to the writing of its ten episodes. In comparison to the large rooms often found on US shows, the writers' rooms at DR are small. In the words of *Borgen* producer Camilla Hammerich, three people is 'the magic number' (2012). We might argue that this could be considered a writing team rather than a writers' room, but in the DR framework this is considered to be the number of writers required for the best conversations around a series.

Whereas US showrunners often oversee the work in the writers' room, rather than actively taking part in all of its discussions, the head writer on a series from DR is usually present throughout the storylining process. The structure for both *Borgen* and *The Killing* has been to have two episode writers taking turns in producing drafts, which are then given notes during meetings and move through several drafts, until the head writer takes over for final rewrites. Developing all of the series' storylines together ensures that writers are literally on the same page, and the collaborative process then allows for specific skills of different writers to be drawn on. In the case of *Borgen*, head writer Adam Price was described by his fellow writers as an 'idea generating machine', one who could always move the story forward and come up with new scenes and situations (Gram, 2012; Larsen, 2012). This was regarded as a positive quality in a head writer by his co-writers, who described their role as very much challenging his ideas to ensure the right choices were made before moving on.

Observing the storylining of episode 25, the process appeared to be highly collaborative, with all writers contributing important points to the material and having a shared responsibility for all aspects of the story. All three writers afterwards described the process as an example of best practice. The head writer was very appreciative of the input from the episode writers (Price, 2012), who in return felt a great sense of ownership of the material, describing the room as 'dynamic', 'generous' and 'egoless', and marked by a sense of 'confidence' and of feeling 'safe' (Larsen, 2012). There was certainly room for bad ideas and disagreement, and Larsen calls Price's approach to this 'collective' (2012).

It could be argued that working in small writers' rooms creates less competition between writers vying for attention. In comparison to depictions of the US writers' rooms in the work of scholars such as Caldwell, the *Borgen* room had two highly satisfied episode writers who described a good working process and even seemed content with both their pay and their working hours. There are, of course, major differences between the DR public service framework in a small nation context and the commercial US production culture that sits behind most major series. Nevertheless, *Borgen* is perceived to be an exemplary production by everyone involved, whilst studying other series from DR could have provided examples of more conflict.

In the case of the DR writers' rooms, there always seemed to be a clear sense of the head writer being in charge of the series as a whole, and Adam Price in particular seemed free to make what he perceived as the best choices for the material when finalising the screenplays for each of the episodes. At the same time, Price's co-writers characterised one of his major qualities as being truly appreciative of the dialogue they had in the room. Larsen describes how some head writers always talk of 'I' rather than 'we', and how it is a common feeling that instead of being open to difficult discussions about challenges in a screenplay, such head writers will simply change things to their liking in later drafts. On the contrary, Larsen found that Price has a talent for giving others a sense of ownership (2012), and Price himself describes work on the series as 'an extremely happy collaboration' marked by 'an incredibly creative room' (2012).

Whilst there are no doubt many dysfunctional writers' rooms, described by Phalen and Osellame as 'functional dysfunctional families' (2012: 12), there are also rooms where writers feel that the process is constructive, and that the collaboration of the room creates material that they could never have produced on their own. Amongst writers, discussions of having the right 'chemistry' seem crucial, and in fact when setting up his own writers' room following his work on *Borgen*, Jeppe Gjervig Gram expressed concern about whether what was perceived as a good chemistry in the *Borgen* room could be recreated for his new series. Writers' rooms are full of complex collaborations, and no writer seems to take for granted that there is a default mode to making a room work. As discussed by Henderson, every show's culture is unique (2011: 1) and so every room needs to find its own way to structure and talk about the work.

Collaborative writing with one vision

As highlighted at the beginning of this chapter, the work in writers' rooms remains a rather unexplored territory, mainly because of problems gaining access to them. For me, there seems to be great value in trying to gain more knowledge about the processes that take place in rooms for different series, not only to better understand the many potential problems related to issues such as developing storylines in hierarchical structures and casting the room, but also to understand better what might facilitate the creative work in these rooms and the ways in which collaborations unfold. Scholars and screenwriters seem to agree that the specific nature of a series and its writers' room always varies, but some issues, such as issues of trust and of feeling safe, do seem always to play a central part. To this end, this chapter has aimed to outline what can be regarded as three fundamental strengths of working with writers' rooms by focusing on the context, the creative space and the collaborations.

All three of these aspects are concerned with facilitating communication around ideas and stories on different levels, between writers as well as between other people who are involved in the production of a series. Having a writers' room seems to encourage a dialogue between personnel, not least since the work in the room becomes an example of how stories are created and refined in a collaborative process on site, rather than being conceived somewhere else and now needing to be executed. The chapter has thus suggested thinking of writers' rooms as potential sites of synergy, opening up the possibility of collaboration inside the room as well as with non-writing members of the crew outside the room. This seems a constructive way to structure television production, where quite specific demands on the writing process are often present from the outset.

There are still few production studies of collaborative screenwriting processes in the European television industry, but the increased international interest in subtitled content might change this in the years to come. Some scholars have described this change in audience appreciation of foreign fare as a 're-orientation' of the marketplace marked by new 'counter-flows' (Weissman, 2012: 191). The industry has similarly noticed this new interest in subtitled series, attempting to pinpoint the reasons behind the sudden appeal of the Danish series.

DR Fiction has earned a strong identity when it comes to its storytelling style or brand, with its in-house so-called 'dogmas', or guidelines for production, recently emerging in the public realm as part of the explanation for recent success. These guidelines contain ideas about always building series on 'double storytelling', regarded as a 'public service layer' that offers stories with ethical and social concerns as well as an entertaining plot. The guidelines also emphasise the value of crossover between people working in the film and television industry (Redvall, 2010). However, the privileged position of the writer and the concept of 'one vision' is continuously raised as the most important aspect for a successful television series. As discussed above, explicitly putting one person at the centre of the process does not necessarily equal a creative dictatorship. A vast number of people, amongst them directors, cinematographers and actors, are important to the process, and whilst writers are presented as *where it all starts* we can argue that the vision for the series truly comes alive through the context, the creative space and the collaborations of the writers' rooms.

Notes

1. The chapter is based on a research project funded by The Danish Research Council, published as the book *Writing and Producing Television Drama in Denmark: From* The Kingdom *to* The Killing (2013b).
2. The observational studies in the writers' room of *Borgen* took place during the storylining of episode 25 in December 2011, followed by observations at note meetings and at the reading of the screenplay during the spring of 2012. Following this, interviews about the process were conducted, referred to in the text by the surname of the respondent.
3. In the US television context, the term 'showrunner' is usually used to describe the role of one individual who has the overall responsibility for a show. How-to books on television writing and production often define the showrunner as the executive producer (e.g. Sandler, 2007: 255), but the showrunner is also described as 'the creative force behind a series' (Del Valle, 2008: 403). The use of the term 'showrunner' is not common in the European television industry, but it is gaining more ground. Christine Cornea has discussed the gradual introduction of the term in the UK in relation to series like *Doctor Who* (2005–2008), where she regards 'the assigning of an American-style showrunner role to Russell T. Davies' as a 'signifier of the BBC's intended "quality" status for the series' (2009: 166). Recent industry events like the 2012 European TV Drama Series Lab have focused on what Europe might learn from the work of US showrunners (Redvall, 2012a).
4. One such example is British screenwriter and scholar Jill Nelmes, who analyses screenwriting and the balance between craft and creativity (2007), and the process of developing, writing and rewriting a specific feature film screenplay (2008).

References

Bielby, D. and Bielby, W.T. (2002) 'Hollywood Dreams, Harsh Realities: Writing for Film and Television' in *Contexts: Journal of the American Sociological Association*, 1(4), 21–27.

Bordwell, D., Staiger, J. and Thompson, K. (1985) *The Classical Hollywood Cinema*, New York: Columbia University Press.

Born, G. (2005) *Uncertain Vision: Birt, Dyke and the Reinvention of the BBC*, London: Vintage.

Caldwell, J.T. (2008) *Production Culture: Industrial Reflexivity and Critical Practice in Film and Television*, Durham: Duke University Press.

Cornea, C. (2009) 'Showrunning the *Doctor Who* Franchise: A Response to Denise Mann' in Vicki Mayer, Miranda J. Banks and John T. Caldwell (eds.) *Production Studies: Cultural Studies of Media Industries*, New York: Routledge, pp. 115–122.

Del Valle, R. (2008) *The One-Hour Drama Series: Producing Episodic Television*, Los Angeles: Silman-James Press.

Finney, A. (1996) *The State of European Cinema*, London: Cassell.

Gilbert, G. (2012) 'How does Danish TV Company DR Keep Churning Out the Hits?' in *The Independent*, 12 May, from http://www.independent.co.uk/arts-entertainment/tv/features/how-does-danish-tv-company-dr-keep-churning-out-the-hits-7728833.html [accessed 29 March 2013].

Gram, J.G. (2012) Interview with the Author, 9 November.

Hammerich, C. (2012) Interview with the Author, 9 November.

Hammerich, R. (2012) Interview with the Author, 7 June.

Henderson, F.D. (2011) 'The Culture Behind Closed Doors: Issues of Gender and Race in the Writers' Room' in *Cinema Journal*, 50(2), 145–152.

Hjort, M. (2005) *Small Nation, Global Cinema: The New Danish Cinema*, Minneapolis: University of Minnesota Press.

Kofoed, R.T. (2012) Interview with the Author, 9 November.

Larsen, M.J. (2012) Interview with the Author, 8 November.

Maras, S. (2009) *Screenwriting: History, Theory and Practice*, London: Wallflower Press.

Meyers, L. (ed.) (2010) *Inside the TV Writer's Room: Practical Advice for Succeeding in Television*, Syracuse, NY: Syracuse University Press.

Nelmes, J. (2007) 'Some Thoughts on Analysing the Screenplay, the Process of Screenplay Writing and the Balance Between Craft and Creativity' in *Journal of Media Practice*, 8(2), 107–113.

Nelmes, J. (2008) 'Developing the Screenplay *Wingwalking*: An Analysis of the Writing and Rewriting Process' in *Journal of British Cinema and Television*, 5(2), 335–352.

Phalen, P. and Osellame, J. (2012) 'Writing Hollywood: Rooms with a Point of View' in *Journal of Broadcasting & Electronic Media*, 56(1), 3–20.

Pham, A. (2012) 'DR's Queens of Drama Give the Ingredients to their Winning Recipe', *News from Nordisk Film and TV Fond*, 11 May, from http://www.nordiskfilmogtvfond.com/news_story.php?cid=3356&sid=10&ptid=4 [accessed 7 November 2012].

Price, A. (2012) Interview with the Author, 20 December.

Redvall, E.N. (2010) *Manuskriptskrivning som kreativ proces: De kreative samarbejder bag manuskriptskrivning i dansk spillefilm*, PhD Thesis, University of Copenhagen: Department of Media, Cognition and Communication.

Redvall, E.N. (2011) 'Dogmer for tv-drama: Om brugen af *one vision*, den dobbelte historie og *crossover* i DR's søndagsdramatik' in *Kosmorama* 248(Winter), 180–198.

Redvall, E.N. (2012a) *European TV Drama Series Lab: Summary of Module 1*, Berlin: Erich Pommer Institut.

Redvall, E.N. (2013a) *European TV Drama Series Lab: Documentation Module 2*, Berlin: Erich Pommer Institut.

Redvall, E.N. (2013b) *Writing and Producing Television Drama in Denmark: From* The Kingdom *to* The Killing, Basingstoke: Palgrave Macmillan.

Sandler, E. (2007) *The TV Writer's Workbook*, New York: Delta Trade Paperbacks.

Staiger, J. (1979) 'Dividing Labor for Production Control: Thomas Ince and the Rise of the Studio System', *Cinema Journal*, 18(2), 16–25.

Stempel, T. (1992) *Storytellers to the Nation: A History of American Television Writing*, New York: Continuum.

Strandvad, S.M. (2008) *Inspirations for a New Sociology of Art: A Sociomaterial Study of Development Processes in The Danish Film Industry*, PhD Thesis, Copenhagen: Copenhagen Business School.

Sveistrup, S. (2012) Interview with the Author, 6 November.

Weissman, E. (2012) *Transnational Television Drama: Special Relations and Mutual Influence between the US and UK*, Basingstoke: Palgrave Macmillan.

14

And the Screenwriter Created Man: Male Characterisation in Bromance and Bromedy

Helen Jacey

Introduction

Recent discussions of gender and screenwriting have largely focused on the perennial problem of the female character, and the continued need for writers to avoid clichés and stereotypical forms of characterisation (e.g. Seger (1996); Francke (1994); Jacey (2010); Silverstein (2013)). However, when the bromance and the bromedy/bromcom are flourishing as recognisable mainstream sub-genres in both film and television series, critical attention to the approaches screenwriters might take in the creation of the male character is remarkably lacking. This absence raises questions about male representation and the screenwriter's role in developing characters that promote positive images of men and male identity.

To what extent this lack of discussion serves to normalise storytelling with a 'boys will be boys' rationale, one that arguably glosses over extreme portrayals of the evolving roles of men and hetero-normative aspects of masculinity, is thus discussed in this chapter. The intention is to help screenwriters consider men from new critical angles, ones that can help them in their creation of male characters. Recent genre categorisations of stories involving men's relationships with one other will be explored in order to understand ways that screenwriters might approach male character development, as well as to learn from existing representations of men in stories with strong male relationships at their heart.

The typecasting of male characters, which sits alongside increased expressions of men's emotional needs in screen narratives, is a hallmark

of the bromance and the bromedy, and so notions of how these contribute to the themes and ideas of male-driven narratives will also be
used. Case studies from recent film and television texts such as *Entourage*
(2004–2011), *House* (2004–2012), *The Hangover* (2009) and *The Hangover 2* (2011) will offer both practical and theoretical approaches to the
characterisation of men across age ranges, all of which will be explored
explicitly from the perspective of the practising screenwriter.

A bromantic challenge for screenwriters

Over the past decade, the bromance has proliferated in mainstream
film and television and is now widely recognised in both industrial and
critical contexts as a sub-genre of comedy, comedy drama and romantic comedy in arguably equal measures. Bromance films include *Y Tu
Mama Tambien* (2001), *Sideways* (2004), *Pineapple Express* (2008), *I Love
You, Man* (2009), *Due Date* (2010), *The Hangover* (2009) and *The Hangover 2* (2011). Television shows include *Entourage* (2004–2011), *Two and
a Half Men* (2003–), *Band of Brothers* (2001), *The Inbetweeners* (2008–
2010) and *House* (2004–2012). Formerly known as the 'buddy movie',
the bromance goes one step further in that it is predicated on notions of
heterosexual men's needs and desires for each other (on a non-sexual
basis) and around the value of such friendships to the protagonists.
For industry, 'bromance' is now a widely accepted term that serves as
a marketing catchphrase for a narrative where male friendships and the
evolution of these relationships are central, in a similar way to how
the term 'chick flick' indicates narratives that are predominantly concerned with conventionally feminine concerns from love, to fashion to
friendship.

For critics, this burgeoning media representation of male friendship
raises interesting questions about male identity, gender roles and the
entrenched and shifting attitudes towards these. Mortimer describes
bromance as 'an ironic take' (Mortimer, 2010) on romantic comedy,
highlighting its audience appeal regarding shifting representations of
men in wider culture. Alberti explores bromance's representation of
masculinity as a site of gender crisis in men which points to an 'obsoles-
cence' of traditional versions of masculine identity (Alberti, 2013), and
usefully offers an in-depth exploration of the films of Judd Apatow to
substantiate his claims.

For the screenwriter, however, 'bromance' is a more complex term as it
refers not only to the sub-genre but also to the nature of male friendship
in a narrative that might not actually be a bromance, for example, *Master*

and Commander (2003). This range of uses of 'bromance' has potentially conflicting agendas, which require 'creative management' when developing a story where men display friendships. For instance, what might be a genre convention for a bromance might severely impact upon or restrict a writer's motivation to depict a more subtle or complex relationship between men. My exploration here focuses on screenwriters' active engagement with critical issues concerning male friendship in the bromance during the script development process and how writers might creatively manage possibilities and limitations for characterisation presented by assumptions around the genre. The driving questions, then, are: what models might be utilised to serve character and story development in the bromance; and, how can the screenwriter usefully employ these models, whether writing 'on spec' and immersed in an individual, non-collaborative stage of screenwriting, or whether in active collaboration with others in more advanced stages of script development? Furthermore, and in the pursuit of creating new and innovative works, how might the screenwriter evaluate values, perceptions and judgements of gender, genre and story at any stage of script development for the good of the project, whilst still maintaining a sense of authorship and voice?

This is a timely study as it builds on the aforementioned feminist screenwriting projects undertaken by myself (2010), Francke (1994) and Seger (1996) to raise awareness of gender issues in screenwriting at the level of script development, encompassing gender issues in an industrial setting and their implications for female characters, female-driven stories and female screenwriters. Whilst critical discussion of male identity and narrative is well established, there has been far less transfer of these ideas to the creation of male characters in bromance films, specifically within a screenwriting context. Screenwriting discourse has yet to turn serious attention to the question of the male character, including the role and responsibilities of the screenwriter. Whilst screenwriters continue to agonise over female characters and how to make them 'multi-dimensional', they potentially risk falling into the trap of letting the male character off the metaphoric hook.

The lack of attention on men and masculinity in screenwriting could be attested to an enduring normative framework prevalent in the film and television industry for narratives with a male protagonist, reflecting feminist concerns about mechanisms in the film industry that perpetuate dominant ideologies that impact negatively on women (Caplan, 1983) and, at a wider level, an ongoing association with masculinity and universality in dominant media platforms. The Screen Idea Work Group

(SIWG) is proposed by McDonald as the stakeholder group for all those with a role in getting a screenplay into production, who subscribe to a set of values and industry norms (the 'doxa') about what makes a good screenplay/film (McDonald, 2010). Whilst McDonald acknowledges that conflicts can abound in the SIWG, creative decision making and status issues affecting the screenwriter, the implication remains that the doxa is broadly subscribed to and formed by prevailing mechanisms about screenwriting such as how-to manuals. At a time when there is little 'out there' for screenwriters about how to develop male characters, the prevailing doxa is potentially extremely limited in opening up questions about gender and representation. This can result in characterisation – eventually in the form of a produced text – that is based on hegemonic notions of masculinity that have been internalised by those collaborating on the development of a screenplay, and that are potentially at odds with feminist or masculinities ideas. For example, female stereotypes abound in mainstream bromances (e.g. *The Hangover* and *Pineapple Express*) implying that somewhere in the development process the incorporation of what could be considered problematic female characters in the narratives was deemed acceptable, if not desirable. Ideas and questions from critical discourse are relevant to screenwriters, and to what extent they can incorporate these in their narratives and within an industrial context that still faces its own challenges in terms of gender discrimination is an interesting dilemma, one I do not seek to resolve. However, the widespread popularity of the bromance and the bromedy offers a timely opportunity to identify and explore both creative and critical issues that a screenwriter might explore and 'creatively manage' in the development of their screenplays.

Authorial intentions for writing bromance

When writing a bromance, whether originating a screenplay, rewriting one that has been developed previously, or adapting from another source, a first step screenwriters might usefully take is to define their authorial intentions and what might largely be termed as their 'subjective value system' when it comes to male characters, masculinity, male identity and even their own understanding of and commitment to feminism. For instance, Chen discusses bromance in the context of the law and the distribution of power in society, examining both the implicit limitations of bromance as a model of friendship that is beneficial to men and women in that it poses questions of exclusivity and privilege, as well as bromance's more useful relevance as a site for the exploration of a male friendship and intimacy that is not based on competition (Chen, 2011). To what extent a writer aligns with either of these perspectives in writing bromance is an interesting question, but one which could probably be considered from the outset of any writing process. Through an identification of their own ideological position regarding masculine identity, screenwriters can be mindful of the replication of hetero-normativity, homophobia and misogyny. In other words, authorial intention can function as a parameter for creative choices at the level of the screenplay narrative.

Clarity and awareness of these 'gender elements' will inevitably affect the decisions that screenwriters make in relation to the matrix of elements that Parker suggests constitute a screenplay narrative (Parker, 1998). These comprise genre, style, plot, theme and story. A story incorporates character and characterisation in terms of character traits, the actions and choices of characters, and the subjective identity of the character even if their point of view is never presented in the narrative. As male friendship is the central and most defining feature of the bromance, the screenwriter's own perspective on this is critical to how they will represent it thematically in their narrative. It is worth exploring here in further depth the conventions of the bromance, to identify critical issues concerning gender and representation that might confront a screenwriter. As will be discussed, articulating these authorial intentions can be useful for later redeployment in the SIWG.

Bromance as genre

Parker presents a model for understanding and writing genre, one that is comprised of 'sets of patterns [and] combinations of narrative elements, which screenwriters and the audience recognize and use in interpreting the screenwork' (1998: 29). His sets of patterns determining primary genres include form, the number of protagonists, the nature and scale of the conflict, dramatic structure, the function of the plot, and tone. From these, secondary types evolve that are differentiated by character and the nature of the dramatic concerns of the protagonists, such as family, institutional or romantic. The bromedy, according to this rationale, could therefore be defined as a secondary genre from the main comedy genre. *Two and a Half Men* might thus be understood as a bromedic sitcom genre (secondary) emerging from sitcom (primary), yet with its central concern of the male protagonist as their living-together friendship. *Entourage* is an ensemble bromedy emerging from ensemble comedy drama, the central concerns of the main characters being the dynamics of their group friendship and their support of each other.

Distinct from bromedy, according to this definition the bromance is a secondary genre that emerges from the primary genre of drama. *House* is a cross sub-genre, mixing the hospital procedural drama with bromance. The bromance shares some conventions with the romance in that the main sources of dramatic conflict in the narrative are the obstacles (internal and external) facing the protagonist and his bromantic interest in the pursuit of their relationship. Significantly, a third female character frequently functions as an off-screen or relatively insignificant corner of the triangle, symbolising the heterosexual union; the real 'love' interest is the secondary male protagonist (or group of friends, in the ensemble bromance). As bromedy and bromance involve either a male protagonist and a dominant secondary male character, or a group of male friends, it is justifiably a sub-genre in terms of screenwriting generic categories, yet for the purposes of industry factors such as marketing and distribution, it is a stand-alone generic category.

Exploring the value of genre to screenwriters, Selbo maintains that 'varying uses of the term genre has led to a misunderstanding of its efficacious place in the screenwriter's toolbox' (2010: 273). She suggests that a definition of genre in the context of screenwriting practice incorporates an understanding of audience anticipation and expectation from certain genres, including a desired emotional response. At the most simplistic level, an audience watching a bromance would expect to see or experience one or several male protagonists who spend a significant amount of the plot in each other's company, with some degree of emotional depth and complexity evolving in the friendship, and resolution of relationship conflicts. These relationships explore emotional growth and inter-dependency in the same way that an audience would expect to visually experience an intimate and/or sexual relationship in a romance. Selbo explores Grodal's biocultural rationale for genre when she suggests that it has relevance for screenwriters as it supports an awareness of deep primal drives in the audience, something that how-to author Blake Snyder has also popularised (Snyder, 2005). Endorsement of the primal argument in genre as corresponding to the drives and urges of the audience is problematic for screenwriters. It can reinforce a simplistic 'boys will be boys' approach, such as Grodal's (2003) argument that the young man's love of computer war games corresponds to brain chemistry and behaviour patterns evolving from species survival behaviour. The problem for screenwriters here is that writing at the primal level, under the guise of it being natural and innate to humans, can be seen as complicit in the oppression of others. It is possible to suggest that the exclusion of homosexuality in the main characters of a bromance, and the reinforcement of emotional experiences that improve the central characters' heterosexual identity, including a sense of 'male bonding' that is exclusive of women, can be seen as a contemporary form of a masculine rites of passage. Such rites of passage prepare men for heterosexual/reproductive requirements, men-only rituals such as stag nights, finding a best man, being there for the birth of a first child, and becoming able to commit to a woman, and are indeed frequent pre-occupations of bromance narratives, particularly bromcoms. Ultimately, however, the primal argument can be an unfortunate obstacle for the screenwriter who wishes to use the bromance to question some of the more negative and restrictive aspects of heterosexuality, heterosexual male identity, and the expectations put upon men that restrict equality and reproduce inequalities between the genders.

Gay men or homosexual encounters are routinely stereotypically drawn in the bromance, which some have suggested are symbolic of the acute paranoia of heterosexual masculinity's fear of desire for men (Becker, 2006; Steenberg, 2014). In *Y Tu Mama Tambien* the two male protagonists end up in bed together after a drunken night, depicting only half-repressed desires. Homosexuality in the bromance would seem to symbolise deeply buried yearnings that only secondary characters are permitted to express openly, whilst a bromantic protagonist must keep any gay encounters, should they occur, secret and hidden due to his subconscious or unconscious self getting the better of his normally well-behaved heterosexual identity, as depicted in the bromance ensemble *The Hangover 2*. When the dentist character Stu has sex with a lady-boy after taking drugs the narrative suggests that being out of control is a legitimate way for men to indulge in forbidden desires, celebrating the animal in men whilst excluding women from the same excesses. A screenwriter intent on breaking down the rigid codes that define sexuality may thus need to question how repression and desire can be represented without the hysterical shenanigans, paranoia or suggestions of moral depravity. A narrative that includes female 'animalistic' urges might go someway to balance the exclusive supremacy of male physical desire and pleasures. Conversely, *Bridesmaids* (2011), arguably an attempt at being the female equivalent of *The Hangover*, depicts sexual desire within the constraints of a heterosexual one-night stand with a female protagonist who ostensibly needs 'a good man' and one that will be committed to her.

Indicators that the bromance can forge increased physical connections between men, albeit within the enduring 'safe' parameters of heterosexuality, are gaining ground. For example, season eight of *House* charts the final stages of Gregory House's close friendship with Wilson, with the last episodes portraying the two men coming to terms with the notion of unconditional respect in platonic love. They take to the open road together to spend Wilson's last five months of life in the great outdoors, on motorbikes and without a heterosexual mating ritual anywhere in sight. Central to the culmination of the series is the importance of this enduring friendship to House's sense of self-worth and his deep desire to change his self-destructive patterns that trap him in compulsive psychological games designed to keep people at arms' length, and which generate distrust and unhappiness not only in his relationship with others but also with himself. Wilson, by embodying customary 'bromantic' opposite traits, serves as a potential role model to House that for most of the series he has resisted and ridiculed. Cancer is the catalyst to House's acceptance of what Wilson can teach him when he nurtures, cares for and supports his friend in the final stages of the illness. Coming to terms with Wilson's death triggers in House a new self-awareness and desire to heal himself. Whilst one man tries to heal/care for the other's body, the other heals his friend's sick mind. In terms of the depth of connection between the men, sexual expression of love could ensue in this highly intimate context. The fact that House and Wilson's intense interaction does not progress to sexual love, but to a road trip, is unsurprising in the context of conventional restrictions to the representation of sexuality in the bromance. However, the series goes some way in exploring emotional intimacy between men. Indeed, the global popularity of *House* indicates that male protagonists that are not interested in or capable of 'normal' heterosexual relationships or kinship behaviours, such as building a family, and who do not resolve this 'problem' (as in many mainstream bromcoms) do not necessarily alienate the audience on a primal level.

Other screenwriting approaches relevant to the consideration of bromance as a genre include McKee's (1999) view that comedy as a genre functions to attack cultural and social institutions. In this respect, bromance and bromedy narratives can be read as poking fun at male bonding and masculine identity formation processes. The bromance is a genre that potentially offers the screenwriter relative freedom to attack and subvert conventional masculinity, at the same time as reinforcing notions that the male (and female) audience might find comfortable or affirming. Alberti, for example, refers to *Knocked Up* (2007) in terms of the contradictions and confusions, as well as new liberations, for men when 'alpha male' constructions of male dominance are unstable, if not crumbling (2013: 163).

Developing the bromantic hero

The bromantic hero is often characterised as a conformist, a man constrained by duty and self-imposed expectations of achievement; in essence, as someone who is 'doing the right thing' but with inner wounds to heal. Alternatively, the bromantic hero is non-conformist, like Gregory House, Walden (*Two and a Half Men*) and Sherlock Holmes in both television series *Sherlock* (2010–) and feature film *Sherlock Holmes* (2009). Issues of self-esteem are usually indicated in both types of men, in terms of how he feels about trust, success, women and friendships. A clear emotional wound, revolving around any one of these issues, is normally set up early in the first act of the narrative.

In the bromcom, the hero is often pursuing or facing the challenge of a 'rites of passage', such as a wedding, fatherhood, divorce or illness. In television series, such as *House*, *The Inbetweeners*, *Two and a Half Men* and *Entourage*, episodes and season arcs deal with multiple incidents that involve women, failed relationships and work responsibilities, in which the evolved self of the hero is challenged to emerge. In terms of race and class, the bromantic hero is frequently white, aspirational and affluent and/or educated: House in *House* is a leading medical consultant; Miles in *Sideways* is a snobbish novelist and would-be oenologist; Vincent in *Entourage* is a talented emerging Hollywood star. Ethnically mixed bromance narratives are beginning to emerge, but normally as relationships within the parameters of other genres. Black/white bromantic pairings appear in the crime drama series *Hannibal* (2013–), in the drama *The Soloist* (2009) and in the comedy drama *The Bucket List* (2007). The common denominator in these narratives however is that the main protagonist is white.

As mentioned, the mandate in popular screenwriting discourse for protagonists to have an inner wound is predominant in most bromances, yet the enduring traits of 'alpha male' status, to reflect Alberti's (2013) use of the term, indicate a trope that limits the range and possibilities for the bromantic hero in terms of race, class, sexuality and physical ability, particularly in bromcoms. This in turn limits the kinds of internal 'wounds' the bromantic hero might have, which is significant for screenwriters who seek to push the boundaries of the bromcom by giving the main protagonist internal conflicts deriving from social inequalities, for example, and friendships which provide emotional support, intimacy and allegiance.

The bromantic 'partner'

As in the construction of conventional romance narratives, the secondary protagonist represents seemingly opposite qualities and traits that the main protagonist is at first challenged by, before learning from them and inevitably supporting maturational growth. The exchange of traits can also be reciprocal in that the bromantic partner learns from, and is ultimately benefited by, traits and values of the protagonist. In bromcoms, this can take the form of the bromantic hero casting aside superficial and judgemental attitudes (towards the bromantic partner in particular), leading to a healing of his inner conflicts that are holding him back in finding happiness, self-mastery and true selfhood, *Due Date* and *Dinner for Schmucks* (2010) being good examples. The familiarity of this classic transformational pattern reflects guidance for creating transformational arcs in many screenwriting manuals such as those by Marks (2009), Vogler (2007), and Snyder (2005).

Often inspired by wildness and an unconventional value system, the secondary protagonist (although sometimes the protagonist) embodies the spirit of liberation. He possesses echoes of the Wild Man or Fool archetype of Jungian mythology; someone on the edge of society, a misfit or a rebel, as in films such as *The Soloist, Dinner for Schmucks, I Love You, Man, Due Date* and *The Hangover*. During the course of the unfolding bromantic relationship, transactional exchanges take place between the two men that gradually impact on the main protagonist's world-view and value system. In *House*, House's extreme irreverence is seen as an essential ingredient of his medical genius but also a factor in his compulsive misanthropy. His understanding of the dark side of humanity enables him to crack medical mysteries whilst also allowing him to affirm his contempt for human weakness – a self-destructive entrapment. Wilson's converse humanity, exemplified by his patience, empathy and capacity to forgive, represents House's ultimate redemption and salvation by acquiring these very traits.

As explored by Chen, the notion of unconditional fraternity is elevated by privileging friendship and loyalty, as well as the lengths that male characters will go to for one another to the exclusion of females. Learning about himself from these emotional and physical challenges provided by the bromantic partner, the bromantic hero evolves but never at the expense or loss of his new buddy or group of friends. The importance of male friendship as the ultimate form of understanding and empathy for men is an implicit theme in the bromance. *Entourage*, for example, centres on actor Vinnie Jones and his motley crew of old friends. As the alpha male of the group, defined by his looks, star status, wealth and sex appeal, Vinnie demands and returns loyalty in return for his magnanimous patronage of his less fortunate male friends. Vinnie's most complex relationship is arguably with best friend and manager E, who embodies many qualities that Vinnie does not possess: he is small, faithful and committed to his girlfriend, and his luck comes through hard work; all features of the polarisation at work in bromantic relationships. However, ensemble bromances such as *Entourage* potentially give more opportunities for screenwriters to dismantle the genre's grip on heterosexual mirroring and to explore group dynamics between men in the same way that *Sex and the City* (1998–2004) explores the dynamics of female friendship (Alberti, 2013). There would appear to be plenty of unexplored comedic explorations of male friendship in the gap between the ubiquitous 'opposites repel until they attract' scenario derived from mainstream romantic comedy, as described by Mernitt (2000), and the repressed forms of male friendship where a permitted heterosexual masculinity bonds the men (as in *Entourage* and *The Inbetweeners*).

The female character

A recurring theme of bromantic narratives is that male friendship, whether in the dyadic bromance or the ensemble, does indeed constitute the most effective and sacred space for the facilitation of a male identity that is unshackled by the complications of sexual relationships and gender baggage. The most apt narrative metaphor for this sacred space is the 'man cave', a retreat that symbolises the freedom needed by the male from any kind of female intrusion. For screenwriters wanting to explore male friendships in bromance narratives, some difficult yet fundamental questions can surface, including: why is the male identity crisis so often triggered and resolved by another male, resulting in a bromantic relationship which takes the form of a love story; is the familiar trope of unconditional brotherly love essential to the success of the genre and its fulfilment of audience expectations; and where and how do women feature in the bromance dyad or grouping?

Perhaps the most problematic challenge to screenwriters developing bromances, a genre described by Chen (2011) as potentially 'harmful' to the feminist project is the role and function of female characters.

Unfortunately, the bromantic relationship in many mainstream texts, particularly bromcoms, seems to necessitate the presence of the female stereotype. Another critical challenge for screenwriters of the bromance, therefore, is dealing with and avoiding the implicit misogyny that can permeate these narratives. Whilst many writers may not consciously choose to create stereotypes, the privileged male friendship of the bromance restricts narrative agency for female characters on a surprising number of levels. From *Entourage* to *House* to *The Hangover*, female stereotypes abound in the form of strippers, models, hookers, victims, seductresses, frustrated housewives, nagging or betrayed wives, good and bad mothers, and the independent career woman who will not let a dysfunctional man get in her way. The female character can take the form of antagonism for the main protagonist, a sexual rival for the secondary bromantic protagonist, an object of lust, or simply a bastion of morality and stability to which the dysfunctional men can only aspire to be good enough. Feminist film and media studies have focused on both psychoanalytic and socio-economic causes for the ongoing dread of women that manifests in stereotypical forms (e.g. Caplan, 1983), yet the persistent appearance of the female stereotype in bromance feels resonant with backlash ideology.

With such limited forms of female characterisation, many bromances reinforce the impossibility of intimate friendship between men and women that is not predicated on sexual attraction. The popularity of bromances would seem to reflect a desire in the primary target audience (heterosexual young men) to derive satisfaction from female characters in stereotypical roles, from sexual objects to patient angels to suffocating harridans, or a combination of all three. Yet, whilst critical discourse points to these types as emblematic of misogynistic reactionary values, Alberti suggests they equally reflect self-loathing and panic as central features of a heterosexual male identity crisis (2013: 163) which the audience might share. The lack of women confidants to whom bromantic heroes expose their fears and vulnerabilities attests to a male identity that is still bound up in pride and male ego, and that has a long way to go before it can see women as anything but 'other'. Screenwriters' representations of female agency in helping the bromantic hero with his self-loathing might involve giving female characters the capacity to be playmates in hedonism, or emotionally available non-sexual friends to whom the hero can expose emotional or physical vulnerability; yet, such characters are few and far between. One notable recent exception is *Identify Thief* (2013), which charts the surprising friendship between a hedonistic woman who falls through the cracks and gains self-worth through the support of a heterosexual man, which eventually also includes that of his wife and daughters. Unlike the wild men and bad boys of bromance who get off scot free, such as Jack in *Sideways*, and the men in *The Hangover*, this female hedonist ends up in prison to resolve the error of her ways. The sex, drugs and rock 'n' roll permissive and celebratory world of *The Hangover*, and the articulation that only men can truly understand and look out for each other, conversely serves to demote women and restrict their modes of representation.

Thus, the bromance truly allows men to 'have it all' whilst women stay at home waiting for their roving bad boy to call. *Bridesmaids* (2011) affords its female characters very limited forms of hedonism or 'having it all' behaviour, reinforcing this notion of a moral and sexual double standard at work in mainstream comedies. Development issues in the SIWG for a bromance might therefore include assumptions of gender around which the screenwriter might have to tread carefully if they are motivated to avoid recreating over-familiar stereotypes in both male and female characters. Discussions of youth and sexual attractiveness in female characters is also a feature of bromances, and thus also potentially an issue in the SIWG. The frequency of young and beautiful women in bromances is highly problematic for feminist writers, yet seemingly a non-negotiable source of pleasure for the male audience. Creating female characters in bromances might therefore entail some collusion and feelings of 'selling out' by a critically engaged screenwriter in the SIWG, particularly when it comes to the creation of the female characters and homosexual expressions of love.

Reclaiming types

Archetypes are a familiar notion to character development in screenwriting (e.g. Vogler (2007); Indick (2004); Hudson (2009)), which supports the notion that familiarity in types attests to a fixed and universal 'truth' about human nature that is recognisable and attractive to audiences. Vogler's suggestion that archetypes, often reflected in other characters, correspond to the diverse potential of the hero to achieve self-mastery is a useful model for character development, yet as a paradigm for characterisation that seeks to question gender roles and issues of representation, they are arguably limited for writers. To counterbalance this, a typological framework of 'the role-choice' (Jacey, 2010) can be broadly defined as a way for screenwriters to think about how a character makes sense of their own situation within familiar 'roles' and expectations of their gender in wider culture, and how characters identify with these according to their own subjectivity. This can be demonstrated in the story through the character's emotional states, attitudes, values and internalisation of hegemonic values, such as gender expectations, in the diegetic world they belong to. Being character-driven, role choice is primarily a narrative form in developing subjectivity and characteristics/traits in protagonists, secondary and even tertiary characters. 'Feminine' role choices include those of mother, wife, sorority, amazon, rival, caryatid, victim, child and healer. 'Masculine' role choices are father, husband, fraternity, warrior, rebel, boss, victim, child and healer. Using role choices, writers can examine their own value system when it comes to the ways they relate role choices with either male or female characters, and more specifically, how they represent them in terms of traits, attitudes, and both personal and cultural values associated with the role choice.

When it comes to the development of both male and female characters in bromances, using role choices also enables a screenwriter to critically question their own implicit values about gender assumptions. If and when developing a bromance, conventional roles traditionally associated with men can be brainstormed to identify the stereotypical ways in which they might be depicted. The conscious choice to subvert negatively clichéd representations, such as male sexual rivalry over an attractive woman, the challenge of a father-in-law-to-be and the would-be husband of his daughter, or men needing to repress emotions when female characters are verbally volatile, can be put to the test, and deliberately avoided, when shaping characters. In certain instances, it can be equally illuminating for screenwriters to attach conventionally masculine attributes such as self-sacrifice, heroism, fraternity, protectiveness and loyalty to female characters, which in the bromance and the bromedy is exceptionally rare.

Another creative strategy for screenwriters seeking to subvert stereotypes can be achieved by the use of the composite character paradigm (Jacey, 2010). This is a device for narrative construction that can be used to link the themes of the story with character. For example, if the themes of a bromance are identity and the value of friendship, the composite character symbolises this overall, combined theme. Individual characters created by the screenwriter are developed according to how they serve and contribute to this central theme, as parts of a whole rather than the simplistic but overused strategy of making secondary characters only function to serve the plot. A female character, rather than being a simplistic causal device such as a nag (the bad wife in *The Hangover*), sexual object (the beautiful hooker/tart with a heart), pinnacle of morality (the waiting fiancée in *The Hangover*, or the wife about to give birth in *Due Date*) to which the errant male must aspire, or ballbreaker (e.g. Cuddy in *House*) would be characterised in terms of her identity and need for friendship, requiring a consideration of her unique traits and agency. This would immediately assist the screenwriter in elevating her from the cipher form that she frequently takes, give her more dimension, and even permit this new version of the female character to go on the metaphoric or literal journey as well. This increased dimensionality is evident in *Y Tu Mama Tambien* where Maribel's agenda and needs are portrayed from her own point of view, resulting in a deeper sense of characterisation.

Bromance and tone

As a genre, personal drama generally allows screenwriters more scope to focus and explore the human condition through the employment of a dramatic tone that conveys realistic characterisation (Parker, 1998). In writing dramatic bromances, the complexity of friendship and the wide-ranging forms which friendship can take between men offers writers great scope to avoid negative stereotyping and hegemonic versions of masculinity which peddles back to the audience somewhat repetitive messages of what men are and should be, that is, the 'boys will be boys' agenda. Emotional intimacy and support, vulnerability, reciprocal care, feelings of loss and inadequacy, and men's experience of nurturing, remain ripe for conscious exploration by writers outside the bounds of what is arguably a prevailing masculine hegemony.

Whilst comedy is a genre where stereotyping can be employed to generate laughter through satire, ridicule and gross-out antics, screenwriters of the bromance invariably need to make a creative judgement call regarding the use of negative stereotyping in their narratives, and how to subvert them to support their overall authorial intentions and values. Bromcoms frequently rely on physical comedy in their narratives, including sex, scatology, alcoholic- or drug-fuelled excesses, shame and ridicule related to uncontrollable bodily functions (farting, erections, failure to perform), sexually devouring unattractive women or persecuting repugnant older women, and humiliating physical procedures. The lack of comedic narratives with female protagonists and extreme physical comedy only reinforces the bromcom's function in cementing outrageousness and masculinity.

Doubt whether female writers can authentically create male bawdy and excess is one possible risk in the SIWG. Questions around the female screenwriter's ability to write a bromedy or other male-driven film screenplays could be symptomatic of a barrier to the employment of women screenwriters in certain male-driven genres targeted at male audiences, and further research into the employment of women screenwriters in male driven narratives is needed. Film producer Tim Bevan claims, in an interview with Shoard, 'For a hard-ass thriller you would instinctively go towards a male writer' (*The Guardian*, 2012), although also claiming Bridget O'Connor's work on *Tinker Tailor Soldier Spy* disproved his assumption. Further research is needed to assess the relationship to gender of the writer and on screen representation of male characters. Stacy Smith suggests that 'entrenched industry perceptions and beliefs about market forces and male audiences contribute to perpetuating the status quo. Unconscious cultural or traditional stereotypes about occupations and sex roles might unwittingly seep into characterisations and fictional, even fantastical, realms' (*The Huffington Post*, 2010).

Conclusion

The collaborative development process of a screenplay inevitably involves a wide range of attitudes and assumptions about 'what works', and the credence given to creative opinions in the SIWG accords, as McDonald has described, to levels of status (McDonald, 2010). In a collaborative development of a bromance, screenwriters can be inevitably required, directly or indirectly, to specifically manage potentially conflicting values around male friendship and masculine identity, including their own ideological motivations and those of the group members. Values in a SIWG may be implicit, covert, hidden or overt in relation to the perceived desirability of male characterisation, particularly for audience satisfaction in a mainstream genre. As such, screenwriters might find themselves in the position of guardian of their own preferred implicit codes for characterisation or theme, particularly when other members of the group call for clichéd or hegemonic modes of representation. To what extent women are employed as writers of bromances is outside the scope of this paper, but judging by statistics of credited screenwriters of produced films alone, it is safe to assume the bromance largely remains the preserve of the male writer.

Whilst the bromance and the bromedy are continually evolving, both as a genre and as a type of friendship in the story, screenwriters will have opportunities for developing new representations of men. As this chapter has highlighted, clarity of authorial intention, strategies to

avoid cliché and stereotyping in characterisation, and a clear articulation of theme can support writers in the creative management of bromantic narratives and their potentially problematic protagonists in the
development process. On the assumption that audience expectations of
the bromance as a genre can be stretched by new representations of
masculinity, male friendship and friendship between men and women,
this chapter encourages screenwriters to rethink the male character and
liberate him from his limiting and lonely hetero-normative man cave.

References

Alberti, J. (2013) ' "I Love You, Man": Bromances, the Construction of Masculin-
ity, and the Continuing Evolution of the Romantic Comedy' in *Quarterly Review
of Film and Video*, 30(2), 159–172.
Band of Brothers (2001) Wrs. Various, Dirs. Various, UK/US.
Becker, R. (2006) *Gay TV and Straight America*, Piscataway: Rutgers University
Press.
Bridesmaids (2011) Wrs. Kirsten Wiig and Annie Mumolo, Dir. Paul Feig, USA,
125 mins.
Caplan, E.A. (1983) *Women and Film: Both sides of the Camera*, London: Methuen.
Chen, E.J. (2011) 'Caught in a Bad Bromance' in *Texas Journal of Women and the
Law*, 21(2), 241–266.
Dinner for Schmucks (2010) Wrs. David Guion and Michael Handelman, Dir. Jay
Roach, USA, 114 mins.
Due Date (2010) Wrs. Alan R. Cohen, Alan Freedland, Adam Sztykiel and Todd
Phillips, Dir. Todd Phillips, USA, 95 mins.
Entourage (2004–2011) Cr. Doug Ellin, Dir. Various, USA.
Francke, L. (1994) *Script Girls: Women Screenwriters in Hollywood*, London: British
Film Institute.
Grodal, T. (2003) 'Stories for Eye, Ear, and Muscles: Video Games, Media, and
Embodied Experiences' in Bernard Perron and Mark J. P Wolf (eds.) *The Video
Game Theory Reader*, New York: Routledge, pp. 129–155.
Hannibal (2013–) Cr. Bryan Fuller, Dir. Various, USA.
House (2004–12) Cr. David Shore, Dir. Various, USA.
Hudson, K. (2009) *The Virgin's Promise: Writing Stories of Feminine Creative, Spiritual
and Sexual Awakening*, Studio City, CA: Michael Wiese Productions.
I Love You, Man (2009) Directed by John Hamburg. Written by John Hamburg and
Larry Levin. US: Dreamworks SKG. 105 mins.
Indick, W. (2004) *Psychology for Screenwriters*, Studio City, CA: Michael Wiese
Productions.
Jacey, H. (2010) *The Woman in the Story: Writing Memorable Female Characters*,
Studio City, CA: Michael Wiese Productions.
Jacey, H. (2010) *Journey to Nowhere: Christopher Vogler's Screenwriting Paradigm and
the Writing of Loy*, Doctoral Thesis, University of the Arts London.
Knocked Up (2007) Wr./Dir. Judd Apatow, USA, 129 mins.
Marks, D. (2009) *Inside Story: The Power of the Transformational Arc*, London: A&C
Black.

Master and Commander (2003) Wrs. Peter Weir and John Collee, Dir. Peter Weir, USA, 138 mins.

McDonald, I.W. (2010) ' " ... So It's Not Surprising I'm Neurotic" the Screenwriter and the Screen Idea Work Group' in *Journal of Screenwriting*, 1(1), 45–58.

McKee, R. (1999) *Story: Substance, Structure, Style and the Principles of Screenwriting*, London: Methuen.

Mernitt, B. (2000) *Writing the Romantic Comedy*, New York: Harper Collins.

Mortimer, C. (2010) *Romantic Comedy*, London: Routledge.

Parker, P. (1998) *The Art and Science of Screenwriting*, Exeter: Intellect Books.

Pineapple Express (2008) Wrs. Seth Rogen and Evan Goldberg, Dir. David Gordon Green, USA, 111 mins.

Seger, L. (1996) *When Women Call the Shots: The Developing Power and Influence of Women in Film and Television*, New York: Henry Holt.

Selbo, J. (2010) 'The Constructive Use of Film Genre for the Screenwriter: Mental Space of Film Genre – First Exploration' in *Journal of Screenwriting* 1(2), 273–289.

Sex and the City (1998–2004) Cr. Darren Star, Dir. Various, USA.

Sherlock (2010–) Crs. Mark Gatiss and Stephen Moffatt, Dir. Various, UK.

Sherlock Holmes (2009) Wrs. Michael Roberts Johnson, Anthony Peckham and Simon Kinberg, Dir. Guy Ritchie, USA, 128 mins.

Shoard, C. (2012) 'Bafta Awards: British Women vie for Writing Prizes' in *The Guardian*, online, available at http://www.theguardian.com/film/2012/feb/10/bafta-awards-british-women-writing [accessed 10 February 2012].

Sideways (2004) Wrs. Alexander Payne and Jim Taylor, Dir. Alexander Payne, USA, 126 mins.

Silverstein, M. (2013) *In Her Voice: Women Directors Talk Directing*, USA: Women and Hollywood.

Smith, S. (2010) 'Female Directors, Writers and Producers in Film Matter' in *The Huffington Post* [online], available from: http://www.huffingtonpost.com/stacy-smith/female-directors-writers_b_480848.html [accessed 1 March 2010].

Snyder, B. (2005) *Save the Cat: The Last Book on Screenwriting that You'll Ever Need*, Studio City, CA: Michael Wiese Productions.

Steenberg, L. (2014) ' "Get More Action" on Gladiatorial Television: Simulation and Masculinity on *Deadliest Warrior*' in Brenda R. Weber (ed), *Reality Gendervision: Sexuality & Gender on Transatlantic Reality Television*, London: Duke University Press.

The Bucket List (2007) Wr. Justin Zackham, Dir. Rob Reiner, USA, 97 mins.

The Hangover (2009) Wrs. John Lucas and Scott Moore, Dir. Todd Phillips, USA, 100 mins.

The Hangover 2 (2011) Wrs. Craig Mazin, Scot Armstrong and Todd Phillips, Dir. Todd Phillips, USA, 102 mins.

The Inbetweeners (2008–2010) Wrs. Damon Beesley and Iain Morris, Dir. Various, UK.

The Soloist (2009) Wr. Susannah Grant, Dir. Joe Wright, USA, 117 mins.

Two and Half Men (2003–) Crs. Chuck Lorre and Lee Aronsohn, Dir. Various, USA.

Vogler, C. (2007) *The Writer's Journey: Mythic Structure for Writers* (3rd ed.), Studio City, CA: Michael Wiese Productions.

Y Tu Mama Tambien (2001) Wrs. Alfonso Cuaron and Carlo Cuaron, Dir. Alfonso Cuaron, Mexico, 106 mins.

15
Gals Who Make the Jokes: Feature Film Screenwriting for the Satirical Female Voice

Marilyn Tofler

Introduction

This chapter aims to contribute to an understanding of satire as it relates to screenwriting. The primary focus is on methods of screenwriting useful for the creation of social satire, featuring a female protagonist. The work stems from my practice-based PhD, *Give the Girl a Line: Methods of Feature Film Screenwriting for the Satirical Female Voice*, developed at RMIT University under the supervision of Dr Lisa Dethridge.

Theorists and critics agree there is a need for strong comedic female roles on screen. British screenwriter and academic, Helen Jacey, argues that the 'vast majority of the screenwriting guides tend to ignore gender difference' (2010); *Boston Globe* critic, Ty Burr, suggests that 'more than ever movies are built around male roles. Increasingly, the pickings for women aren't just slim but nonexistent' (Burr, 2005: 9); and *The New Yorker* film critic, David Denby, argues that the female protagonist in many contemporary romantic comedies 'doesn't have an idea in her head, and she's not the one who makes the jokes' (Denby, 2007: 2). The issue of comedic roles for females is not a new one. Eighteenth-century poet and critic, Samuel Johnson, pointed out that the history of satire was predominantly written by men and displayed women in a less than favourable light (cited by Hodgart, 1969: 79). This work thus addresses the issue directly by examining how a screenwriter can create a female protagonist who is, in the end, more witty, intelligent and humorous than her male counterpart.

In order to achieve this, the chapter first analyses and defines the generic features of satire, focusing on the work of Northrop Frye, Gilbert

Highet, Molière and others. Frye's principles of satire are then offered in application to the acclaimed feature screenplay *Something's Gotta Give* (Meyers, 2002), a classic romantic comedy screenplay with a satirical sensibility, focusing on the relationships of several multi-generational couples. This work aims to determine more about both the structure of satire and screenwriting method. As such, it is important to analyse how screenwriter Nancy Meyers has used a satirical writing method to create her female protagonist in the hope that by doing so, we can understand how such theories and techniques may useful to any screenwriter developing strong and funny female characters.

Definitions of satire

An initial search for theory relating to satire found most references were within the fields of literature and theatre. These included texts by literary theorists and historians such as Matthew Hodgart, Gilbert Highett, David Worcester, Edward Rosenheim and Northrop Frye. More recently, however, film scholar Mark Hamilton has applied Northrop Frye's theories to a discussion of the feature film (2006). That said, there is still very limited research relating to satire and the practice of screenwriting, and an even greater lack of practice-based theory relating to the actual techniques of writing satire for female roles.

Let us begin then by defining the guiding features of satire, as written about by various authors. Matthew Hodgart suggests that 'satire on women is a comic recording of deviations from the ideal [...] and traditionally it has been centred on the cardinals of docility, chastity and modesty' (1969: 79–81). He argues that satirists traditionally lampoon women who stray from the boundaries placed upon them by society around submissiveness, modesty and humility.

Seventeenth-century playwright Molière is often seen as the 'originator of modern satirical comedy' (Norman, 1999: 1). In the preface to his theatrical satire of religion, *Tartuffe*, Molière argues: 'the most forceful lines of a serious moral statement are usually less powerful than those of a satire; and nothing will reform most men better than the depiction of their faults'. He suggests that the satirist can deliver 'a vigorous blow to vices' simply by exposing them to public laughter, pointing out that once people see their faults attacked and exposed to public laughter, they are more likely to correct them (1965: 2–3).

Gilbert Highet distinguishes between satire and other comic forms including farce, pure comedy, invective and lampoon. He claims that in nearly every satire there are some elements of comedy and farce, and asserts that the author of comedy always wishes to evoke laughter. In contrast, the author of farce focuses upon elements of the 'ridiculous' and 'ludicrous', using exaggeration and slapstick in order to create 'gaiety' and a 'joke' (1962: 155–156). Highet defines pure comedy as 'a story which merely amuses or thrills us, with no aftertaste of derisive bitterness' (1962: 150) and thus points out that satire is defined by the use of invective and lampoon (1962: 155). Invective, according to the *Concise Oxford Dictionary*, is a 'violent attack in words' or 'abusive oratory'. The author of a lampoon uses invective to criticise or ridicule a person, group or institution. Like Molière, Highet also alerts us to what is perhaps the key function of satire: to attack a target that represents an 'evil' deserving of audience contempt (1962: 156).

Highet also suggests that authors of comedy and farce have kindly motivations, 'rich with liking' and wanting to 'appreciate and enjoy'. In contrast, authors of invective and lampoon 'are full of hatred, and wish only to destroy' (1962: 154–155). He argues that the writer of satire strives for emotional effects within an audience somewhere in-between these two polar emotions.

David Worcester would seem to agree with Highet on the distinction between satire and pure comedy. Worcester asserts that comic wit is loose, casual and 'relatively purposeless'; in contrast, 'the laughter of satire is focused toward a preconceived end'. Furthermore, Worcester asserts that a tone of harsh derision denotes satire whilst gentle banter and mild amusement denotes comedy (1940: 37–38). Like Worcester and Highet, Edward Rosenheim asserts that satire goes further than pure comedy, in that satire not only intends to make an audience laugh but also aims to raise concerns and allow an audience to question their belief systems (1971: 317).

If these are the features of satire, then we can turn to the work of Sigmund Freud in order to understand its underlying principles. In *Jokes and Their Relation to the Unconscious*, Freud suggests that a joke can be a powerful swayer of beliefs, because jokes and laughter impair the critical judgement of an audience (1960: 142). He also argues that by combining a joke with an attack of social injustice, a writer is able to 'bribe the hearer [...] into taking sides with us without any very close investigation' (1960: 103). Where aggressiveness may fail in exposing social injustice, the use of wit and humour by the satirist may soften an attack but still hit and ridicule or punish the target. According to Freud, jokes provide a persuasive method 'which is psychologically the more effective' (1960: 133). Humour can thus be used to align an audience with a screenwriter's viewpoint and 'bring the laughers over to our side' (Freud, 1960:103).

From the features and principles offered, then, we can understand that the satirist attacks social injustices by using comedy and lampoon, and that the satirist may examine issues that convince an audience to question their own beliefs, particularly in relation to social vanities and inequality. Frye goes even further in his definition of satire with his discussion of the use of additional techniques applied by the author of satire. In other words, the practice of satirical writing. This includes the satirist's use of irony, moral viewpoint, degradation of character or belief alongside the techniques of wit and humour, a sense of attack, and an absurd and grotesque fantasy. We will now examine the theory of Northrop Frye to further understand specific techniques of satirical writing.

Northrop Frye: Anatomy of criticism

Frye attempts to formulate an overall view of the scope, theory, principles and techniques of literary criticism (1957: 3), however he has been criticised by some as being difficult to understand (Hart, 1994: 2). According to Hamilton, although there is no doubt that Frye's theories are groundbreaking, they are often problematic to apply (2006: ii).

Hamilton cites that within his theory of Myths, Frye describes the genres of Comedy, Romance, Tragedy and Irony/Satire by identifying typical narrative characteristics and structures for each of these genres (2006: 1). Let us now look closely at this discussion of satire in order to gain a clear understanding of this genre.

Frye describes satire as a form that includes phases of both comedy and tragedy (Frye, 1957: 236). Satire may present outrageous situations in an ironic fashion to reinforce the author's moral position. He claims that 'satire shows literature assuming a special function of analysis, of breaking up the lumber of stereotypes, fossilized beliefs, superstitious terrors, crank theories, pedantic dogmatisms, oppressive fashions, and all other things that impede the free movement [...] of society' (Frye, 1957: 233). In this sense, Frye's theory clearly aims for cultural reform.

In the absence of any clear categorisation by Frye, I have identified six basic characteristics in his discussion of satire. These characteristics are designed to enable an examination of Frye's theory in the hope that they can be applied to a screenplay case study; and, in turn, then be applied in practice, by the screenwriter.

In short, Frye emphasises the following: that the author must identify a moral viewpoint in order to select an object of attack; and that, in
order to make a sharp assault on unreasonable beliefs or social injustice,
a cache of satirical weapons including wit, humour, irony, degradation,
the absurd and farcical fantasy elements must be used. Armed with
these, we can observe and analyse Nancy Meyers' screenplay for *Something's Gotta Give* in order to understand not only what satirical elements
exist but also how and why they have been written.

Satire and *Something's Gotta Give*

Nancy Meyers is known for critically and commercially successful
screenplays that feature strong female heroines. She has written over ten
produced screenplays, including *Private Benjamin* (1980), *Protocol* (1984),
Father of the Bride (1991), *The Parent Trap* (1998) and *The Holiday* (2006).
Her 2003 film *Something's Gotta Give*, a satirical romantic comedy dealing with gender and the sexual conduct of characters in their late middle
age, grossed $124,590,960 in the USA (The Internet Movie Database,
2011).

In the film, Harry Sanborn, a 63-year-old perpetual playboy, and his
20-something girlfriend, Marin Barry, intend on having a weekend fling
at Marin's mother's beach house in the Hamptons. Harry suffers a heart
attack during foreplay with Marin and is nursed to health by her disapproving mother, divorced playwright Erica Barry. In the process, Harry
and Erica fall in love, but Harry finds it hard to commit. Erica is heartbro-
ken to discover that Harry has returned to his philandering ways in the
city, once again dating younger women. The relationship is complicated
further when Erica starts to date Harry's much younger doctor, Julian.
Erica satirises Harry, the playboy, in her latest play and he is forced to
come to terms with his womanising ways. They are finally reunited in
Paris where he declares his love for her.

Let us now observe Frye's key terms to analyse how screenwriter
Nancy Meyers has used satirical writing techniques in the development
of her screenplay for *Something's Gotta Give*. By doing this, it is hoped
that techniques specific to screenwriters interested in writing satire for
the strong female protagonist will emerge, with the intention that they
can then be practised.

The satirist's use of wit or humour

Frye argues that wit or humour is 'essential to satire' (1957: 224).
A screenplay will, however, evolve from a work of 'pure' comedy to a

satirical comedy by focusing upon an object of attack, comparable to the lampoon. An author of satire may ridicule a victim but does so with wit, humour and irony (Frye, 1957: 224–229). In examining Meyers' screenplay, it is clear to see these techniques in abundance. Meyers shows her protagonist Erica using wit and humour rather than mere aggression to attack Harry's penchant for womanising, sexist behaviour and failure to commit to a relationship.

Erica attacks Harry in a restrained way. For instance, in the film's first act, dramatic conflict is shown when Erica describes Harry's genre of hip-hop music as 'violent and crude...not to mention just a tad misogynistic' (Meyers, 2002: 15). After Harry replies that 'a lot of people see rapping as poetry', Erica is able to restrain her attack. She replies wittily, 'Yeah, but come on, how many words can you rhyme with "Bitch"?'

Meyers also ensures that Erica is able to tame Harry with humour when he is being shallow or rude. For instance, in the film's second act, Harry is unable to commit to saying 'I love you' and instead delivers a paltry 'I love ya'. Erica responds with a dry '...I don't know if it ends in "ya" if it's an official I love you' (Meyers, 2002: 86). Meyers also portrays her female protagonist as smart and genuine by contrasting her with a male protagonist who is often shallow and insincere, thereby using Frye's principle of wit or humour to hold injustices up to an audience for their judgement.

The satirist's focus upon an object of attack

Frye clearly states that the writer of satire should focus upon an object of attack. To do so, he or she should show a sense of aggression towards a social injustice. This may take the form of an attack of unreasonable beliefs of characters created by the satirist to magnify what he or she believes to be unjust. Rather than a direct verbal attack, Worcester argues that generally within satire, the 'emotion is controlled, the blow is softened and the approach is indirect' (1940: 17).

In *Something's Gotta Give*, Meyers attacks those who are insincere and unjust in their attitudes towards women. To set up the comedy, Meyers ensures that Harry gives Erica plenty of fuel to use in her attack on him. Meyers has constructed Harry as a womaniser who has never been married. Erica may then attack him for being chauvinistic, too old for Marin and the fact that he cannot commit to marriage. In the process, Harry's suave playboy image is shattered. Nobody is immune from Meyers' attack, however, even Erica is a figure of ridicule. In the first act of the film, Harry playfully attacks Erica for always covering her body, insinuating that she is uptight and repressed (Meyers, 2002: 45–48). In this way, Meyers is using the antagonist to satirise what Frye would see as the compulsive behaviour of her female protagonist (1957: 226).

Later in the film, Erica is deeply hurt by Harry's philandering and failure to commit. She wreaks revenge, humiliating Harry and attacking him in a restrained way by killing off a character 'like' him in her Broadway play. Erica exacts a true writer's revenge, humiliating Harry as she makes him 'the laughing stock of Broadway' (Meyers, 2002: 110).

In the third act of the film, Harry visits a number of his former lovers to ascertain where he went wrong. Meyers subsequently reveals more of Harry's backstory when he is attacked by generations of women that he has previously wronged. He learns that a 'conventional life' of monogamy is preferable to being hated. Harry subsequently decides to give up on his 'compulsive' dating and settle down with Erica, which supports Frye's first phase satire: where 'conventional life' is recommended with an avoidance of 'compulsive behaviour' (1957: 226).

The satirist's use of irony

The third of Frye's characteristics concerns the satirist's application of irony, a complex term that requires further focus. The *Concise Oxford Dictionary* defines irony as:

> expression of one's meaning by language of opposite or different tendency, esp. simulated adoption of another's point of view or laudatory tone for purpose of ridicule; ill-timed or perverse arrival of event or circumstance in itself desirable, as if in mockery of the fitness of things; use of language that has an inner meaning for a privileged audience and an outer meaning for the person addressed or concerned.

This suggests that the ironic tone is one of artifice, whereby the author may adopt a contemptible character's point of view before distorting and bewildering them with comic capriciousness.

Frye defines irony as a 'technique of saying as little and meaning as much as possible' or 'a pattern of words that turns away from direct statement or its own obvious meaning' (1957: 40). A writer who uses irony may refrain from clearly stating the truth; however, to an audience, that truth will nevertheless be evident. In this way, the satirist uses irony to make a literary attack more indirect and subtle.

Meyers uses comic irony in the first act of her screenplay when Harry is rushed to hospital. As Hodgart argues, irony is the 'normal device for exposing the comedy of human pretensions' (1969: 131) and in this scene, Harry is forced to confront his age and mortality under the gaze of his young girlfriend, Marin. At first, Dr Julian mistakes heart attack patient Harry as Marin's father. When told that this is not the case, Julian assumes that he must surely be Marin's grandfather. Here, Meyers avoids stating the obvious in that Harry is too old for Marin. Instead, she ironically and subtly states it through the character of Dr Julian, making Harry look like a fool.

Prior to this scene, we learn that Harry is looking forward to eventually having sex with Marin. However, after his heart attack, Marin clearly has other ideas and merely kisses him on the cheek (Meyers, 2002: 35). The irony here is that whilst Harry still sees himself as a potential suitor for the young woman, she now perceives him as an old man.

Meyers uses additional irony in the film's second act when Harry is forced to live with Erica, whom by now he despises. It is ironic, then, that these two people who appear to be the enemy and the antithesis of what each other are looking for end up falling madly in love.

A further use of irony occurs when Harry, described by Erica's sister, Zoe, as 'a real catch' (Meyers, 2002: 19), cannot even climb a flight of stairs after his heart attack, let alone chase after younger women (Meyers, 2002: 50). This supports Frye's phase one of satire in which, despite the humour within this scene, there is a 'sense of nightmare and demonic' (1957: 226).

Meyers has ironically drawn Harry as believing he could be happy dating numerous younger, carefree women until he meets the mature and desirable Erica. Meyers also ironically shows that Erica believes she can be happy alone and sober until she meets the fun-loving Harry. In addition, Erica assumes that because Harry has many girlfriends, he is shallow. It is ironic, however, that after Erica has spent time with Harry, she discovers that 'He's soulful when you don't expect it.' (Meyers, 2002: 68) Likewise, Harry assumes that because Erica wears skin-covering turtlenecks and is disapproving of his womanising, she must be frigid. After their first sexual encounter together, Harry rather ironically discovers otherwise.

On a more macro level, Meyers uses irony in the plotting of *Something's Gotta Give* in that her characters' fears become a reality when they turn into exactly what they are trying to avoid. Both characters believe they can be at their happiest if they remain unattached. When Erica and Harry fall in love, however, their compulsive desire for remaining single cannot survive. As Worcester purports, whereas 'pure' comedy demands little of the audience, satire 'makes the brain reel with the continuous effort of unravelling the irony' and subtext (1940: 37–38).

The satirist's implicit moral standard

Frye claims that satire requires an implicit moral standard: 'The satirist has to select his absurdities, and the act of selection is a moral act' (1957: 224). Meyers chooses themes within her screenplay that may reveal her moral stance towards various social issues, her personal beliefs being hinted at through the attitudes of her characters and the conflicts played out amongst them. Such moral standards are explored in the first act when Zoe derides society's belief that a single, older, successful man is 'a real catch' whereas an unmarried woman is known as 'an old maid, a spinster'. Meyers continues with this theme when Zoe then describes the injustice of older men who find older women, who are productive and interesting, less desirable than younger women (Meyers, 2002: 19–20).

Meyers also displays her moral standard when the 'chauvinist older guy' is punished with a heart attack for fooling around with a younger girl (2002: 108). In the film's second act, Erica explains to Harry that she decided to kill the character in her play based on him because the character 'screwed around with our heroine, so it won't be too sad' (Meyers, 2002: 109). This dialogue highlights Meyers' belief that it is unacceptable for a man to be physically intimate with a woman without any lasting commitment.

Meyers' own moral standard is displayed as her characters judge and deride Harry's various social vanities and faults centring on his hunger for young women. She has focused on the ageing playboy character of Harry and the 'spinster' character of Erica to demonstrate various forms of social hypocrisy using wit, humour, a sense of irony and the absurd.

The satirist's reduction or degradation of character or belief

Frye argues that the protagonist may devalue an incorrect belief system or degrade an unjust person in order to reduce his or her stature or dignity (1957: 233). He emphasises that satire goes beyond mere ridicule or invective with the use of unique wit and attack on social injustices. He also notes the prevalence of the Omphale archetype in literary satire, which he describes as a particular form of comic degradation typified by 'the man bullied or dominated by women' (1957: 228).

There are several examples of the Omphale archetype in *Something's Gotta Give*. Early on in the first act, for example, Erica and Zoe discover

Harry, half naked, in Erica's kitchen. The women mistakenly believe him to be an intruder, and a mad conflict ensues where Erica threatens Harry with a knife and falsely claims that Zoe was in the Israeli army. Erica then demonstrates an example of what Frye would call the overbearing Omphale stereotype, warning Harry that Zoe will 'break you in half' (Meyers, 2002: 9). Meyers emasculates Harry, even undressing him down to his boxer shorts, as he is dominated by Erica and Zoe.

Later in the film, Harry sinks into further degradation when hospitalised after his heart attack. He 'stumbles into the corridor in his Hospital Gown, pretty out of it [...] Confused [...] a little lost, giving the women a FULL VIEW OF HIS BARE ASS' (Meyers, 2002: 31). In this scene, Harry is again emasculated, dressed in a 'feminine' hospital gown.

Meyers continues to degrade Harry by making him 'the laughing stock of Broadway' with Erica's play showing him as a foolish old man, needing Viagra to keep up with the young women he dates and also magnified in a 'chorus line of balding 60-year-old men in hospital gowns and socks' (2002: 112). Frye argues that within the third phase of satire, a satirist 'will change his hero into an ass and show us how humanity looks from an ass's point of view' (1957: 234). An example of this occurs when Meyers has Erica describe the character in her play, based upon Harry, as 'a schmuck who screwed around with our heroine, so it won't be too sad' when he dies of a heart attack. Harry (the ass) retaliates by arguing, 'Schmucks are people too, you know. Death doesn't seem a little harsh?' (Meyers, 2002: 109) The use of Jewish humour by Meyers here may enable an audience to maintain compassion for the 'schmuck', a derogatory Yiddish term, literally translated as 'prick,' 'jerk' or 'moron' (*Urban Dictionary*, 2011).

The final humiliation of Harry occurs in the third act when he travels all the way to Paris to find Erica so that he can proclaim his love for her. Harry discovers her embracing the handsome Dr Julian, quickly seeing himself as 'a sap, a stupid old sap, standing on a bridge in Paris, crying my eyes out [...] Look who gets to be the girl.' (Meyers, 2002: 127) At this point, Meyers ensures that Harry is seen to be tragic, broken-hearted and degraded.

Erica is also subject to degradation in the screenplay. For example, Meyers explores the idea that Erica shutting herself off sexually is cause for satire. Meyers allows Erica's dignified composure to unravel when, in the first act, Harry accidentally sees her naked. Erica, highly embarrassed the next day, takes to covering herself up even further. Harry responds with the line, 'You saw my ass, you don't see me acting nuts, wearing hats and glasses and weird get ups' (Meyers, 2002: 48). This humiliation allows Erica to be ridiculed by Harry until she changes her sexual frigidity. Later, we see that Harry is successful in breaking down Erica's defences when she finally meets him at his request for a 'pajama party' in her living room (Meyers, 2002: 63).

Frye describes satire as requiring both tragic and comic elements. This is clearly displayed at the mid-point of the screenplay when Myers progresses the plot from comic revelry towards a more tragic mood. Both Erica and Harry fall dramatically from being tough and independent singles to being 'needy' (Meyers, 2002: 102). Meyers lampoons Erica, putting her in a montage with exaggerated crying and despair after she discovers Harry dining with another woman. Harry suffers from one humiliation after another until he decides to sell the majority of his business interests. Frye would describe this as 'the fall of the tragic hero' (1957: 236).

The satirist's use of token fantasy; the absurd and the grotesque

The last of Frye's six characteristics of satire concerns the satirist's application of a token fantasy that the reader can recognise as grotesque, farcical or absurd. Satire should include an element of the imaginary, recognised as absurd, farcical or ridiculous. Frye argues that satire 'breaks down when its content is too oppressively real to permit the maintaining of the fantastic or hypothetical tone' (1957: 224).

I have already described how Meyers portrays the normally dignified Erica sobbing like a baby over Harry. I have also discussed the humorous irony of the ageing playboy, Harry, having a heart attack during foreplay. In scenes like these, Frye argues that the use of the absurd and the grotesque is important in preventing the tone from being 'too oppressively real' (1957: 224). Had Meyers made such scenes more realistic, they may have come across as tragic; however, by adding the elements of fantasy and farce, Meyers succeeds in maintaining a satirical tone. The screenwriter's use of absurd fantasy can make moments like those featuring Harry's heart attack and Erica's weeping the funniest rather than most heartbreaking in the screenplay.

Meyers also uses grotesque or absurd humour in the first act when Erica, who according to Harry is an old shrew, proceeds to give Harry mouth-to-mouth resuscitation, his eyes widening in horror. Harry's revulsion of the idea of close proximity with Erica, exaggerated for comic effect, makes the scene somewhat farcical and thus prevents the scene from becoming too 'oppressively real' (Frye, 1957: 224). Meyers also uses humour founded on fantasy to satirise the hypocrisy of her female characters. The Barry women are not known for being sweet and demure; however, Meyers humorously and farcically transforms both Marin and Zoe into 'the Step Sisters trying on the Glass Slipper' as they flirt with the handsome Dr Julian (2002: 29). This has the effect of exaggerating the double standards of these strong and forthright female characters, who compete for Julian's affections by softening to appear more attractive.

Conclusion

As this chapter has demonstrated, Frye's theories of satire have been useful in understanding the satirical techniques utilised by Nancy Meyers in her screenplay, *Something's Gotta Give*. By association, this analysis also provides a set of principles that can be useful for any screenwriter wishing to employ satire: areas to consider when developing a screenplay, and techniques to employ when writing it.

As highlighted, satire differs from a broad comedy in that its spotlight is firmly on an object of attack. In the case of Meyers' screenplay, Harry is an aging playboy who is lampooned by the screenwriter and her alter ego, the female protagonist Erica, using the satirical techniques of irony, wit and humour.

The screenplay demonstrates what Frye calls 'an implicit moral standard' (1957: 224). The various female characters all use irony in their witty and humorous degradation of those who do not fit their moral codes. The characters created by Meyers are used to devalue the 'fossilized belief' that a woman loses her sexual appeal once she reaches a certain age. In doing so, Meyers has discredited what Frye would call the stereotypes and 'oppressive fashions' (1957: 233) of those who believe that a powerful and successful woman cannot be sexy.

The character of Erica is mature, strong and witty, which contrasts with the familiar stereotypes of 'docility, chastity and modesty' (Hodgart, 1969: 79–81). Meyers' protagonist rejects the traditional view of women as subordinate and inferior to men and is therefore a more than equal match for her male counterpart. She does not acquiesce to disparaging male humour and patriarchal ideology, but is able to give as well as she gets. Using wit, humour and irony rather than direct invective, Erica has emerged as victor rather than victim. As a female protagonist, she is presented as smart and witty in comparison to her shallow and insincere male counterpart, Harry. She seizes power from him, humiliating him in the process. Following her own fall from grace,

Erica then compromises and manages to build with him a relationship based upon the freedom and equality of both sexes (Young, 1997: 251).

Meyers has been able to effectively expose her characters' social pretensions with a strong ironic sensibility, giving the screenplay an additional layer of wit. In this capacity, by using irony an audience is able to derive pleasure from reading between Meyers' lines and the screenplay's hidden layers of meaning.

Reduction or degradation of character or belief gives a satirical work its sting. Meyers has degraded those in society who hold back the spirit and progress of women. She also uses the principles of reduction or degradation and a token fantasy by humiliating her female protagonist with exaggerated crying and despair, after she believes her love interest has been unfaithful, for example. This is important in depicting Erica's humility. In this sense, Meyers has created a heroine who is strong and feisty, yet one who audiences can sympathise with and relate to.

Finally, Meyers' characters are based upon real people yet are heightened with elements of the grotesque or absurd. This, a token fantasy which the audience can recognise as such, gives satire its fun and emits a sense of frivolity and humour, with a fine balance between what is real and what is imaginary. For example, an audience can laugh at some of Harry's sexist attitudes whilst at the same time judging him.

It is my suggestion that Meyers has moved beyond what feminist theorist Mary Russo describes as the 'grotesque' female (1994: 65), and instead has created a protagonist who uses wit and humour for laughs, not grotesquery. Unlike the characters in *Bridesmaids* (2011), for example, Meyers did not intend for her protagonist to be funny just because she is considered grotesque; instead, she has created a protagonist who is funny as a consequence of her clever and amusing dialogue.

Sol Saks, ex-Network Supervisor of Comedy at ABC, asserts that those who are oppressed may use humour to outwit the enemy. He argues: 'Ridicule is a powerful weapon [...] When used against injustice it can bring the malefactor to his knees quicker than physical force' (1985: 19). As this chapter has shown, satire has the power to be used in a positive way: to explore the injustice in the battle for equality for women. As Felicity Collins argues, Frye's phase of comedy 'requires the bride to be little more than the hero's prize [...] bereft of her own desire' (2003: 168–169). In addition, Brian Henderson argues that 'there can be no romantic comedy without strong heroines' (1978: 8). For the romantic comedy to progress and thrive, then, female protagonists must move on to be more than the pining female or damsel in distress.

Importantly, the focus on Frye's theory of satire outlines explicit comic angles and techniques that may be utilised by the practising screenwriter. Just like Meyers, he or she can use such techniques to attack social injustices in a witty, humorous and ironic satirical style. Frye argues that 'in Old Comedy, when a girl accompanies a male hero in his triumph, she is generally a stage prop' (1957: 173). With a greater understanding and application of these theories and techniques of satire, we may, and expect, to see in the future more screenplays featuring 'gals who make the jokes' (Denby, 2007: 2).

References

Bridesmaids (2011) Wrs. Kristen Wiig and Annie Mumolo, Dir. Paul Feig, USA, 125 mins.

Burr, T. (2005) 'Hollywood Leaves Ladies in Waiting; Trend Toward Male-Centred Films Puts Actresses in Background' in *Boston Globe*, Boston, 4 December 2005, 9.

Collins, F. (2003) 'Brazen Brides, Grotesque Daughters, Treacherous Mothers: Women's Funny Business in Australian Cinema from *Sweetie* to *Holy Smoke*' in Lisa French (ed.) *Womenvision: Women and the Moving Image in Australia*, Melbourne: Damned Publishing, pp. 167–182.

Denby, D. (2007) 'A Fine Romance; A Critic at Large' in *The New Yorker*, 23 July, 59.

Freud, S. (1960) *Jokes and Their Relation to the Unconscious* (trans. James Strachey), New York: The Norton Library.

Frye, N. (1957) *Anatomy of Criticism*, Princeton, NJ: Princeton University Press.

Hamilton, M.A. (2006) *Categorizing Twentieth Century Film Using Northrop Frye's Anatomy of Criticism: Relating Literature and Film*, New York: Edwin Mellen Press.

Hart, J. (1994) *Northrop Frye: The Theoretical Imagination*, London: Routledge.

Henderson, B. (1978) 'Romantic Comedy Today: Semi Tough or Impossible' in *Film Quarterly*, 31(4), 11–23.

Highet, G. (1962) *The Anatomy of Satire*, Princeton, NJ: Princeton University Press.

Hodgart, M. (1969) *Satire*, London: World University Library.

Jacey, H. (2010) 'Finding the Woman's Voice' in *The Writers' Store*, available at http://www.writersstore.com/finding-the-womans voice-helen-jacey [accessed 16 November 2010].

Meyers, N. (2002) '*Something's Gotta Give*' *The Daily Script*, available at http://www.dailyscript.com/scripts/SomethingsGottaGive.pdf [accessed 10 November 2008].

Molière. (1965) 'Preface to *Tartuffe*' (trans. and ed. by Haskell M. Block) in Robert W. Corrigan (eds.) *Comedy: Meaning and Form*, San Francisco, CA: Chandler Publishing Company, pp. 1–7.

Norman, L. (1999) *The Public Mirror: Moliere and the Social Commerce of Depiction*, Chicago, IL: The University of Chicago Press.

Rosenheim, E.W. (1971) 'The Satiric Spectrum' in Ronald Paulson (ed.) *Satire: Modern Essays in Criticism*, New Jersey: Prentice-Hall Inc., pp. 305–329.

Russo, M. (1994) *The Female Grotesque*, New York: Routledge.

Saks, S. (1985) *The Craft of Comedy Writing*, Cincinnati: Writer's Digest Books.

Something's Gotta Give (2003) Wr./Dir. Nancy Myers, USA, 128 mins.

The Internet Movie Database, *Nancy Meyers*, available at http://www.imdb.com/name/nm0583600/[accessed 21 November 2011].

The Internet Movie Database, *Something's Gotta Give*, available at http://www.imdb.com/title/tt0337741/ [accessed 21 November 2011].

Tofler, M. (2011) *Give the Girl a Line: Methods of Feature Film Screenwriting for the Satirical Female Voice*, Doctor of Philosophy, Melbourne: RMIT University.

Urban Dictionary, *Schmuck*, available at http://www.urbandictionary.com/define.php?term=schmuck [accessed 21 November 2011].

Worcester, D. (1940) *The Art of Satire* (2nd ed.), New York: Russell & Russell.

Young, D.M.(1997) *The Feminist Voices in Restoration Comedy*, Maryland: University Press of America, Inc.

16

Self-Reflexive Screenwriting and LGBT Identity: Framing and Indirectly Reading the Self

Christopher Pullen

Introduction

In the 1995 documentary *The Celluloid Closet*, based on Vito Russo's celebrated book of the same name, Richard Dyer tells us:

> Most expressions of homosexuality in most of movies are indirect. And what is interesting about that, is that it is of course what it was like to express homosexuality in life. That we could only express ourselves indirectly, just as people on the screen could express themselves indirectly. And the sense that the characters on the screen are in the closet, the movie is in the closet, and we are in the closet.

Dyer illuminates the key context of screen representation for LGBT (lesbian, gay, bisexual and transgender) identity: that historically, overt expression has been denied, and this offers impact not only on senses of self but also the witnessing of the self, which is potentially a covert experience. Despite this, screenwriters have involved themselves in the process of self-representation, evident in their screenplays and cultural disseminations. They are involved in speaking to mainstream audiences about the context of their identity and, in the case of gay and lesbian identity, this involves a personal intimate subjectivity, presented to a public world. Whilst Dyer attests that historically Hollywood has offered an indirect relationship to gay and lesbian identity, increasingly more direct routes are offered, relating advocacy, affirmation and social inclusion. For example, the screenwriting practice of Lisa Cholodenko and Tom Ford, respectively, in their films *The Kids Are All Right* (2010) and *A Single Man* (2009), offer self-reflexive visions of contented or devoted same-sex couples, framing aspects of their own lives and establishing productive narratives for LGBT identity (Lucia and Porton, 2010; Pullen, 2013).

However whilst the analysis of affirmative texts can be productive, involving a celebration of identity ideals, the purpose of this chapter is to consider theoretical contexts of LGBT identity engaging with historical foundations. In doing this, I wish to consider the potential for indirect readings that do not necessarily display an obvious positive meaning relative to the self-reflexive processes within screenwriting. In order to consider this, I will look specifically at the work of Tennessee Williams and Joe Orton who, as playwrights, may be seen to have offered contentious representations of homosexuals within the then mainstream cultural domain. As gay-identified men themselves,[1] their personal lives inevitably impacted on the audience's reading of a text, and whilst many would consider these authors as expressing the problem of queer identity, I argue that their writing offers a contemporary sophistication in the potential to embed the self in the production of identity.

Screenwriting as a creative practice thus offers the opportunity to present contemporary visions of identity. In this chapter, then, I consider aspects of personal agency within the writing process, which might be related to the potential of 'queer theory' (Butler, 1999) where those involved in media production stimulate new opportunities for identification. Although I am not specifically relating to the context of 'New Queer Cinema' (Aaron, 2004), similar issues of personal agency are central here in the desire to simulate new narratives. In this chapter I also wish to consider the audience's engagement with the iconic identity of the screenwriter in reading such potential. This is related to an historical foundation that supressed homosexual identity, yet also stimulated interest in finding evidence of queer lives.

Histories, covert reading and stereotypes

Vito Russo (1987) records in *The Celluloid Closet* that gay men and lesbians were evident in early Hollywood cinema, however they were often assigned identities that were covert or subliminal. This was due to the Motion Pictures Production Code, where the representation of homosexuality was forbidden (Gross, 2001). Screenwriters thus had to conceal homosexual identity, ensuring that censors would not edit out 'queer' characters. For example, as discussed by Richard Dyer in *The Celluloid Closet*, in *The Maltese Falcon* (1941) the character of Joel Cairo (played by Peter Lorre) is coded as homosexual in reference to his connection with the perfume Gardenia and, in a key scene in which he encounters Humphrey Bogart, he holds his walking cane handle close to his mouth to signify a desire for phallic oral sex. In another incidence, in the film *Rebecca* (1940) the character of Mrs Danvers, as housekeeper, is obsessed with the memory of her now deceased employer Mrs De Winter, which is represented as covert lesbian desire. This is played out in the film where Mrs Danvers, preserving the memory of her deceased female employer, takes sensual pleasure in caring for her clothing. More specifically, this is apparent in a scene where she demonstrates the translucence of Mrs De Winter's underwear to the new Mrs De Winter, sliding her hand in the garment to demonstrate its potential transparency and also caressing her face with a garment.

Such covert representations are not only connected to Hollywood's influence on gay character types (as Russo reports) but also apply to conditions in British theatre that contributed to the concealment of gay identity. These restrictions, executed by The Lord Chamberlain's Office between 1737 and 1968 and that concerned punishment for playwrights who represented homosexuality, engendered queer characters to be practically invisible (Clum, 2000). However, in a similar manner to the Motion Pictures Production Code, queer characters would often appear but would be covert and sometimes contorted. Thus, through the necessity of playwrights having to avoid open depictions of homosexuality, character types became recognised as outsiders, seeming like veiled apparitions.

As such, audiences were not provided with representations of the homosexual as an everyday social type. Instead, they were provided with covert homosexual types that became fixed to specific performative traits. Clum points out that in order to replicate homosexual identity without verbal affirmation or physical juxtaposition, a repertoire of male homosexual stereotypes are thus used (2000: 77). These include:

- effeminacy (mincing, limp wrists, lisping, flamboyant dress)
- sensitivity (moodiness, a devotion to his mother, a tendency to show emotions in an unmanly way)
- artistic talent or sensibility (an emblematic sign reinforcing the idea that gay men belong to distanced artistic worlds, rather than normative productive social worlds)
- misogyny (this contextualised the perceived failure of gay men to outgrow their bond with maternal figures and become sexually interested in females)

- pederasty (this became the stereotypical formula for homosexual relationships, with its connotations of arrested development and pernicious influence)
- isolation (the homosexual's fate, if he or she remained alive at the final curtain).

Through engagement with these traits or devices, playwrights would construct a covert homosexual character type that was recognisable, but was not directly connected to issues of acceptance. Consequently, through presenting the homosexual character as a covert identity (only visible by reading the signs), an unnatural spectre emerged which seemed distanced from realism. The homosexual character thus became a marginalised entity, unable to integrate or engage with realistic contexts. Evidence of this can be seen in numerous plays where the homosexual character had to die or be punished in service of returning the narrative to a normal world (Clum, 2000), such as in Tennessee Williams's *Suddenly, Last Summer* (1959), discussed below. Whilst contemporary screenwriters may not be obliged to offer such narrative closure, inevitably the context of 'the other' and 'the outsider' remains a key issue of engagement in mediating the historical and contemporary representation of LGBT lives.

Episteme, the individual and author function

Issues around representation are clearly problematic. Visibility itself, even the covert reading of visibility, relies on knowledge of dominant narrative ideals. For the representation of gay men and lesbians in theatre, Hollywood film, or even later in television, the use of stereotypes became essential in constructing a sense of identity. Clearly, as Clum considers with regards to the covert reading of queerness, there must be some understanding from the audience about the nature of representation itself in order to understand the *context* of representation. Therefore, a double edge may be considered to exist in the representation of 'queerness': that on the one hand, there is an expectation to see the signs of difference in order to mediate the 'otherness', but also that there must be some political understanding of problems in representation itself. For screenwriters to mediate a coherent gay and lesbian identity, it is natural that signs of difference will be exhibited. However, depending on the context of the screenwriter, different approaches may be 'successful'.

Whilst more recently we have experienced a proliferation of openly gay writers creating powerful texts (such as the work of Lisa Cholodenko and Tom Ford, discussed earlier), either expressing an overt political context or at least challenging order through subversion within theatre (Sinfield, 1999), television (Capsuto, 2000) and film (Benshoff and Griffin, 2004), what I want to consider in this chapter is a more complex representation, relative to the self-identity of the writer themselves.

Such a process is related to the potential of discourse, and Foucault's (1973) concept of 'episteme', which he considered as the production of knowledge at a specific point in time. This might relate to the processes within society where ideas are coherently organised, and there is a sense of understanding, through issues such as representation. For diverse sexuality, as Foucault notes in the *History of Sexuality* (1998), it was not until sexuality and desire were explored in the late 19th century that an identity was specifically assigned to homosexuality. In this sense, as David Gauntlett (2002) tells us,

> It was precisely the discourses about sexuality, in Victorian times and the early twentieth century, which sought to *suppress* certain kinds of behavior, which simultaneously gave an *identity* to them, and so (ironically) launched them into the public eye.
>
> (2002: 121)

In this way, the power used by institutions and authorities against those involved in prohibited sexual behaviour, such as prohibitive legislation and the scientific examination of allegedly deviant sexual practices (such as non-procreative sex), actually resulted in defining an identity for those who became subjects for examination. Hence, although the 'episteme' of the cultural and historical period framed the problem of homosexuality, at the same time such engagement provided an opportunity for resistance and creation.

Foucault's (1992) notion of 'discursive formations' is also useful in considering the contexts of the 'episteme'. For gay and lesbian representation in theatre and, beyond, in screenwriting, clearly the 'discursive formations' have been produced around issues of fear within society, and the problem of the 'other'. It is perhaps then understandable that representation within culture will evoke these issues. Foucault considers that disciplines, commentary and the author are key aspects in attempting to make sense of diverse identity and its representations.

Disciplines involves the organisation of legitimate knowledge, which will be enabled by dominant orders; commentary might involve the support or critique of these ideologies; and the author might be the individual voice that we put into context with regards to our evaluation.

With regard to the author in 'the author function', Foucault tells us that, 'The coming into being of the notion of the "author" constitutes the privileged moment of *individualisation* in the history of ideas, knowledge, literature, philosophy, and the sciences' (1991: 101). This sense of the individual emerging as a key narrative force thus becomes central in shifts in the production of knowledge. Foucault considers that

> it would be worth examining how the author became individualised in a culture like ours, what status he has been given, at what moment studies of authenticity and attribution began, in what kind of valorization the author was involved, at what point we began to recount the lives of authors rather than heroes, and how this fundamental category of 'man and his criticism' began.
>
> (1991: 101)

Although we are unable here to consider the historical emergence of the author in this way, within an examination of gay and lesbian authors, the notion of the individual is a key context in the claiming of identity through writing. For example, the writings of Oscar Wilde (Cohen, 1993) might be related to the idea of the individualised author-oriented narrative force. Although Wilde's stories offer depth in exploring heroes and heroines, we are more likely to consider the author identity of Wilde himself in an evaluation of the narrative. Hence, the life story of the author plays a central role in our reading of discursive formations that might simulate the episteme and the production of knowledge at a particular point in time.

At the same time, I would like to argue that the agency of the individual might be related to self-reflexivity in producing an individualised author identity. Anthony Giddens (1992) uses the term 'reflexive project of the self' to relate to the potential of modern citizens to reflect on their own ideas of identity, rather than for an individual to necessarily conform to and reaffirm the dominant order. The notion of self-reflexivity is thus a contemporary construct that offers scope for change. This is specifically evident in the process of 'autobiographical thinking', which Giddens describes not only as a central element of self-therapy but also something that should be considered as a process by which to engender change. As he tells us,

For developing a coherent sense of one's life history is a prime means of escaping the thrall of the past and opening oneself out to the future. The author of the autobiography is enjoined to go back as far as possible into early childhood and set up lines of potential development to encompass the future.

(1992: 72)

In terms of embedding a homosexual identity in the practice of screenwriting, this relates to constructing a modified future through personal narrative inventions. For example, if we consider the writing of Christopher Isherwood, who expressly presented an openly gay identity, he integrated his personal identity within diary, novel, play and film works that produced discursive moments reflecting and reproducing Isherwood as the integral personal narrator (Berg and Freeman, 2000; Pullen, 2012). This practice involving a kind of challenge not only questions what constitutes appropriate textual form, including whether or not the author should integrate their personal identity, but also who should capture and frame the narrative by placing the homosexual as the dominant storyteller. By challenging dominant forms and heterosexual authority, Isherwood may thus be considered as working towards change through intimate self-reflexive storytelling.

Isherwood and many contemporary openly gay screenwriters embed this idea of positive representation, or the context of equality. This is evident in recent work by Tom Ford (discussed briefly above), who adapted Isherwood's *A Single Man* as a Hollywood film and embedded his own political ideology to offer a mainstream representation of gay male affirmation (Pullen, 2013). In this film, heterosexual authority is challenged though presenting gay male sexuality as positive and constructive, such as the central romantic characters being seen to form a loving household together, alongside eternal bonding. This is also evident in Jonathan Harvey's ground-breaking film *Beautiful Thing* (1996), where the story of two gay male teenagers who fall in love on a London council estate offers a connection to the Romeo and Juliet narrative as an eternal foundation, framing it within the cinematic stylistic structure of British social realism (Pullen, 2012).

Although these are clearly powerful cinematic texts, I would like to consider in more detail the work of Tennessee Williams' *Suddenly, Last Summer* and Joe Orton's *Entertaining Mr Sloane* and their film adaptations. Whilst these are older texts, they are worthy of examination for their relationship to self-reflexivity and the indirect potential of representation within screenwriting.

Suddenly, Last Summer and Entertaining Mr Sloane

Suddenly, Last Summer (1959) and *Entertaining Mr Sloane* (1970) appear as oppositional texts, the former being the product of an iconic American playwright known for an intense and literature-based approach, and the latter produced by a contentious figure in British theatre, known for humour and the grotesque in his writing. The two texts also come from different time periods and different political and social cultures. However, these texts have been selected not for their similarity, or even their difference, but because they represent key textual products of gay-identified writers whose personal lives were as much reported as the plays that they wrote. My intention in bringing them together is to consider the author function process in relation to issues of self-reflexivity, employing textual analysis of the films that were adapted from the original plays. *Suddenly, Last Summer* was adapted for the screen by Tennessee Williams and Gore Vidal. *Entertaining Mr Sloane* was adapted for the screen by Clive Exton. My point here, then, is to explore these texts as products of queer scriptwriters able to contextualise the episteme and potentially influence ideas.

Although Tennessee Williams wrote a diverse range of plays, and *A Streetcar Named Desire* (1951) and *Cat on A Hot Tin Roof* (1958) are the key adapted films that mainstream audiences are likely to think of when considering his work, I have selected *Suddenly, Last Summer* for its direct connection with Tennessee's life story. This is mostly apparent in the representation of a young girl in the play, Catherine, who is constructed in direct reference to Williams' own sister, specifically in relation to her psychological problems and the surgical operation of the lobotomy. As Raymond Hayman reports, 'more autobiographical than they seem [Williams'] plays are full of outcasts, misfits, and fugitives' (1993: xv), and the representation of himself and problematic issues surrounding his family are key aspects of his work. Hence, *Suddenly, Last Summer* is a key self-reflexive text that offers recognition of themes in Williams' personal life.

Not only does Catherine in some ways represent Williams' sister, Catherine's aunt Violet may be related to his own mother, specifically in reference to her suspected madness and Williams' mother suffering from psychological problems. The persona of Williams himself is also apparent in the two main male characters of the film, Dr Curcowicz and Sebastian: Dr Curcowicz is represented as the central male force concerned for the female characters, and Sebastian is represented as free spirited and sexually liberated.

The basic plotline of *Suddenly, Last Summer* concerns the troubling psychological state of Catherine, after she has witnessed the death of her cousin Sebastian whilst on holiday abroad. Catherine's wealthy aunt, Violet, is aware that Dr Curcowicz is involved in groundbreaking surgery (the lobotomy) to cure troubled psychological states, and so she desires that Catherine undergo this treatment to resolve her disturbed state. Dr Curcowicz experiences a professional moral dilemma when Violet offers to fund the building of a wing for the hospital where he works, in return for the operation on Catherine. The central narrative theme concerns the inappropriate intimate relationship between Violet and Sebastian, as mother and son, and Catherine's intrusion in this relationship when she goes on holiday with Sebastian, as Violet is unable to travel with them.

Sebastian is coded as homosexual in that he desires the company of young men whilst on holiday, and he uses his mother, and later his cousin, to attract them. Due to the Motion Pictures Production Code, Sebastian could not be expressly presented as homosexual, hence in the documentary *The Celluloid Closet* Gore Vidal tells us about his concerns in working with Williams to adapt the play for Hollywood. Vidal relates problems in engaging with the censors who wanted to extinguish any direct references to homosexuality. According to Vidal, when the film was eventually finished, Williams' original story was almost unrecognisable. Nevertheless, despite this reworking I would like to argue that the character of Tennessee Williams is not only apparent in the covert reading of the text but also played out through the notion of difference and the story of 'the outsider' that is expressed in key aspects of the film.

Notably, the film focuses on the idea of the primeval, and the deeply instinctive, rather than the ordered and civilised. Hence the contrast between the Dionysian and Apollonian drives within tragedy, as explored by Friedrich Nietzsche (2008), is apparent, the former representing the shift to senses, indulgence and emotion, and the latter concerning stability, the adherence to order and good citizenship. This is vivified in the adaptation through the representation of the garden at Violet's house, which was the design of Sebastian. In an early sequence of the film, Violet takes Dr Curcowicz on a tour of the garden and not only states that the primitive plants go back to the 'dawn of time' but also demonstrates the idea of the primitive by feeding a Venus flytrap with insects she has already prepared. Such a focus on the primitive, the instinctive and the carnal is also apparent when Violet recalls the memory of Sebastian to Dr Curcowicz, of an afternoon overlooking a beach whilst on holiday, relating predators and their prey.

> Violet
> I saw the sand; all alive, and all dark,
> as the new-hatched sea turtles made their
> dash for the sea, while the birds hovered
> and swooped to attack, and hovered and
> swooped to attack. They were diving down
> on the sea turtles, turning them over to
> expose their undersides, tearing their
> undersides open, and rending, and eating
> their flesh. Sebastian guessed that
> possibly only 100th of one per cent
> would escape to the sea.

> Dr Curcowicz
> Nature is not created in the image of
> man's compassion.

> Violet
> Nature is cruel. Sebastian knew it all
> along. He was born knowing it. Not I, I
> said no; no those are only turtles and
> birds, not us. I didn't know that it was
> us, that we are trapped in this devouring
> creation.

This focus on the primeval, the instinctive and the Dionysian also references the carnal in relation to theology. This is evident not only when Violet considers the problem of 'devouring creation', but is also apparent in references to Sebastian 'seeing the face of God' in establishing the context of this sequence. Therefore, Williams relates the Dionysian and the carnal to the actions of God, framing the vulnerable as innocent, faceless and worthy of care.

This reading is also contextual by considering the film's final sequence where Catherine recalls the death of Sebastian. Rather than a heart attack, as she had earlier recalled, she recounts the murder of Sebastian whilst on holiday by local boys, pursued in a similar manner to the newborn sea turtles. Written into the film is a flashback of Sebastian being pursued by young men, his face hidden as offering no identity. After a long sequence that is accompanied by an emotive voice-over, where Catherine describes the pursuit, the young men chase Sebastian up a hill in the manner of pursuing a monster. He is held down, like prey, and without visual representation we hear from Catherine that they had cut up his body and consumed it. In this sense, Sebastian is represented as an innocent creature desiring to find life, or at least vulnerable within life, and in his failing to recognise his predators is consumed by the natural and the theological order. This juxtaposition of man, as an agent of individual and untrammelled desire, subject to nature but also consumed by it, is a key theme within the play.

It is my argument, then, that this foregrounds the identity of the author not only in our knowledge of the identity of Williams' sister and his mother (Catherine and Violet) but also in the representation of Sebastian, which is relative to Williams' own instability. Such instability may be evident when considering Williams' enduring relationship with lover Frank Merlo, which ended tragically when Merlo died of cancer at a time when, although they had been apart earlier, Williams cared for him at the end. As Hayman reports,

> It had been too easy to take Frank for granted; nothing short of bereavement could have taught his lover to appreciate him fully. Writing a letter to the dead man, Tennessee said his sleep was full of dreams about suffocation, and describing himself as too sick to know the truth, he thanked his good friend for having told no lies.
>
> (1993: 196)

Such a focus on devotion and truth, yet framed with insecurity and restlessness, is evident in Williams' desire not to settle in any place for long. Williams' relationship with Merlo presented a moment of security within the framework of a life where he desired little stability. This presentation of human nature as insecure, rootless and subject to desire is also apparent in Joe Orton's *Entertaining Mr Sloane*.

Entertaining Mr Sloane is the story of outsider Mr Sloane, who is befriended by an older woman of a simple nature named Kath. Mr Sloane is represented as an object of sexual desire, not only to Kath but also to her brother, Ed. The story is set within the iconic signifiers of death and religion, evident in the domestic environment in which Kath invites Mr Sloane to live with her, a converted church next to an old graveyard. The film version of *Entertaining Mr Sloane*, with the screenplay written by Clive Exton, was released three years after the death of playwright Joe Orton, who was murdered by his partner Kenneth Halliwell (Lahr, 1980). The casting of Peter McEnery as the central character in the film adaptation contextualises the historical representation of gay men in film, apparent because McEnery also played the character of

Barrett, a gay youth who is blackmailed and thus commits suicide, in the ground-breaking film *Victim* (1961) (Bourne, 1996; Pullen, 2013); an era when male homosexuality was illegal, and there existed many blackmail cases before the legalisation of male homosexual acts in 1967 (Weeks, 1990). As such, the film of *Entertaining Mr Sloane* offers an engaging conflation of historical film contexts and author life politics, engaging specifically with representation of the male body.

As reported in the biography of Joe Orton, *Prick Up You Ears* by John Lahr (and later a film, screenplay by Alan Bennett, 1897), before he was famous, Orton and his partner Kenneth Halliwell defaced library books and were sent to prison for this and other offences.[2] The couple took books from their local library and modified their appearance by writing in them and/or changing the visual images. For example, a book entitled *The Queen's Favourite* subtitled as 'a ward lock romance' by Phyllis Hambledon was modified to include an image of two wrestling semi-clad young men (Joe Orton, 2013). They produced a proliferation of images and texts in this manner, recasting the covers and content in a subversive or carnivalesque manner. Following their prison sentences, Orton in time became a celebrated subversive playwright, inspired by and surpassing the potential of Halliwell in this area. Orton's death is represented in *Prick Up Your Ears* as stimulated by jealousy on Halliwell's part, for not only failing to achieve the success of Orton in his own writing but also with regards to sexual jealousy; Orton was promiscuous and he flaunted this in public (Lahr, 1986).

As such, the iconic identity of Joe Orton is framed within *Entertaining Mr Sloane* offering contexts of objectification, desire, the uncontainable, death, guilt and loss. Specifically here I would like to focus on the representation of the male body with regards to desire and objectification. This, I argue, is framed within the film in reference to the body of Mr Sloane, a body that is desirable and sensual. For example, early in the film when Kath first meets Mr Sloane sunbathing on a grave in the manner of using it as a sunbed, she testifies, 'What a smell of skin you have on you.' This is followed up with later sequences whereby Sloane's body is on display for the pleasure of the viewer, and there is intimation that the engaging character is enthralled by such a display. As an example, when Kath's brother Ed meets Sloane for the first time, it is in a darkened bedroom on a sunny afternoon. Ed enters the bedroom with a desire to tell Sloane to leave his sister's house as he considers him to be a threat to his sister, and by token his financial and emotional security. As Ed engages in conversation with Sloane in the darkened room, we sense that Sloane is lying on the bed wearing only underwear. Ed gradually draws the curtains and the conversation changes. At the moment when Ed draws the curtain, allowing bright sunshine to illuminate Sloan's youthful and fit physical form, and with the sunshine resting on his body in the manner that medieval religious paintings use light to signify sainthood, there is a moment of realisation and engagement. On finding pleasure in looking at Sloane's body, Ed changes his intents: he comments on the fitness of Sloane's body, and offers him a job as a chauffeur.

Dyer (1993) has explored the objectification of the male body with relation to underwear, considering the case of Nick Kamen who advertised Levi Jeans on UK television in the 1980s. The casting of Peter McEnery as Mr Sloane occurring many years in advance of Dyer's case foregrounds a similar prospect. Notably with regards to underwear, the fabric clings to the male sensual form, which 'is likely to make explicit the part of the male body too often associated with boredom, obligation and rape' (Dyer, 1993: 124), in a way that prioritises consumption, use and a willingness to be used, in order to navigate a way through life.

This is particularly evident in the close of *Entertaining Mr Sloane*, where desire and culpability are merged in uncomfortable alliances. When Sloane has murdered Kath and Ed's father (following the father's threat to expose Sloane for a murder he knows him to be culpable of), rather than report him to the police Kath and Ed see it as an opportunity to use him, both marrying him and embarking on an arrangement of sharing him for six months of each year. Whilst in many ways this parodies the institution of marriage, I suggest that it frames the problem of desire as bound up in responsibilities and everyday uses. Therefore, I suggest that *Entertaining Mr Sloan* foregrounds this narrative to signify Joe Orton's own problematic life, relating to Orton's use of Halliwell and the problem of monogamy. This is self-reflexive practice in that it refers to Orton's own self-vision. It also offers discursive commentary on the alliances that we make in everyday life, here presented to the extreme.

Furthermore, McEnery's identity as leading actor in the film and object of sexual desire echoes the political discourse of his earlier appearance in *Victim*, making further connections to Orton's personal and political life. I argue that this stimulates new contexts for gay male identity, transforming an abject victim of blackmail who is punished within *Victim*, into an everyday, if somewhat troubled, object and agent of sexual desire within *Entertaining Mr Sloane*. Such drive to accept desire and to act on it is evident in Orton's work, challenging histories of shame connected to gay male identity.

Conclusion

Although seen in entirely different contexts, both Tennessee Williams and Joe Orton reproduce a gay identity that extends from their personal lives. As writers and the subject of their work being adapted for the screen, the iconic identity of the author plays a major part in the production of their narratives. Williams and Orton may offer different ways of presenting themselves in their texts, or at least the identities we associate with them seem different, but I would argue that they both similarly expose their personal lives, revealing the raw and the unprocessed as engaging ways of looking.

Whilst the murder of Joe Orton by his partner, and the failure of Tennessee Williams to find security even though he had a loving partner, fit more with tragedy and instability than affirmation and hope, these writers and their works do offer a means of communication which appears unmediated and processed. My point is not that the actual lives of screenwriters should embed a literal or positive message that we can all learn from, but more that it is a process of writing about oneself: a journey that all writers might take. The message about screenwriting practice here is not to try and find answers to questions such as 'Who am I?', 'Who am I like?', 'Where do I come from?' and 'Where am I going?' but rather to be willing to explore your environment and to find a pathway for potential audience engagement.

LGBT screenwriters might have to explore 'problems' and 'issues' in order to relate their identity, framing the cultural moment and the production of knowledge evident in the 'episteme'. Despite this, the drive for stability and sameness should be less important than the opportunity of self-reflection and self-investigation, which potentially challenges and extends representational possibilities. Orton's exposure of the male physical form in relation to objectivity, desire and identity transformation in *Entertaining Mr Sloane* predates our contemporary consumption and reinterpretation of masculinity (Anderson, 2011). Williams' examination of the impossibility of innocence and the oppression of the dominant voice offers insight that is rarely seen in contemporary affirmative texts. Their work remains modern, evident in a lack of compliance and a need to meet specific standards of identity, not necessarily following trodden pathways.

Although many would argue that we have moved beyond an era of self-hate, self-devaluation and self-destruction, I would argue that LGBT identity is better served in the presentation of diversity that is uncontained. Recent affirmative films do offer hope, but they also offer simplicity and in some way deny history. The work of Orton and Williams might seem bleak, involving death, culpability and naivety, bound up with guilt, desire and selfishness; however, it is the recognition of history, and the contexts of abject positioning, that remain central contexts of engagement. Orton's focus on the pleasure of the male body, and Williams's focus on the impossibility of innocence, taken in context with our knowledge of their culturally performed actual lives, offer ways of seeing, not necessarily ways of being.

Screenwriting is a personal process where, inevitably, one's identity is wound up in the work produced. Whether directly or indirectly, screenwriters write about themselves; or at the very least, they frame their personal ideas, contexts and skills in the mediation of a narrative. Writers such as Tennessee Williams and Joe Orton may have appeared to be more concerned with formal styles, celebrity and the achievement of an audience (Hayman, 1993) rather than the politics of self-representation; however, I argue that the iconography of their social worlds and the evidence found in their scripts and screenplays offer ways of looking forward, or looking through. In screenwriting practice, it is this unknowable 'indirect' relationship between the production of self and the ability of the audience to read the self that offers opportunity for change and re-thinking.

Notes

1. Although Joe Orton presented an identity that may be read as homosexual (evident in his demeanour, as being seductive to male audiences, and by association of the work that he produced), he did not expressly promote himself as homosexual. This is partially evident in the fiction that he created with regards to his personal life, as presenting himself as someone who was married earlier in life. In comparison, Tennessee Williams freely discussed his homosexuality.
2. As reported in *Prick up Your Ears*, it is likely that Orton and Halliwell were imprisoned as much for their suspected homosexuality as for the offences that they were charged with.

References

A Single Man (2009) Wrs. Tom Ford and David Scearce, Dir. Tom Ford, USA, 99 mins.
A Streetcar Named Desire (1951) Wrs. Tennessee Williams and Oscar Saul, Dir. Elia Kazan, USA, 122 mins.
Aaron, M. (ed.) (2004) *New Queer Cinema: A Critical Reader*, New York: Rutgers.
Anderson, E. (2011) *Inclusive Masculinity: The Changing Nature of Masculinities*, London: Routledge.

Beautiful Thing (1996) Wr. Jonathan Harvey, Dir. Hettie Macdonald, UK, 90 mins.

Bennett, A. and Lahr, J. (1987) *Prick Up Your Ears: The Screenplay*, London: Faber and Faber.

Benshoff, H. and Griffin, S. (eds.) (2004) *Queer Cinema: The Film Reader*, New York: Routledge.

Berg, J.J. and Freeman, C. (eds.) (2000) *The Isherwood Century: Essays on the Life ands Work of Christopher Isherwood*, Madison: University of Wisconsin Press.

Bourne, S. (1996) *Brief Encounters: Lesbians and Gays in British Cinema 1930–1971*, London: Cassell.

Butler, J. (1999) *Gender Trouble*, London: Routledge.

Capsuto, S. (2000) *Alternate Channels: The Uncensored Story of Gay and Lesbian Images on Radio and Television*, New York: Balantine Books.

Cat on a Hot Tin Roof (1958) Wrs. Richard Brookes and James Poe, Dir. Richard Brookes, USA, 108 mins.

Clum, J.M. (2000) *Still Acting Gay* (rev. ed.), New York: St Martin's Griffin.

Cohen, E. (1993) *Talk on the Wilde Side: Towards a Genealogy of a Discourse on Male Sexuality*, London: Routledge.

Dyer, R. (1993) *The Matter of Images: Essays on Representations*, London: Routledge.

Entertaining Mr Sloane (1970) Wr. Clive Exton, Dir. Douglas Hickox, UK, 94 mins.

Foucault, M. (1973) *The Order of Things: An Archaeology of Human Sciences*, New York: Vintage.

Foucault, M. (1991) 'What is an Author?' in Paul Rabinow (ed.) *The Foucault Reader*, London: Penguin, pp. 101–120.

Foucault, M. (1992) *The Archaeology of Knowledge*, London: Routledge.

Foucault, M. (1998) *The History of Sexuality* Vol. 1, London: Penguin.

Gauntlett, D. (2002) *Media, Gender and Identity: An Introduction*, London: Routledge.

Giddens, A. (1992) *Modernity and Self Identity: Self and Society in the late Modern Age*, Cambridge, Polity Press.

Gross, L. (2001) *Up From Visibility: Lesbians, Gay Men, and The Media in America*, New York: Columbia University Press.

Hayman, R. (1993) *Tennessee Williams: Everybody Else in an Audience*, New Haven: Yale University Press.

Joe Orton (2013) *Gallery*. Retrieved 23 September 2013, from http://www.joeorton.org/Pages/Joe_Orton_Gallery23.html.

Lahr, J. (1980) *Prick Up Your Ears: The Biography of Joe Orton*, London: Penguin.

Lahr, J. (1986) *The Joe Orton Diaries*, London: Methuen.

Lucia, C. and Porton, R. (2010) 'Gay Family Values: An Interview with Lisa Cholodenko' in *Cineaste*, 35(4), 14–18.

Nietzsche, N. (2008) *The Birth of Tragedy* (translated by Douglas Smith), Oxford: Oxford University Press.

Pullen, C. (2012) *Gay Identity, New Storytelling and The Media* (rev. ed.) Basingstoke: Palgrave Macmillan.

Pullen, C. (2013) 'Tom Ford's *A Single Man* and Don Bachardy's *Chris and Don*: The Aesthetic and Domestic Body of Isherwood' in Pamela Demory and Christopher Pullen (eds.) *Queer Love in Television and Film: Critical Essays*, New York: Palgrave Macmillan, pp. 233–243.

Rebecca (1940) Wrs. Robert E. Sherwood and Joan Harrison, Dir. Alfred Hitchcock, USA, 130 mins.

Russo, V. (1987) *The Celluloid Closet* (rev. ed.), New York: Harper & Row.

Sinfield, A. (1999) *Out on Stage: Lesbian and Gay Theatre in the Twentieth Century*, New Haven: Yale University Press.

The Celluloid Closet (1995) Wrs. Rob Epstein, Jeffrey Friedman and Sharon Wood, Dirs. Rob Epstein and Jeffrey Friedman, USA, 102 mins.

The Kids Are All Right (2010) Wrs. Lisa Cholodenko and Stuart Blumberg, Dir. Lisa Cholodenko, USA, 106 mins.

The Maltese Falcon (1941) Wr./Dir. John Huston, USA, 100 mins.

Suddenly, Last Summer (1959) Wrs. Tennessee Williams and Gore Vidal, Dir. Joseph L. Mankiewicz, USA, 114 mins.

Victim (1961) Wrs. Janet Green and John McCormick, Dir. Basil Dearden, UK, 90 mins.

Weeks, J. (1990) *Coming Out: Homosexual Politics in Britain from the Nineteenth Century to Present* (rev. ed.), London: Quartet Books.

Index